MW00721038

SEXUAL ASSAULT IN CANADIAN SPORT

SEXUAL ASSAULT IN CANADIAN SPORT

Curtis Fogel and Andrea Quinlan

UBCPress · Vancouver

32 31 30 29 28 27 26 25 24 23   5 4 3 2 1

Printed in Canada on FSC-certified ancient-forest-free paper (100% post-consumer recycled) that is processed chlorine- and acid-free.

Library and Archives Canada Cataloguing in Publication

Title: Sexual assault in Canadian sport / Curtis Fogel and Andrea Quinlan.
Names: Fogel, Curtis, author. | Quinlan, Andrea, author.
Description: Includes bibliographical references and index.
Identifiers: Canadiana (print) 20230495877 | Canadiana (ebook) 20230495990 |
    ISBN 9780774869126 (hardcover) | ISBN 9780774869140 (PDF) |
    ISBN 9780774869157 (EPUB)
Subjects: LCSH: Violence in sports—Canada. | LCSH: Sexual harassment
    in sports—Canada. | LCSH: Athletes—Sexual behavior—Canada. |
    LCSH: Rape—Canada. | LCSH: Rape—Prevention. | LCSH: Rape
    culture—Canada. | LCSH: Sports—Moral and ethical aspects—Canada. |
    LCSH: Sports—Social aspects—Canada.
Classification: LCC GV706.7 .F64 2023 | DDC 796.0971—dc23

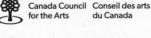

UBC Press gratefully acknowledges the financial support for our publishing program of the Government of Canada, the Canada Council for the Arts, and the British Columbia Arts Council.

This book has been published with the help of a grant from the Canadian Federation for the Humanities and Social Sciences, through the Scholarly Book Awards, using funds provided by the Social Sciences and Humanities Research Council of Canada.

UBC Press
The University of British Columbia
Vancouver
www.ubcpress.ca

For our fiery one

Contents

Acknowledgments

This book is the culmination of over a decade of research on sexual assault in sport, in which time we have moved between different universities, all of which we thank for providing resources and support that contributed to this research. For Curtis, this list includes Lakehead University, the University of California–Berkeley, and Brock University. For Andrea, this list includes Cornell University, the University of California–Berkeley, Trent University, and the University of Waterloo.

We also gratefully acknowledge the Social Sciences and Humanities Research Council of Canada for providing funding for this research. Through this funding, we have been fortunate to work with several research assistants who contributed to finding and organizing thousands of media articles, case files, and legal documents, many of which are cited in the pages of this book. We owe our thanks to them for the dedication that they brought to the project. These research assistants include Emily Buehlow, Bailey Mason, Chadd Sine, Jess Running, Ethan Mask, Sarah McCullough, and Jessica Woollings.

Our deep gratitude goes to James MacNevin at UBC Press for his ongoing support of and belief in this project as well as his patience as we navigated the challenges of pandemic parenting through the process of revising this book. We are also indebted to the two anonymous reviewers who provided thoughtful and detailed feedback on earlier drafts of the manuscript. We extend our thanks to the staff at UBC Press, and Katrina Petrik in particular, for their work in bringing this book to print.

Finally, a very special thank you goes to our family and friends, whose unwavering support and love made this work possible.

SEXUAL ASSAULT IN CANADIAN SPORT

1

Sport, Sexual Assault, and the Law
An Introduction

In May 2022, news broke that Hockey Canada, the major governing body for amateur hockey in Canada, had settled a lawsuit with a woman who reported that she was sexually assaulted by eight hockey players, including members of the Canadian junior men's national team, in 2018 (Westhead 2022a). The story threw Hockey Canada under a media spotlight as details emerged about the settlement as well as twenty-one other settlements totalling $8.9 million that the organization had made with sexual assault victims between 1989 and 2022 (Raycraft 2022). In a parliamentary hearing, at which federal politicians pressed Hockey Canada officials for more details, the officials disclosed that the organization maintains a fund – to which minor hockey league registration fees contribute in part – to handle sexual assault settlement payments out of court (Robertson 2022c). The revelation generated significant public outcry. Dubbed in the national news as "an explosive scandal that is shaking the sports world" (Burke 2022), the story of Hockey Canada's settlements with sexual assault victims propelled a national conversation about sexual assault in sport and the continued failure of sport organizations to address it (Ewing 2022b; S. Moore, Fowler, and Skuce 2022; M. Ross 2022).

Why and how the reported sexual assault in 2018 was kept out of public view for so long are questions that many have asked (Stinson 2022). At the time of this writing, no information has been released about the identities of the hockey players involved in the reported sexual assault in 2018; however, some investigative journalists have suggested that several, if not all, of the players are currently playing in the National Hockey League (NHL) (Wegman 2022). What has become clear is that Hockey Canada silenced information on the 2018 incident until the lawsuit was settled in 2022. It was not alone in doing so. The sexual assault was reported to the London, Ontario, police in 2018, but they closed the investigation without pressing charges or issuing a media release (Friesen 2022). Media reports have also revealed that Sport Canada, the major governing body and funding source for amateur sport in Canada, was aware of the incident in 2018 and did not press for details, follow up with Hockey Canada on how it was being handled, or provide any public transparency on its handling of the incident (McKenzie 2022).

In July 2022, another revelation about a group sexual assault reportedly perpetrated by members of the 2003 Canadian junior men's national hockey team was made public. In a public statement, Hockey Canada wrote that it had "heard a rumour about 'something bad' at the 2003 World Juniors" in Halifax (Hockey Canada 2022). As reports would later suggest, the incident that Hockey Canada was referring to involved a video recording of several players from the junior men's hockey team reportedly sexually assaulting a nonresponsive woman (Westhead 2022b). Under significant public pressure, Halifax police are now investigating the reported 2003 incident, and London police have reopened their investigation of the reported 2018 incident (McGran and Leavitt 2022).

Hockey Canada is not the only sport organization that has received considerable recent media attention and public scrutiny over its handling of sexual assault. In March 2022, groups of Canadian bobsleigh and skeleton athletes and gymnasts spoke publicly about the abuses that they experienced in sport and the failure of their sport organizations to protect and support them (Ewing 2022a; Robertson 2022a). Similar allegations were made by Canadian artistic swimmers in a lawsuit filed in March 2021 (Laframboise 2021). In May 2022, a group of gymnasts filed a class-action lawsuit against Gymnastics Canada and six affiliated provincial organizations alleging that the governing bodies failed to protect athletes by ignoring the rampant sexual abuse in the sport perpetrated by coaches and team officials (Robertson and Brady 2022a).

In March 2022, federal minister of sport Pascale St-Onge stated that there is a "crisis" (Robertson 2022b, para. 3) in the Canadian sport system. Despite the heightened attention that abuse in sport is seemingly now receiving, this "crisis" is not new. A look into the past reveals the enduring problem of sexual assault in sport and the systemic failure of institutions to take it seriously. As this book illustrates, reports of sexual assault perpetrated by and against athletes in Canadian sport historically have been met with silence, inaction, and tolerance within sport organizations and often in the Canadian criminal legal system.

This book traces a thirty-year span of publicly documented cases of reported sexual assault in Canadian sport from 1990 to 2020. Through a detailed examination of 307 publicly reported cases of sexual assault that have appeared in news media and legal documents from across Canada, we explore how sport organizations and the Canadian criminal legal system have responded to reports of sexual assault in sport and the structural and cultural elements of Canadian sport that promote, facilitate, and normalize sexual assault by and against athletes. Our analysis reveals the continued institutional tolerance and silencing of sexual assault in Canadian sport and the forms of institutional betrayal that often result for victims and their communities.

The 307 sexual assault cases analyzed in this book involved over 350 alleged perpetrators – athletes, coaches, and other authority figures in sport – and over 1,100 victims, nearly all of whom were women and children and many of whom reported being sexually assaulted multiple times by the same alleged perpetrators. Although thirty-six sports are represented across the analyzed cases, 118 of the 307 cases (38 percent) occurred in ice hockey – a number that reflects the long history of reported sexual assaults in the sport. As we argue, the details of the cases expose an ongoing pattern of a lack of accountability for sexual assault in sport. Many athletes accused of sexual assaults, including violent group sexual assaults, have advanced their playing careers and moved between teams and to higher playing levels with minimal to no interruption, and many coaches and other authority figures have sexually exploited athletes over years and sometimes even decades with relative impunity and little to no accountability. We show that, within the Canadian sport system, sexual assault is not only tolerated but also promoted and normalized as part of a competitive culture of masculine violence in sport. We illustrate how criminal legal responses to sexual assault in sport have failed to ensure safety for victims and their communities and impose harms that ultimately undermine sexual assault prevention. In the concluding chapter, we look beyond carceral responses to violence to explore ways of mobilizing communities, governments, policies, activism, sexual assault research, and civil and human rights law to increase safety in sport.

Notes on Method

Sexual assault in sport is a particularly challenging topic to study. The normalization of sexual violence and rape culture in sport and athletes' team loyalties and fears of reprisal for reporting sexual assaults present significant barriers for researchers studying sexual assault in sport contexts. Research-ing sexual assault in any context is difficult due to low reporting rates for sexual assault as well as the potential risks of retraumatizing victims through the process of research. Studying how institutions and organizations respond to sexual assault is made more complex by the institutional silencing of sex-ual assault in these contexts. Responding to these known methodological challenges in sexual assault research within and outside sport, we employ an unobtrusive method of data collection (E. Webb et al. 2000).

Given the unique challenges of studying sexual assault in sport, unob-trusive methods are particularly well suited for research on this topic. Such unobtrusive methods rely on existing texts that have not been created for the purposes of academic research. This approach has been exemplified in other Canadian research on criminal legal responses to gender-based vio-lence that rely primarily on legal case files and other unobtrusive data (e.g. Backhouse 2008; Sheehy 2014).

We used two online databases to locate the Canadian legal documents and media articles on reported sexual assault cases in Canadian sport from 1990 to 2020 that we analyze in this book: CanLII, a free database of court reports of judges' decisions on significant legal cases in Canada, and Canadian Major Dailies, a database of print news articles from over twenty of Canada's most widely circulated newspapers. We located additional articles and documents through internet searches to supplement the available information on each case. The 307 legal cases included in this analysis are those for which there was sufficient information available on who was involved, when the incident happened, at which playing level it occurred, and if any disciplinary or legal sanctions resulted. We chose 1990 as the starting point of this study since it marked a turning point in sexual assault activism and law reform in Canada, which we will discuss in more detail in Chapter 5.

This methodological design does not capture all cases of sexual assault that occurred in Canadian sport during this thirty-year span. It includes only those cases that were reported in one of Canada's twenty most-read newspapers and/or were reported to police, went to trial, and resulted in a written legal decision. Existing data on sexual assault victimization suggest that as few as 5 percent of sexual assaults in Canada are reported to police (Department of Justice 2019b). Of those reported to police, fewer become known to journalists and are reported in the media. Even fewer are pros-ecuted. Canadian statistics indicate that only 0.3 percent of perpetrators of sexual assault are convicted (H. Johnson 2012). Existing research has also shown that police are more likely to dismiss and doubt reports of sexual assault compared with any other reported crime (Crew 2012). One in five sexual assault reports is deemed unfounded by police (Doolittle 2017). These trends are exacerbated when a sexual assault complainant is Indigenous, a person of colour, disabled, poor, 2SLGBTQI+, and/or from any other group experiencing marginalization (Du Mont, Miller, and Myhr 2003; A. Quinlan 2016; Tasca et al. 2012). Despite the known obstacles that victims face in reporting sexual assaults in Canada, and the resulting low reporting rates for sexual assault, our search for publicly accessible texts on reported sexual assaults in Canadian sport still resulted in 307 legal cases. Although these data reflect a small fraction of the cases of sexual assault in sport in Canada, they simultaneously reveal the sheer magnitude of the problem.

We have aimed to triangulate the study's data by relying on multiple sources of unobtrusive data, including legal case files and media reports, as well as other publicly available legal documents such as victim impact statements, police releases, and parole board decisions, and first-person accounts of sexual assault in sport in the form of victim autobiographies. Following Norman Denzin's (1978) suggestion that data should be triangulated across time and space, we have analyzed legal cases occurring over a thirty-year period from 1990 to 2020 across Canada. Several of the cases in this book involve sexual assaults that occurred before 1990 but were reported and/or prosecuted between 1990 and 2020, such as cases in which coaches and other authority figures committed multiple sexual assaults over decades.

Since we have relied on an unobtrusive method of collecting and analyzing media and legal case files, the cases that we discuss are not representative of the totality of cases, occurrences, and experiences of sexual assault in Canadian sport. Our analysis is limited to the details reported in the data, which primarily feature reported sexual assaults by men against women and children. This is not to suggest that athletes who identify as trans, nonbinary, or gender queer do not experience sexual assault or that women in sport do not perpetrate sexual assault. These forms of sexual assault in sport are undoubtedly in need of more scholarly attention and await a more detailed study. This book focuses on reports of sexual assault that have been brought to light in the criminal legal system and media, which reflect the selective decision making in both institutions on which cases are seen as deserving of such attention. Despite these limitations, the cases in this book provide a unique look at trends in sexual assault in Canadian sport and how sport organizations and the criminal legal system have responded to the problem over the past three decades.

Notes on Language

This book is about sexual assault. To better illustrate, analyze, and understand some of the diversity of sexually violent acts, sport cultures, victims, and perpetrators in Canadian sport, we include some descriptions, including first-person accounts of sexual assault from legal reports and media files. Some of the content undoubtedly will be disturbing, upsetting, and potentially traumatizing for some readers. However, we have chosen to include some of these details to facilitate a deeper analysis and understanding of some forms and experiences of sexual assault in Canadian sport. As another Canadian researcher who examines legal responses to sexual assault, Elaine Craig (2018, 17), states in her book on sexual assault law, "while this makes some parts of the book difficult to read, the cost of sanitizing this content would be too great." That said, the chapters are organized in such a way that readers can opt for different levels of enagement with the empirical details of the cases. For readers more interested in focusing on theoretical discussions of sexual assault in sport, these can be found in the "Making Sense" sections in the chapters that follow.

Given our attention on the criminal legal system and its handling of sexual assault cases in sport, we discuss legal definitions and understandings of sexual assault throughout this book. We provide more depth and detail on sexual assault law and legal reforms where relevant in the chapters that follow. To reflect the study's empirical context, we deliberately use the term *sexual assault* rather than broader related terms such as *sexual violence* and *gender-based violence*. Laws pertaining to sexual assault in Canada are found in the Criminal Code of Canada, which outlines each act that can be tried as a criminal offence as well as the range of possible penalties that accompany the offence.[1] Sexual assault is currently defined in Canadian law as "an assault committed in circumstances of a sexual nature, such that the sexual integrity of the victim is violated."[2] There are three tiers of sexual assault listed in the Criminal Code, based upon physical injury to the victim: (1) sexual assault, (2) sexual assault with a weapon or causing bodily harm, and (3) aggravated sexual assault. Most of the cases discussed in this book are classified as sexual assaults, which carry a maximum sentence of up to ten years in prison.[3]

The Criminal Code also includes child-specific sexual assault offences relevant to some cases analyzed in this book, including sexual interference, invitation to sexual touching, and sexual exploitation. Sexual interference in the Criminal Code is defined as touching of a person under sixteen years old, by someone more than five years older, for a sexual purpose, and it carries a maximum sentence of ten years and a minimum sentence of ninety days.[4] Invitation to sexual touching refers to the act of inviting or counselling a person under sixteen years of age to touch the body of any other person for a sexual purpose and carries a maximum sentence of ten years and a minimum sentence of ninety days.[5] Sexual exploitation is defined in law as an individual in a position of trust who invites sexual touching or engaging in sexual contact with a person under eighteen years of age, and it carries a maximum sentence of fourteen years with a minimum sentence of ninety days.[6] These child-specific sexual offences differ from other sexual assault offences because sexual consent cannot be used as a legal defence. As a result, and as we will identify in the chapters to come, authority figures who sexually assault young athletes are more likely to be convicted compared with athletes accused of sexually assaulting other adults or their peers.

In this book, we use the term *victim* to refer to individuals who have experienced sexual assault. The term has long been criticized by feminist scholars for suggesting passivity and denying the agency of individuals who have experienced sexual assault (Allard 1997; Kelly 1988; Wolf 1993). As a result, many sexual assault scholars, activists, and advocates employ the term *survivor* to better capture the strength and agency of people who have experienced sexual assault (e.g., Ontario Coalition of Rape Crisis Centres 2015; Ullman 2010). Other feminist scholars, however, have criticized both terms for implying a passive female body that is either victimized by or survives an active male body (e.g., Doe 2012; Spry 1995). The term *survivor* can also wrongly imply that a person has moved past and recovered from the experience of sexual assault, which might not be the case for all who have experienced it. As this analysis will show, sexual assault in sport can have long-lasting effects on the lives of those who are harmed by it. These effects are often exacerbated by forms of "institutional betrayal" (Fitzgerald 2017, 483), such as when the criminal legal system and sport organizations ignore, silence, and tolerate sexual assault committed by coaches, athletes, and other authority figures in sport. These experiences of trauma are not always clearly recovered from or "survived." Neither term, *victim* or *survivor*, effectively captures the breadth and diversity of experiences of sexual assault. However, to reflect the language most often used within the sport and legal contexts that we are analyzing, we have chosen to use the imperfect term *victim* to refer to those who have experienced sexual assault.

In media sources, the term *accuser* is commonly used to describe a person who reports a sexual assault. Jackson Katz (2019, 129) argues that this term undermines the credibility of victims and conveys "skepticism and suspicion" about the violence that they report. We thus do not use the term *accuser* in this book. Existing research has consistently shown that false reporting rates for sexual assault are low. Using both qualitative and quantitative analysis, Melanie Heenan and Suellen Murray (2006) examined 812 reports of sexual assault and concluded that the false reporting rate for sexual assault is approximately 2.1 percent, which is consistent with false reporting rates for other crimes in Canada (Greenland and Cotter 2018). Police estimates of false reporting rates for sexual assault are often inflated. Some police classify a report as false, which implies that "no crime was committed or attempted" (IACP National Law Enforcement Policy Center 2005, 13), when there is insufficient evidence that a crime occurred, when the victim is deemed uncooperative, or because of trauma-induced inconsistencies and memory lapses in the victim's statement (A. Quinlan 2016). As a result, many reports are likely classified incorrectly as false. As such, even in cases that have not resulted in convictions in a court of law, we use the term *victim* to describe individuals who have reported that they have experienced sexual assault.

We use the terms *alleged* and *reported* throughout the book to describe all other aspects of cases that have not been established in a court of law. This language is not meant to imply that the alleged or reported incidents did not occur; instead, it indicates that the high burden of proof of *beyond a reasonable doubt* required of criminal cases in Canada was not met or that the trial has not yet happened. In cases in which an alleged perpetrator has been found not guilty, but certain facts have been agreed on in the trial, we do not use the term *alleged* or *reported* for those specific facts. The descriptions of cases, events, and individuals involved are accurate to the best of our knowledge based on publicly reported information at the time the manuscript was written. Some cases discussed may be subject to re-interpretation through court appeals, new factual developments, government actions, or legal reforms.

The two focal points of this book are the criminal legal system and the sport system. We refer to the Canadian criminal legal system as the procedures, processes, and practices aimed at enforcing criminal law in Canada. We have chosen not to use the similar term *criminal justice system* as, for many people, including many victims whose experiences are recounted in this book, the system has not, historically, provided anything resembling justice. We refer to the Canadian sport system as a network of sport organizations across Canada that predominantly utilizes a hierarchical model of governance featuring national, provincial, and local levels and is geared to the development of athletes for the purposes of increasing competitiveness at higher levels of play. Sport organizations in Canada are largely autonomous and govern themselves, but often they are required to adhere to some overarching government regulations. Although independent from government, national and provincial sport organizations typically receive public financial support in what Bruce Kidd (2013, 362) refers to as a "state-financed system of sport development." Most of the cases discussed in this book, even those involving victims who are young athletes, are situated at highly competitive levels of Canadian sport. By examining the problems with sport organizations and the sport system in Canada, we are not suggesting that every sport organization is complicit in the institutional tolerance and silencing of sexual assault, just as we are not arguing that all competitive male athletes or coaches are perpetrators of sexual assaults. We do argue, however, that sexual assaults have been tolerated and normalized in many competitive sport organizations in Canada and that significant changes both within and beyond the Canadian sport system are necessary to better respond to and prevent sexual assault in sport.

Organization of the Book

The chapters in this book are organized around different forms of sexual assault in Canadian sport: athlete-perpetrated sexual assault against women and girls, athlete-perpetrated group sexual assault, sexually violent hazing, and sexual assault perpetrated by coaches and other authority figures in sport. We conclude with a chapter that explores the interconnections among these different forms as well as strategies to enhance sexual assault prevention, accountability, and safety in sport.

Chapter 2 focuses on reports of sexual assaults perpetrated by individual, predominantly white, male athletes against women and girls. We discuss thirty cases, involving male athletes and at least forty-eight victims identified in legal documents and media reports as women, to generate a broader discussion of rape culture in competitive men's sport in Canada. We look specifically at how sexual assaults, particularly when committed by white male athletes, are routinely tolerated by other athletes and team and league officials and often ignored or excused in the Canadian legal system. We explore how this culture is fostered and maintained in the hierarchical environment of competitive men's sport, which places value on sexually aggressive definitions of masculinity, and the tolerance and promotion of violence, including sexual violence.

Chapter 3 builds upon the previous chapter and examines twenty-two cases of reported group sexual assault perpetrated by two or more competitive male athletes against single victims identified in reports as women or girls. As the chapter shows, within the twenty-two cases, at least seventy athletes, all of whom are men's hockey or football players, have been reported for participating in group sexual assaults against women and girls. Building upon the theoretical discussions in Chapter 2, in this chapter we explore the social currents that fuel the disproportionately high rates of reported group sexual assaults in men's competitive sport and how sport organizations and the criminal legal system have responded to them. This chapter illustrates how Canadian hockey and football organizations commonly stand behind their young and often white male athletes, providing them with support and care after they have been accused of violent sexual acts against women and girls while offering no support to victims who are frequently blamed and shamed.

In Chapter 4, we turn to a different form of group sexual assault perpetrated by competitive male athletes: sexually violent hazing rituals targeting younger male teammates. Despite the difference in the form of sexual assault, similar themes are revealed through our analysis of reports of twelve sexually violent hazing incidents across Canada. To contextualize these cases, we discuss the intersections of precarious, violent masculinities in a hierarchical sport system, in which athletes often have limited bodily autonomy and opportunities to provide uncoerced consent to physical violence and harm, and the broader forms of privilege and entitlement that lead to the social, legal, and institutional tolerance of sexual assault in sport.

Shifting away from a focus on athlete-perpetrated sexual assaults, in Chapter 5 we examine cases in which athletes and other young persons in sport are victims of reported sexual assaults by coaches and other authority figures in sport, including team doctors or trainers, managers, directors, facility staff, billet hosts, drivers, and/or referees. The chapter is based on the analysis of reports of 243 authority figures accused of sexual assault against and sexual exploitation of over 1,000 victims, spanning a wide range of team and individual sports. Departing from individualized, psychological perspectives on offender behaviour that tend to dominate child sexual abuse literature, we consider the structural conditions and power dynamics embedded in competitive, hierarchical sport environments that disempower and silence victims and provide ample opportunities for coaches and other authority figures to commit sexual assaults largely without consequences for long periods of time.

In the concluding chapter, we explore the interconnections among the different forms of sexual assault in sport discussed throughout the book and identify a cycle of sexual assault in Canadian sport. We conclude by examining how and why sport organizations' continued reliance on the criminal legal system to solve the persistent problem of sexual assault in Canadian sport is problematic, ineffective, and untenable, and we propose alternative avenues for addressing this complex, multidimensional problem.

2

Athlete-Perpetrated Sexual Assault
Misogyny, White Male Privilege, and Entitlement in Competitive Men's Sport

In the 1990s, researchers at the Center for the Study of Sport in Society at Northeastern University in the United States were commissioned by the National Collegiate Athletics Association (NCAA) to conduct a pioneering study of sexual assaults perpetrated by male university athletes against women. The authors of the study surveyed reports of sexual assault at twenty NCAA universities with football and basketball programs perennially ranked in the top twenty in the United States (Crosset, Benedict, and McDonald 1995). Although athletes comprised only 3 percent of the university student populations, the researchers found that male athletes were responsible for nearly 20 percent of reported sexual assaults on the university campuses.

Following their lead, other researchers in the United States and a few in Canada have illustrated the link between competitive male university sports and sexual assaults against women (e.g., Caron, Halteman, and Stacy 1997; Chandler, D. Johnson, and P. Carroll 1999; Fogel 2017; Volkwein-Caplan et al. 1997). Largely missing from this literature have been analyses that extend beyond university sport to examine how sport organizations and the criminal legal system respond to these cases. In this chapter, we focus on reported cases of individual male athletes in Canadian high school, junior, university, and professional sport who have sexually assaulted women and girls, and we reveal how the Canadian criminal legal system and sport organizations have routinely minimized, excused, and tolerated this form of gender-based violence.

The exact prevalence of athlete-perpetrated sexual assaults is difficult to determine. Sexual assault reporting rates are systemically low, with estimates suggesting that only 5 percent of sexual assaults in Canada are reported to the police (Department of Justice 2019b). Compounding this problem, police statistics and national victimization surveys in Canada do not capture specific rates of athlete-perpetrated sexual assaults. However, all existing evidence suggests that there is a link between competitive men's sport and sexual assault and that male athletes are disproportionately reported for sexual assaults against women compared with nonathletes.

Much of the North American literature on sexual assault by male athletes is focused on an American context (e.g., Boeringer 1996, 1999; Chandler, D. Johnson, and P. Carroll 1999; Cheever and Eisenberg 2020; Murnen and Kohlman 2007; Young et al. 2016). Scot Boeringer (1996, 134) surveyed 477 male undergraduate students, 16.2 percent of whom were athletes, and concluded that male athletes displayed a "greater rape proclivity." Similarly, according to another study (Chandler, D. Johnson, and P. Carroll 1999), of the 342 American college students sampled, male athletes were significantly more likely than nonathletes to perpetrate sexual assaults. These findings have been supported more recently in a meta-analysis (Murnen and Kohlman 2007) that focused on sexually aggressive behaviours and attitudes of college men and found significant correlations among men's athletic participation, hypermasculinity, and sexual aggression. Another study (Young et al. 2016) surveyed 379 male college students in the United States and found that male athletes were 77 percent more likely to engage in sexually coercive behaviours than male nonathletes. Most recently, Jamie Cheever and Marla Eisenberg (2020) surveyed 122,501 high school students in Minnesota and found that male students who were highly involved in sports were significantly more likely to coerce another person into sex than any other group.

In a Canadian study, Curtis Fogel (2017) found that male athletes frequently appear in media reports of sexual assaults on university campuses as accused perpetrators. In fact, 23 percent of media reports of sexual assaults on Canadian university campuses from the past ten years involved male athletes as alleged perpetrators. This number appears to be significantly out of proportion compared with sexual assaults perpetrated by nonathletes, particularly given that competitive male athletes comprise less than 2 percent of the Canadian university student population. Although revealing, these findings are not definitive since drawing statistical conclusions about criminal behaviour from media reports is problematic. Most crimes, especially those of a sexually violent nature, are not reported in the media, and thus they are not captured in data derived purely from media reports. It can also be argued that athlete-perpetrated sexual assaults on university campuses are seen as more newsworthy and therefore receive more news coverage than sexual assaults committed by nonathletes. Although 23 percent cannot be taken as a precise measure, it does point to a problem of sexual assault in competitive male university sport in Canada.

Other research on competitive men's sport in the United States has drawn attention to the cultures and ideologies supporting sexual assault in sport. This literature has shown that sexist, misogynist, and homophobic views are held by many male university athletes. One study (Volkwein-Caplan et al. 1997) found that 27 percent of male university athletes reacted positively to derogatory, violent, and sexist remarks about women. Similarly, Boeringer (1996, 1999) concluded that students on men's athletic teams and in fraternities were significantly more likely to have attitudes that support rape. Likewise, in a sample of a group of college freshmen in the United States (Forbes et al. 2006), another study found that men who played contact sports in high school were significantly more likely to approve of rape, sexist attitudes, violence, and negative, homophobic views of gay men.

The connections among sexist, misogynist, and homophobic attitudes and higher rates of sexual assault are well documented. Research by Peggy Sanday (1981, 1990) identified that high levels of tolerance for sexist attitudes correlate with high rates of sexual assault. Murnen and Kohlman's (2007) meta-analysis illustrated a strong relationship among athletic participation, hypermasculinity, and sexually aggressive attitudes and behaviours. Capturing this trend succinctly, Robin Warshaw (1988, 112) argued that "athletic teams are breeding grounds for rape [because they] are often populated by men who are steeped in sexist, rape-supportive beliefs."

Taken together, this evidence suggests a high prevalence of sexual assaults perpetrated by male athletes as well as cultural belief systems in much of competitive men's sport that normalize and celebrate rape. Although these studies undoubtedly have their limitations – many focus on self-reports, utilize samples limited to university student populations, and do not include in-depth qualitative analyses – they suggest a connection between competitive men's sport and sexual assault against women. This predominantly American literature raises new, underexamined questions about athlete-perpetrated sexual assaults against women in the Canadian context and how the Canadian criminal legal system and sport organizations have responded to this form of interpersonal, gender-based violence.

Taking up this focus, in this chapter we examine thirty publicly reported cases of male athlete–perpetrated sexual assault against women in Canada between 1990 and 2020, and we explore the relevant Canadian laws and policies shaping institutional responses to these cases. In so doing, we shed light on why sexual assaults against women appear to be disproportionately common among competitive male athletes, and how the Canadian criminal legal system and sport organizations commonly minimize, excuse, and tolerate this form of violence, particularly when it is committed by white male athletes. In this chapter, we focus on cases involving individual athletes, and in the next chapter we examine cases of male athletes who have sexually assaulted women in groups. Together these chapters reveal the ties between violent masculinities and sexual assault as well as the unique social dynamics and institutional and organizational contexts that normalize and excuse sexual assaults against women and girls.

In this chapter, we refer to reported perpetrators of sexual assaults as men, and reported victims as women, since the thirty publicly available reported cases from 1990 to 2020 reflected this gender dynamic. This language is not meant to suggest that women cannot be perpetrators of sexual assaults or that men, or people who identify as trans, nonbinary, or gender queer, cannot be victims of sexual assaults. It does reflect, however, the glaring trend that there were no publicly documented reports of female or publicly identifying nonbinary/gender queer athletes in Canada perpetrating sexual assaults.[1] To frame the following discussion of athlete-perpetrated sexual assault cases, we turn first to the wide-reaching consequences of sexual assaults against women.

Consequences of Athlete-Perpetrated Sexual Assault against Women

Sexual assault can result in serious, long-term harms for victims. Existing research on the physical, emotional, and psychological harms of sexual violence shows that victims disproportionately experience depression (Au et al. 2013), sleep disorders (Krakow et al. 2001), eating disorders (Ganson 2020), substance abuse (Kilpatrick et al. 2007), sexual dysfunction (D. Elliott, Mok, and Briere 2004), self-harm (Brooker and Tocque 2016), poor academic performance (Stermac et al. 2017), disassociation (Temple et al. 2016), anxiety and panic attacks (Hassija and Gray 2013), and suicide (Bryan et al. 2013). Many of these emotional and psychological harms have also been shown to affect secondary victims of sexual violence, such as victims' friends and family members (R. Davis, Taylor, and Bench 1995).

Beyond consequences to victims and their communities, athlete-perpetrated sexual assault can also lead to reputational harm for teams and organizations for which the athletes play. Sport organizations are currently under increased scrutiny in the wake of the #MeToo movement, which was founded by American activist Tarana Burke in 2006 and grew to global proportions in 2017, resulting in media attention on institutional responses to sexual assault on university campuses, or in the military, entertainment industry, and other institutional contexts. In this context, sport organizations have greater potential to face reputational damages if they are seen to be failing to appropriately acknowledge and respond to sexual assault allegations against athletes on their teams. Indeed, there are a few contemporary examples of such scrutiny, such as recent public dismay with the Chicago Blackhawks for failing to respond to the sexual assault of an athlete by a team trainer (Draper 2021) and calls for Hockey Canada executives to step down after their sexual assault settlement fund became publicly known (Sadler 2022). However, as the cases in this chapter illustrate, such examples are exceptions when set against the long history of sport organizations' apparent immunity from public scrutiny for their handling of sexual assaults.

In addition to possible reputational harms, teams can lose athletes from their rosters if they are suspended or incarcerated, causing team performance to suffer. In leagues in which there are salary cap restrictions in place, an athlete who is suspended for disciplinary reasons or cannot play because of a criminal trial or imprisonment often still has their salary counted toward the salary cap, which creates challenges for the team to add a new player. Athletes and sport organizations can also face financial consequences from athlete-perpetrated sexual violence. For example, sponsorship and endorsement deals can be terminated because of morality clauses in athletes' contracts.

Athletes and organizations can also be found legally liable for the harms of sexual assault. The American university sport context provides some recent examples. In 2020, an American class-action lawsuit was filed against the NCAA by women who had been sexually assaulted by male athletes at NCAA institutions. In the lawsuit, the women argued that the NCAA, as the governing body for college athletics in the United States, has a duty to "supervise, regulate, monitor and provide reasonable and appropriate rules to minimize the risk of injury or danger to student[s]" (cited in Lavigne 2020, para. 3). They further asserted that the NCAA "knew or should have known that their actions or inaction in light of the rate and extent of sexual assaults reported and made known to [the NCAA] by male student-athletes ... would cause harm to female student-athletes and non-student-athletes at NCAA member institution campuses in both the short- and long-term" (cited in Lavigne 2020, para. 3). Similar lawsuits have been filed and won by victims of athlete-perpetrated sexual violence in the United States, even before the rise of the #MeToo movement and the resulting public attention to sexual violence. For example, in 2016, the University of Tennessee–Knoxville paid US$2.48 million to students victimized by male football players (Rau and Wadhwani 2016). And, in 2007, a female student at the University of Colorado was awarded US$2.5 million after being sexually assaulted by football players at the university.[2] Although the resolution of these cases suggests a move toward some accountability for some victims, the details of the cases in this chapter reveal the far more common trend of a lack of institutional responsibility that many sport organizations take for the sexual assaults that athletes perpetrate and for the enduring harms for the victims of this violence.

Relevant Laws Governing Athlete-Perpetrated Sexual Assaults in Canada

Most of the reported cases of individual male athletes who perpetrated sexual assaults against women discussed in this chapter fit within the legal definition of sexual assault as outlined in Section 271 of the Criminal Code of Canada. The cases that we describe and analyze all involved a single alleged perpetrator over twelve years of age, which means that the perpetrator could be held criminally responsible, and a single victim, most of whom were over sixteen years of age, which is the current legal age of sexual consent in Canada. The reports described assaults of a sexual nature that violated the sexual integrity of the victims. Nearly all thirty cases discussed in this chapter involve charges of sexual assault. In the one exception, *R v Smith*, the athlete was charged and convicted of aggravated sexual assault, defined as sexual assault that can cause serious, life-altering physical harm.[3] Smith was charged with aggravated sexual assault since he failed to disclose to the women with whom he was sexually active that he was HIV-positive, and the prosecution argued, controversially, that this posed significant health risks to the women.

Although typically straightforward in legal application, cases of individual athlete-perpetrated sexual assault against women can become complicated in criminal proceedings because evidence typically is limited to witness testimonies, and the trial often revolves around the question of whether the sexual activity was consensual. When forensic evidence, such as the athlete's semen found on the victim's body or underwear, is available, it can demonstrate that sexual activity occurred but not that a sexual assault definitively took place (A. Quinlan 2017). In most cases analyzed in this chapter, the male athlete did not deny that sexual activity occurred and argued instead that it was consensual. In Canadian law, consent refers to "the voluntary agreement of the complainant to engage in the sexual activity in question."[4] In these cases, the primary legal question is whether the complainant voluntarily agreed to engage in sexual activity with the athlete. When there is a shred of doubt, the accused can be found not guilty as the prosecution must prove its case beyond a reasonable doubt.

Reports of Athlete-Perpetrated Sexual Violence against Women

The thirty cases of reported athlete-perpetrated sexual assault discussed in this chapter occurred between 1990 and 2020, and all involved a single male athlete reported for sexually assaulting a woman or girl. In the section that follows, we separate cases by playing level and discuss them in chronological order from the date of the reported sexual assault.[5] These cases collectively reveal some of the commonalities of reported and prosecuted athlete-perpetrated sexual assaults against women in Canadian sport over the past three decades and provide a foundation for the subsequent theoretical discussion of what fuels this form of gender-based violence in sport. Additionally, the cases illustrate the routine tolerance of sexual assault in sport organizations and how it is often minimized in the criminal legal system. The cases are divided by playing levels (junior, university, and professional men's sport in Canada[6]) to allow for a more nuanced understanding of how and why sexual assaults are perpetrated by male athletes in these varying age groups and contexts.

Junior Sport

Junior sport in Canada primarily involves athletes between sixteen and twenty-one years old. Although many junior athletes are still high school students, junior-level sports teams form a bridge to university and professional playing levels and typically are run on a for-profit basis. In some communities in Canada, junior sports teams inspire much fanfare, particularly in regions that do not have a major professional sports franchise.

Junior playing levels occupy a unique, and in many ways controversial, place in Canadian sport. There is currently a legal debate about the amateur status of junior sport in Canada, particularly in relation to junior hockey. A major class-action lawsuit was recently filed by former junior hockey players against the Canadian Hockey League (CHL) and its subsidiary leagues in which it was argued that junior hockey players are employees and should be fairly compensated according to labour and employment laws.[7] A partial settlement agreement was reached to compensate eligible players in the amount of $30 million.[8] This lawsuit has exposed that junior sport in Canada, and especially junior hockey, generates significant profit and is not amateur, recreational-level sport. Although many male junior athletes in Canada are celebrated and given athlete celebrity status in their communities, they are not compensated financially like professional athletes. Given the relatively small numbers of athletes who make it to professional levels, most male junior-level athletes are unlikely to reach high-level professional leagues in their sports.

Male junior athletes were significantly overrepresented across all three forms of athlete-perpetrated sexual assaults examined in this book, including individual male athletes assaulting women, groups of male athletes assaulting women, and male athletes assaulting each other during hazing rituals. Of the three categories, junior athletes were most commonly involved in reported group sexual assaults against women or against male teammates during hazing rituals, as Chapters 3 and 4 detail.

In 1993, the Sault Ste Marie Greyhounds won their first Memorial Cup, the equivalent of the NHL's Stanley Cup in the context of junior hockey. The Greyhounds were led by a star player named Jarrett Reid, who scored fifty-five goals in the season. Although he was promoted by the team as the face of the junior franchise and encouraged to represent the team at community events by signing autographs for fans, Reid also faced charges of multiple sexual and physical assaults involving two former girlfriends (Robinson 1998). The team did not publicly address the charges. After their championship season ended, Reid pleaded guilty to three charges of sexual assault, among several other violent offences, and was sentenced to nine months in prison. He was released three months into his nine-month sentence (Robinson 1998). Upon release from prison, he joined the St. Francis Xavier University men's hockey team, on which an assistant coach from Reid's previous team was coaching. Reid had a successful on-ice season and was given the St. Francis Xavier X-Men Athletic Leadership Award. Off the ice, however, there were continued reports of his violence against women, and he was subsequently charged with three counts of assault against his girlfriend and two breaches of parole. After he was charged, the Canadian Olympic Committee awarded him a Petro-Canada Athletic Leadership Scholarship (Robinson 2008). Reid eventually withdrew from St. Francis Xavier University and the men's hockey team when he was sentenced to five months in prison plus two years on probation. He then continued his hockey career playing professionally in

Europe for several seasons (*Soo Today* 2008). Despite his history of criminalized violence against women, once his playing career ended, Reid went on to coach young women's hockey in Burlington, Ontario (Alphonso and Robinson 2008).

In 2000, shortly after being cut during training camp with the Toronto Maple Leafs and returning to his previous junior team, the Ottawa 67's, Lance Galbraith was charged with sexually assaulting a young woman whom he met at a Byward Market night club (Rupert 2001a). He was released on bail, promising that he would return for his hearing. The day after he was charged, he played and scored the team's first goal. When asked by journalists about Galbraith's status with the team given the charges of sexual assault, team president Jeff Hunt stated that "Lance is one of our leaders ... The charge doesn't affect his status with the team. We're going to support Lance through this ... Hopefully this will only be a minor distraction. As was evident in the game, it appears he is carrying on business as usual" (quoted in Sands 2000). During the trial, the victim testified that Galbraith misled her to believe that a house party with other players would be taking place, but she found herself alone with him. She testified that she consented to some sexual activity with Galbraith, but that she did not consent to the vaginal intercourse that he forced on her (Rupert 2001a). She reported that, after the sexual assault, she escaped from the house and was seen by a passing police car (Rupert 2001b). Galbraith did not deny that sex had occurred, but he argued that the woman consented to all of the sexual activity (Rupert 2001a). Controversies about the admissibility of evidence in the case led to trial delays, which prompted his legal defence team to argue that his right to a speedy trial under the Charter of Rights and Freedoms was violated and caused interruptions to his professional hockey career (Rupert 2002). As a result, the charges were stayed. No disciplinary action by the team or league related to the alleged sexual assault was reported.

At eighteen years old, Cass Rhynes from Prince Edward Island (PEI) had a promising future in baseball and had been drafted to play for the Los Angeles Dodgers in Major League Baseball (MLB). In 2003, however, he was convicted of two counts of invitation to sexual touching after engaging in sexual activity with two girls who were in grade seven at the time (Morris 2003). Since they were only twelve and thirteen, under Canadian law, they could not legally consent to the sexual acts with the eighteen-year-old baseball player. At trial, Rhynes admitted to engaging in sexual activity with the girls on multiple occasions but asserted that he thought they were above the legal age of sexual consent. The prosecution successfully argued that Rhynes did not take steps to ascertain their ages, and he was sentenced to forty-five days in prison plus probation and 100 hours of community service (Benedet 2010a). However, in 2004, he successfully appealed the decision by arguing that he "did not intimidate or incite the girls to have sex," which overturned the original decision (*CBC News* 2004, para. 6). In overturning the decision, the judge suggested that, had the RCMP charged Rhynes with sexual inter-ference instead of invitation to sexual touching, a conviction would have been upheld, as the girls could not have legally consented to the sexual acts regardless of whether they were intimidated or incited to perform those acts (Joyce 2008). There are no reports of Rhynes being formally disciplined by any sport organization for his sexual involvement with the girls. However, his athletic scholarship to a university in Florida was rescinded because the institution was unable to defer it indefinitely while his criminal trial and appeal trial took place (Joyce 2008). He eventually received a scholarship to play baseball for a junior college in the United States but never played in the MLB league.

Another junior athlete originally from PEI, David Herring, was charged with sexual assault in 2004. Police reported that Herring trapped a woman in a bathroom at a Peterborough, Ontario, house party and sexually assaulted her (*Sudbury Star* 2004). At the time, he was a member of the Erie Otters junior hockey team. Over a year later, charges of sexual assault and forc-ible confinement against Herring were dismissed by a judge (*Charlottetown Guardian* 2005). Like many of the other cases discussed here, there are no reports of any team or league disciplinary action taken against Herring. However, records show that he actively played for the Erie Otters in 2005, after having been charged with sexual assault and before the charges were dismissed (*Globe and Mail* 2005b).

Also in 2004, an unnamed seventeen-year-old male basketball player from the Vancouver area reportedly sexually assaulted a sleeping seven-year-old girl.[9] While staying at his friend's house, he sexually touched his friend's sister, causing the girl to wake up and alert her mother. Although he pleaded guilty to sexual assault, the presiding judge determined at sentencing that an abso-lute discharge would be most appropriate for the offender and the offence. This meant that the basketball player would have no criminal conviction tied to his sexual assault of a young girl or any condition to fulfill, such as counsel-ling or community service. Reflecting on this sentence, the judge questioned,

is a discharge an appropriate sentence? Looking at the evidence and sub-missions before me, I consider as to whether it is in [the unnamed perpetrator's] interest to not have a conviction recorded. The evidence is that he is of good character and that it would be in his interest to not have a conviction. Given the absence of evidence that the conduct here is likely to reoccur, his prospects for a productive non-offending future, and the adverse inference of a conviction for a sexual offence would have on his future potential of good character, it is not contrary to the public interest to grant a discharge.[10]

Because the offender was seventeen years old at the time of the offence, he has not been named under Canadian law. It is not publicly known which basketball team he played for or whether he was disciplined by his team or league.

In 2007, junior football player Tyler Stephens of the Okanagan Sun was charged with nine counts of sexual assault. Marking a noticeable change in the typical nonresponse to sexual assault charges from sport organizations, after hearing about the charges, the team issued a statement to the media: "The Okanagan Sun Football Club is shocked by today's arrest of one of its players, defensive back Tyler Stephens, on the charges regarding the well-publicized sexual assaults that occurred in Rutland last year. The Okanagan Sun cannot state strongly enough the anger, contempt and distaste the organization feels towards anyone guilty of such charges" (quoted in W. Moore 2008, para. 17). The organization did not mention that Stephens was previously convicted of sexual assault while playing for the team and continued to play while serving time on house arrest (Hayes and W. Moore 2008). The team later indicated that at the time they were not certain why he was on house arrest. Stephens reportedly assaulted ten women on eleven different occasions between May and October 2007, during which time he was playing football and on house arrest (W. Moore 2008). He pleaded guilty to six counts of sexual assault and three counts of sexual assault causing bodily harm, and he was sentenced to five years in prison in addition to the thirty-two months already served at the time of his sentencing (*CBC News* 2010b).

In 2013, junior hockey player Mitchell Vandergunst, who played for the Stratford Cullitons, was charged with three counts of sexual assault against his friend's girlfriend. Vandergunst met his friend and the young woman at a bar in the town of Grand Bend. At the trial, the young woman testified that in the cab ride home from the bar Vandergunst groped her. She said that her boyfriend was reportedly very intoxicated and that Vandergunst helped him to bed before sexually assaulting her.[11] She underwent a forensic sexual assault exam, during which forensic evidence was collected with a sexual assault evidence kit. Forensic analysis of the kit's contents confirmed the presence of Vandergunst's DNA in her vagina and revealed various bruises on her body.[12] After originally denying it, Vandergunst later confessed to sexual activity with the young woman but argued in court that it was consensual. He was convicted of two counts of sexual assault. While awaiting sentencing, Vandergunst was made an assistant captain of the Cullitons team and played in a game the same day that he was convicted (Robinson 2016). He remained on the team for four months until he was sentenced to one year in prison plus two years on probation (Fleming 2015b). Vandergunst appealed the conviction, and while out of prison during the appeal process he joined a new team, the Clinton Radars, and continued his hockey career. The president of the Radars, Steve Campbell, said Vandergunst's conviction on two counts of sexual assault was a "non-issue" (Broadley 2015, para. 1). In 2016, Vandergunst successfully appealed his conviction, arguing that the trial judge failed to consider evidence that the taxi driver did not see any overt sexual touching during the cab ride. As a result, the previous court's decision and sentence were overturned (*Midwestern Newspapers* 2016).

Another junior hockey player, Ben Johnson of the Windsor Spitfires, sexually assaulted a sixteen-year-old intoxicated young woman in a bathroom stall in a Windsor nightclub in 2013 during the team's end-of-season party. She was later found on the floor of the stall, barely conscious, with significant vaginal bleeding (Sacheli 2016). Johnson denied having sex with her, but forensic evidence later contradicted this claim (Sacheli 2017). However, his legal defence team successfully argued that the forensic evidence, collected with a penile swab, should be excluded from the trial because it was collected without a warrant.[13] During the investigation, another young woman came forward and accused Johnson of sexually assaulting her in a bathroom stall at a different nightclub a few weeks earlier, which led to a second sexual assault charge. Johnson was found guilty and sentenced to three years in prison (Pazzano 2017). Like Vandergunst, he appealed the decision, but his effort was unsuccessful (Pazzano 2017). Johnson was drafted by the New Jersey Devils of the NHL in 2012 but never played in an NHL game. He went on to play for the Cincinnati Cyclones in the East Coast Hockey League.

At the beginning of the 2015 season, the Gananoque Islanders junior hockey team held a rookie initiation party. Young women were invited to attend and witness the hazing activities involving the rookie male athletes. At one point during the party, a veteran player on the team, Chance Macdonald, trapped a sixteen-year-old young woman in a room and sexually assaulted her (Krishnan 2017). Her friend interrupted the sexually violent encounter. When the victim reported the sexual assault to the police, Macdonald was charged with sexual assault and forcible confinement. His lawyers arranged a plea deal in which he pleaded guilty to assault, rather than sexual assault, with a sentence of eighty-eight days to be served on weekends (O'Reilly 2017). The judge approved the plea deal. Explaining his rationale, the judge stated that

> I played extremely high-end hockey and I know the mob mentality that can exist in that atmosphere. I'm sure you disappointed not only a lot of people including your parents, but yourself. Not everyone has the talents that you have, and you have them. If there was a trial and you were convicted of a sexual offence, I have no doubt that would have dramatically changed the course of your life. That would have been extremely unfortunate given how accomplished you were at the time, and your potential. (quoted in Gibson 2017, para. 11)

Macdonald delayed serving his sentence for four months while completing an internship through the business program at Queen's University (Yanagisawa 2017). There are no reports of the league disciplining the team for holding a rookie hazing party or Macdonald for assaulting a young woman at the party.

While playing for the Nipawin Hawks in the Saskatchewan Junior Hockey League, Garrett Dunlop was charged with sexual assault and sexual interference in 2015. On two occasions, he reportedly engaged in sexual acts, including oral and vaginal sex, with a thirteen-year-old girl when he was nineteen (MacPherson 2017b). At his trial, he argued that he assumed she was older because she mentioned drinking, smoking, and having friends in high school (MacPherson, 2017a). Dunlop was found not guilty on both counts (Oleksyn 2017). There are no reports that he was ever disciplined by his team or the league. He went on to play for the Vancouver Island University men's hockey team and was named a First Team League Allstar for the 2019–20 season (Vancouver Island University Athletics 2022).

In many of the sexual assault cases involving junior-level athletes, sport organizations responded with silence, and trial judges in the criminal legal system made statements that minimized, dismissed, or excused the reported sexual assaults. Many of the junior athletes successfully challenged the sexual assault charges in court and subsequently moved with relative ease between teams and sport organizations. Their capacity to successfully launch criminal defences while maintaining their mobility within sports is a mark of the relative privilege that many of these athletes carry. Even when convicted, they were able to continue their playing careers. All of the junior-level athletes discussed here present as white and thus carry privilege stemming not only from their gender and status as athletes but also from their whiteness. The impact of these intersecting privileges of race, gender, and athletic status can be seen in some of the trial judges' deliberate mention and consideration of athletes' "potential" (cited in Gibson 2017, para. 11) and "good character"[14] in the justifications of their rulings. Sport organizations' characterization of some of the reported sexual assaults as "a minor distraction" (cited in Sands 2000) or a "non-issue" (Broadley 2015, para. 1) likewise reflects the privilege and institutional protection that many of these athletes are granted, regardless of the outcome of a criminal investigation and trial. At the junior playing level, unpaid athletes are often considered valuable commodities who can generate significant profits for their organizations. In this context, it is perhaps not surprising that junior-level sport organizations commonly choose to ignore or minimize reports of athlete-perpetrated sexual assaults. With few exceptions, these cases illustrate how both sport and legal institutions can work in ways that normalize and excuse sexual assaults against women and girls.

College and University Sport

Canadian college and university sports are played by athletes who are typically eighteen to twenty-six years old. Although there can be overlap in the ages of some junior-level athletes, college and university athletes are usually a few years older. In contrast to junior sports in Canada, college and university sports are generally not seen as launchpads to being drafted or signing high-paying contracts in major men's professional sport leagues (Ellis 2022). College and university sports, however, can still carry much fanfare at postsecondary institutions and often receive significant support from the college and university communities.[15] Many of the athletes do continue their playing careers in semi-professional leagues in North America and other professional leagues in Europe and around the world. College and university sports are highly competitive and involve fierce competition between athletes for limited scholarships and a degree of celebrated status on campus and in the community.

As a junior hockey player, Jarrett Reid was convicted of sexual assaults against women and sentenced to serve prison time. Upon his release, he secured an athletic scholarship to St. Francis Xavier University in Nova Scotia to continue playing hockey. While there, he was again charged and convicted of sexual assault. Reid voluntarily withdrew from the university after he was sentenced to five months in prison plus two years on probation (*Soo Today* 2008). In the same season, 1997–98, his teammate Andrew Power was charged with two counts of sexual assault stemming from two separate incidents (Robinson 1998). Power was convicted, but his sentence has not been reported. He has reportedly gone on to coach boys' hockey (R. Ross 2019).

In 2000, Michael Hofstrand captained the Southern Alberta Institute of Technology (SAIT) Trojans to a national collegiate championship and was named the national collegiate player of the year. A year later he was charged with the sexual assault of a woman on SAIT's women's hockey team (Slade 2002a). The victim reported that she and others went back to Hofstrand's home after a night of drinking at a Calgary bar. She testified that she fell asleep and awoke to find Hofstrand sexually violating her (Slade 2002c). At the trial, an additional player from the SAIT women's hockey team testified that she too was sexually violated by Hofstrand the same night (Slade 2002b). She indicated that her memory of exactly what happened was not clear enough to file a complaint with the police. Hofstrand testified that he had no memory of what transpired from the time he left the Calgary bar to the time he awoke the next morning (Slade 2002c). After two days of deliberations, a jury found Hofstrand not guilty (*Charlottetown Guardian* 2002). After he was charged and before the trial, he received the national player of the year award and continued playing hockey (Slade 2002b). No disciplinary measures by SAIT or the Canadian Collegiate Athletics Association for the alleged sexual assaults against the two female SAIT hockey players were reported.

In 2001, a female wrestler reported that Terry Nixon, a male wrestler for the Bisons Wrestling Club at the University of Manitoba, sexually violated her on multiple occasions (McIntyre 2008b). In 2004, she notified the police. She reported that she also told the club director, Nat Brigante, what happened, and that he threatened her to remain quiet (McIntyre 2008b). At the trial, Brigante testified that she never told him about the sexual assaults. Nixon was found not guilty (McIntyre 2008a). After the trial, the club was disbanded, and Brigante was dismissed from his position at the University of Manitoba. It is unclear in public records whether this dismissal was related to the reported sexual assaults.

Mark Yetman, a goaltender for the Brock University Badgers hockey team, was convicted of sexually assaulting three women in December 2009 and January 2010. After meeting two women at a St. Catharines bar, he and a teammate went back to Yetman's residence. Reports suggest that, after breaking off into two rooms, Yetman and his teammate engaged in consensual sexual activity with the women. However, one woman later recounted that Yetman became increasingly violent; she asked him to stop, but he refused (Walter 2012). He then reportedly entered the other room, asked his teammate to leave, and proceeded to violently sexually assault the other woman (Walter 2012). Media accounts suggest that Yetman remained a member of the Brock University hockey team throughout the investigation of the reported sexual assaults. The following January he was accused of a third sexual assault of another woman whom he met at a St. Catharines bar (Dakin 2013). In a jury trial in 2012 for the first two sexual assaults, Yetman argued that, though the sex was what he called "rough," it was consensual (Dakin 2012). Members of the jury disagreed and found him guilty on both counts of sexual assault. Released on bail while awaiting sentencing, Yetman returned to his home province of Newfoundland and continued to play hockey. In the days before his sentencing, he won a senior men's league championship. He was sentenced to two years less a day, with strong encouragement from the judge to pursue anger management counselling while incarcerated. Shortly thereafter, he faced a second trial for the third sexual assault, during which he pleaded guilty. Over forty coaches, teachers, and acquaintances wrote character references for Yetman claiming that he was of good character. He was sentenced to three years to be served concurrently with his previous sentence (Dakin 2013).

The University of Saskatchewan (U of S) Huskies men's volleyball team recruited Matthew Alan Meyer in 2017 after he played for Medicine Hat College (MHC). The U of S coach reportedly did not tell university officials that Meyer was charged with sexual assault of another MHC student in 2016 (Yard 2018). The young female student attended a party at the college residence where Meyer lived. After consuming alcohol, she passed out on a couch. She awoke to find Meyer sexually assaulting her and taking pictures on his cell phone. When Meyer was arrested, police found 147 images of the sexual assault on his phone (Deibert 2018). He confessed to police, then pleaded not guilty at his trial, but then changed his plea to guilty. He was sentenced to two years in prison (Revell 2018). After sentencing, he voluntarily withdrew from the U of S. The university fired the coach, Brian Gavlas, who defended Meyer, whom the coach thought should "be supported and part of a passion and a sport that he enjoyed and a group of guys that could support him" (quoted in Deibert 2018, para. 7).

In 2016, another male university athlete, Patrick Walsh, recorded images of an intoxicated young woman whom he sexually assaulted. Walsh reportedly streamed a FaceTime video of her while she was naked and vomiting in a bathroom after the sexual assault (B. Powell 2018). Before the assault, Walsh had returned home from Detroit Mercy University, where he played on the lacrosse team. He met the young woman, a student at Ryerson University (now Toronto Metropolitan University), at a Toronto bar and invited her back to his mother's downtown condo, where, the victim testified, he sexually assaulted her (B. Powell 2019). A jury found Walsh guilty of sexual assault. He was sentenced to two years in prison (Pazzano 2019). Records show that Walsh continued to play lacrosse for Detroit Mercy University in 2018 and 2019 while awaiting his trial and sentencing, and he withdrew from the team only once he was incarcerated.

While playing for the Laurentian University Voyageurs men's hockey team in 2016, Blake Luscombe was charged with one count of sexual assault (D. MacDonald 2016). Although details of the reported sexual assault have not been released publicly, the coach of the team, Craig Duncanson, suspended Luscombe from the team following the charges. Explaining this relatively rare sanction against an athlete accused of sexual assault, Duncanson stated that "[Luscombe] has been suspended for breaking the team's code of conduct" (quoted in Moodie 2016, para. 8). The sexual assault charges were withdrawn in February 2017 (D. MacDonald 2018). Luscombe continued his hockey career in Europe and never returned to play for Laurentian University.

In 2018, Davonte Provo, a basketball player at St. Francis Xavier University, was charged with sexual assault in what the university described as a "drug-facilitated sexual assault at an off-campus location" (cited in Lowthers 2019a, para. 3). Similar to Luscombe, Provo was immediately suspended from the university and the basketball program. No updates on the status of his criminal charges have been publicly reported at the time of this writing.

In 2019, Edward "Eddie" Ekiyor, a basketball player at Carleton University in Ottawa, was charged with sexual assault after a woman reported to police that he allegedly gave her a date rape drug and sexually assaulted her (L. Carroll and Crawford 2019). Having just won a national championship with the university, Ekiyor was named the MVP of the championship tournament. One week before his criminal charges were published in the news, Ekiyor announced that he would be leaving Carleton University to pursue a pro contract (Silva 2019). Records suggest that the university did not impose any disciplinary measures against him for the reported drug-facilitated sexual assault. Ekiyor was found not guilty at his trial since the judge was unable to determine that it was Ekiyor who gave the woman the date rape drug before they engaged in sexual activity, which Ekiyor argued was consensual (Duffy 2021).

Like many of the cases involving junior-level male athletes, many of the college- and university-level athletes accused of and prosecuted for sexual assaults received significant support and accolades from their coaches and in some cases sport organizations. In a few notable cases, however, accused and prosecuted athletes were suspended by their teams and/or colleges or universities and convicted in criminal trials. Despite these suspensions and prosecutions, in most cases the athletes were able to maintain their playing careers, continue to accrue markers of athletic achievement, and move easily to other teams and sport organizations. In this context, being accused or convicted of sexual assault seemingly does not reduce the relative privilege that many of these athletes carry within sport contexts. As with junior-level athletes, most of the accused athletes present as white, except for the two basketball players, Davonte Provo and Eddie Ekiyor, both of whom, it is worth noting, were unable to continue playing for their university teams, unlike most of the white male college and university athletes discussed.

Professional Sport

There are two types of men's professional sport leagues in Canada. American men's professional leagues that have franchises in Canada – such as the National Hockey League (NHL), National Basketball Association (NBA), and Major League Baseball (MLB) – are billion-dollar industries, featuring athletes commonly paid in the millions of dollars, in addition to their endorsement contracts. In contrast, Canadian-specific professional sport leagues are smaller in scale and generate significantly less revenue. Of all the Canadian professional leagues, the Canadian Football League (CFL) appears to be most often represented in reported sexual assaults.

The CFL has a long history in Canada. It was established in 1958 and has built a significant spectator following (Fogel 2012). Although CFL players are not paid in the millions of dollars like their National Football League (NFL) counterparts, their games are featured on national television stations in Canada and played in large fan-filled stadiums, with regular-season games averaging over 25,000 fans in attendance (Ralph 2021). Although their paycheques might be one-tenth or less of an average NFL player's salary, CFL players are considered athlete celebrities in many Canadian communities. A recent survey conducted by Reginald Bibby identified that 21 percent of Canadians follow the CFL, making it one of the most popular spectator sports in the country (Ralph 2021).

Professional athletes in Canada typically range in age from twenty-one to thirty-eight. Eleven of the thirty cases analyzed in this chapter featured professional athletes. However, as we will identify in subsequent chapters, there are only a few cases of reported group sexual assault by professional athletes against women and no cases of sexually violent hazing against a professional male teammate. This is not to say that these forms of violence do not occur in professional men's sport in Canada, but they are not commonly reported in the media or prosecuted in the criminal legal system.

In 1994, NHL player Petr Nedved was charged with sexually assaulting a woman in her Vancouver-area home while the NHL was in a labour lockout (*AP News* 1996b; *Orlando Sentinel* 1996). Shortly after, Nedved was traded from the Vancouver Canucks to the Pittsburgh Penguins. When the Penguins were in Vancouver to play the Canucks, Nedved turned himself in to police. Few details have been released on the case; however, the charge was eventually stayed (Let's Go Pens 1997). There have been no reports of any disciplinary action by his team or by the NHL.

In 1995, Calgary Stampeders player Toney Bates was arrested for sexually assaulting a woman at the University of Calgary, near McMahon Stadium, where the Stampeders play (Murray 1995a). After he was charged and released by police, Bates moved to California, where he faced new charges for sexual battery against his former girlfriend's sister (Clarridge 2008). Before joining the Stampeders, Bates played for the University of Iowa, where he also faced multiple charges related to sexually violent acts against women. He has since been accused in more than two dozen incidents of sexual misconduct (Green 2008). Although he has never faced trial in Canada for the reported sexual assault at the University of Calgary, Bates has spent much of his adult life in and out of prison for other subsequent sexual assaults (Clarridge 2008). A rookie at the time of the sexual assault allegations in Calgary, Bates was cut from the roster when he left the country (Murray 1995a).

Just a few months after being named World Boxing Championships (WBC) super middleweight champion in 2000, Dave Hilton Jr. lost his title when he was sentenced to seven years in prison for sexually assaulting two young women (Mulvaney 2007). In 2004, they came forward publicly and revealed their identities as his daughters. While on parole in 2007, Hilton returned to the boxing ring and won a match in Montreal. In 2009, he was again charged with sexual assault, this time of an adult woman (*CBC News* 2009a). The woman refused to testify against Hilton, which led to his acquittal. He has since faced additional charges for allegations of

violence against women; none have led to convictions (Sutherland 2014).
There are no reports of any repercussions or formal discipline of Hilton
by the WBC for perpetrating sexually violent acts against his daughters or
reportedly against other women.

CFL player Bernard Williams was accused of sexually assaulting a woman
in 2006. After his arrest, bail was set at $100,000 for his release. Reports sug-
gest that the Toronto Argonauts president at the time, Keith Pelley, wrote
the cheque to secure Williams's release (O. Moore 2006). The woman testified that she met Williams at a Toronto nightclub before they and other
players from the team went back to her friend's home. She fell asleep and
reportedly awoke to Williams sexually violating her. At the trial, she stated
that "I threw myself out of bed (and) started screaming at him. I don't even
know you. How could you do something like this to me?" (quoted in Lorrigio 2009, paras. 10–11). The judge found Williams not guilty (Kari 2009).
He was not suspended or disciplined by the CFL or the Argonauts. Instead,
reports indicate that he was supported by the team throughout the judicial
process (O. Moore 2006).

Around the same time, another CFL player, Trevis Smith, was charged
with aggravated sexual assault after he had unprotected sexual intercourse with multiple women without disclosing that he was HIV positive.[16]
According to the evidence at his trial, Smith received notification from a
public health authority in 2003 that one of his previous sexual partners
tested positive for HIV and that he should get tested. The woman believed
that she contracted HIV from Smith (Warick 2005). He tested HIV positive and was asked to disclose a list of his sexual partners. He reported that
he was involved in sexual relationships with eight or nine women in the
past but did not mention the two women with whom he was currently having ongoing sexual relationships.[17] One of those women confronted him,
and he reportedly asserted that he was not HIV positive (Walton and Maki
2007). Smith was found guilty of aggravated sexual assault and sentenced
to five and a half years in prison.[18] He was suspended by the Saskatchewan
Roughriders at the time of his arrest (Hutchinson and Bellett 2005).

Like many of the other athletes discussed in this chapter, Josh Boden,
who played for the BC Lions and Hamilton Tigercats in the CFL, has been at
the centre of many reported incidents of violence against women. In 2008,
while playing for the BC Lions, he was charged with assaulting his girlfriend.
However, the charges against him were dropped after his defence counsel
identified inconsistencies between the woman's testimony on the witness
stand and her previous report to police. The Lions released Boden from

the team after he was charged. Once charges were dropped, he resumed his playing career with the Tigercats (Little 2008). When the Tigercats released him to create a roster spot for another player, Boden returned to Vancouver. His girlfriend, whom he reportedly blamed for ruining his football career, was found murdered in March 2009. Police began to conduct surveillance on Boden and observed him sexually assaulting a woman at a Vancouver SkyTrain station. He was also later charged with sexually assaulting a woman in an office building elevator (D. Ward 2009), and he was a suspect in at least four other reported sexual assaults, for which he was never charged (Bolan 2009). In 2011, Boden was found guilty of the two counts of sexual assault and sentenced to one year in prison. He has since been charged for other acts of violence against women, and in 2018 he was charged with the 2009 murder of his girlfriend, Kimberly Hallgarth, when police discovered new evidence linking him to the crime (K. Larsen 2018). In 2021, Boden was convicted of that murder (Fraser 2021).

In 2006, Adam Braidwood was drafted first overall in the CFL Canadian draft and nominated for most outstanding rookie in the season. Over the next few seasons with the Edmonton football team, knee injuries limited his on-field participation and performance, which hampered a seemingly promising football career. Then, after reports that he committed acts of domestic violence against his girlfriend in 2010, he was released from the team in 2011 (Blais 2013). As revealed in the trial, during the domestic violence, Braidwood brought out a firearm, threatened to kill his girlfriend, choked her, and sexually assaulted her (Kornik 2013). He pleaded guilty to sexual assault and was sentenced to four and a half years in prison (Parrish 2013). Upon release from prison, he became a professional boxer and won the World Boxing Union (WBU) heavyweight title.

In 2015, a player for the development team of the Vancouver White-caps soccer team, Sahil Sandhu, was charged with sexual assault (Canadian Press 2015b). In a separate incident, another player from the Whitecaps, Anthony Blondell, was charged with sexual assault in 2018 (Adams 2020). Both players received indefinite suspensions from Major League Soccer (MLS), subject to the outcomes of their criminal proceedings. The details of both sexual assaults have not been reported in the media. However, it is known that Sandhu pleaded guilty to assault, rather than sexual assault, and received an absolute discharge. He has since rejoined the Whitecaps farm team. Blondell's trial was scheduled to begin in January 2021, but he did not appear, leading to an active warrant for his arrest (Johal 2021). He is currently playing professional soccer in Venezuala (*ESPN* 2023).

Since 2011, the BC Lions of the CFL have taken some measures to publicly denounce gender-based violence through their Be More Than a Bystander Campaign. In 2018, however, media reports indicated that the team signed defensive lineman Euclid Cummings to a $150,000 contract plus a $70,000 signing bonus even though he faced multiple criminal charges for incidents of violence against women (Edwards 2018b). Cummings was charged with the sexual assaults of two women, as well as assaults and threats to cause death or bodily harm, stemming from incidents in Vancouver in 2016 while he played for the Winnipeg Blue Bombers (Adams 2018). The Blue Bombers have acknowledged that they were aware of the investigation and informed the league. However, two years after the alleged acts and a year after being criminally charged, Cummings played the entire 2017 season before he signed with the BC Lions in 2018 (Edwards 2018b). In 2018, the CFL voided his contract with the Lions. The CFL did allow Cummings, however, to keep the $70,000 signing bonus (Edwards 2018a). No updates on the status of his criminal charges have been publicly reported at the time of this writing.

Also in 2018, the CFL issued a statement that another player, Teague Sherman, who played for the Ottawa Redblacks, would be released from his contract and unable to sign with any other team after he was charged with two counts of sexual assault after three women in Ottawa filed police reports against him (Yogaretnam 2018). According to a statement issued by the league office, "the league will not register a contract for Sherman should any team attempt to sign him. The Canadian Football League has and abides by a policy on violence against women and condemns violence against women in all its forms" (cited in *CBC News* 2018, para. 8). Details of the alleged sexual assaults have not been released publicly. However, reports suggest that Sherman pleaded guilty to assault in exchange for having his sexual assault charges removed and received a suspended sentence of two years on probation (*3DownNation* 2021).

The context of the CFL's public condemnation of Cummings's and Sherman's reported violence against women in 2018 is significant. Around the same time, the #MeToo movement, shining light on the commonality of sexual assault and institutions' failure to respond to it, was gaining momentum across North America and internationally. Institutions and organizations seen not to be taking sexual assault seriously were receiving significant public scrutiny (Case 2019). It was in this context that the CFL seemingly took such decisive action against these two players. In the years before #MeToo, professional sport leagues' responses to reported and prosecuted cases of sexual assault were largely inconsistent; in most cases, leagues responded with silence; in others, they responded with either public support for or suspension of the athlete. Most notably, however, in many cases, athletes moved with apparent impunity between teams and across sport organizations.

In contrast to most of the cases involving junior- and university-level athletes, in many cases involving professional athletes, the criminal legal system seemingly responded with more severe sentences. Unlike many of the white-presenting athletes accused of sexual assault at junior and university levels of play, the majority of the professional male athletes prosecuted and convicted for incidents of violence against women are Black men or men of colour. It is also worth noting that, of all the cases discussed in this book, the criminal charge of aggravated sexual assault, which carries the longest sentence of all sexual offences, appeared in the case of Trevis Smith. He was criminalized for not disclosing his HIV status – a widely criticized criminal charge in Canada[19] – and is a Black man. The disproportionate criminalization of Black men, Indigenous men, and people of colour in Canada is well documented (Neugebauer 2000; Owusu-Bempah et al. 2021; Owusu-Bempah and Wortley 2013). Decades of work by feminists of colour have pointed to the racism that fuels the heightened criminalization of men of colour for violence against women compared with white men (see Critical Resistance and INCITE! Women of Color against Violence 2016; A. Davis 1983; Gruber 2020; Richie 2012). Although the criminal legal system seemingly delivered more convictions and longer sentences in cases involving professional athletes compared with athletes at lower playing levels, the broader context of racism in the criminal legal system sheds critical light on the legal responses in these cases.

Making Sense of Athlete-Perpetrated Sexual Assaults

The reported cases of sexual assault at junior, college, university, and professional playing levels point to an enduring rape culture in competitive Canadian men's sport, in which sexual assaults are routinely tolerated by other athletes, teams, and league officials and in some cases ignored or excused by the Canadian criminal legal system. Although undoubtedly there are cases that deviate from this trend, many reflect an institutional tolerance of sexual assaults perpetrated by male athletes, particularly white male athletes. Most significantly, regardless of whether an athlete was suspended or criminalized, most of the athletes in these cases retained the ability to move seamlessly between teams and sport organizations. Organizations that ignored or excused the sexual assaults committed by their athletes were not held accountable for their ongoing tolerance of gendered violence.

Rape culture has been defined as being characterized by "attitudes and cultural messages that continually downplay the extent of sexual violence, stigmatize those who are assaulted, and celebrate male sexual aggression" (Whitlock and Bronski 2016, 38). When sport organizations fail to respond to reports of sexual assault, and choose instead to ignore or minimize them and celebrate the accused athletes, they become complicit in maintaining and reproducing a rape culture in competitive men's sport.

The culture that condones and normalizes sexual assault in Canadian competitive men's sport organizations is fostered and maintained through a unique set of gendered social relations and institutional practices. The dynamics of a competitive, hierarchical, social institution of sport, as well as competitive athletes' complex social status within and outside sport, fuel rape culture in these spaces. Within the total institution of competitive sport, male athletes' worth is highly conditional on their athletic success, and athletes possess limited bodily autonomy and opportunities to consent to physical harm to their bodies during play (Fogel 2013). Paradoxically, male athletes carry societal privilege because of their gender, athletic status, and in some cases their race, and often they are given entitlements that result in the social, legal, and institutional tolerance of violence that they commit. Considering the significant number of reported cases of male athletes who perpetrate sexual assaults against women, these unique social relations and institutional practices that uphold rape culture in competitive men's sport warrant further investigation.

Masculinity and Consent in the Total Institution of Competitive Men's Sport

There is an obvious gendered element of the perpetration of sexual assaults by individual athletes. In all thirty reported cases discussed in this chapter, the alleged perpetrators are identified in public records as male and the victims as female. Any explanation of athlete-perpetrated sexual assault must account for this gendered dynamic. As Anne Cossins (2000, 44), along with many other feminist scholars, argues, "rape arises from culturally specific gender practices." Gender is thus pertinent to understanding sexual assault in sport.

Significant sociological and feminist theorizing and research have been done on how male athletes learn to "do gender" (Messerschmidt 1993, 83) through developing contextually appropriate and valued masculinities in and through sport. Masculinities are not inherent, fixed, or stable but are continuously developed and maintained. As Michael Kimmel and Michael Messner (1995, xx) explain,

> men are not born, growing from infants through boyhood to manhood, to follow a pre-determined biological imperative, encoded in their physical organisation. To be a man is to participate in social life as a man, as a gendered being. Men are not born; they are made. And men make themselves, actively constructing their masculinities within a social and historical context.

Competitive men's sport environments have long been identified as significant social and historical contexts in which boys and young men learn and develop masculinities (Burstyn 1999; Kidd 1987; Messner 1995, 2007; Messner and Sabo 1994; Sabo 1985). Raewyn Connell (1987, 84–85) describes sport as an "organizing institution for the embodiment of masculinity ... [in which] images of ideal masculinity are constructed and promoted most systematically."

All of the athletes discussed in this chapter, as well as in the next two chapters, which feature different forms of athlete-perpetrated sexual assaults, were teenage boys and young men at the times of the reported sexual assaults. It could be argued that, as members of competitive sport teams, these athletes exist in a space that Kimmel (2018, xix) has termed "Guyland," which he describes as "both a social arena and a stage of life between adolescence and adulthood." Guyland is a formative space in which masculine identities are developed alongside high levels of social and peer pressure to conform to masculine ideals and expectations. A primary task of adolescents in Guyland is to overcome a general "fragile sense of manhood" (Kimmel 2018, 18) among young men. Kimmel (2018, 9, 10) describes Guyland as a social space in which "guys gather to be guys" and "shirk the responsibilities of adulthood and remain fixated on the trappings of boyhood, while at the same time struggle heroically to prove they are real men despite all the available evidence to the contrary." Teenage boys and young men commonly face such a social space when they enter the world of competitive men's sport.

There is not a single masculinity formed or expected across all competitive men's sports. Rather, different masculinities emerge in different sport contexts in which young men shape, reaffirm, and develop masculine identities. In 1987, Connell argued that multiple masculinities within social spaces are organized on a social hierarchy in which one form gains hegemony over all others. Explaining this further, Connell (1987, 183) wrote that "hegemonic masculinity is always constructed in relation to various subordinated masculinities as well as in relation to women." For Connell (1995), gender and power are largely interconnected and inseparable. Connell and James Messerschmidt (2005) clarified and expanded the concept of hegemonic masculinity, identifying that it is not singular, fixed, or static but must be accomplished continuously and is variable by social context.

Connell and Messerschmidt's (2005) reconception of hegemonic masculinity is valuable for understanding sexual assault in Canadian sport. There are indeed idealized or "exalted" (Carrigan et al. 1985, 592) masculinities in competitive men's sports. These masculinities are shaped in relation to the unique contextual factors of those settings and in turn contribute to shaping those settings. Importantly, continuous work by male athletes is required to accomplish hegemonic or exalted masculinities in competition with their peers.

The cases of athlete-perpetrated sexual assault against women examined in this chapter all occurred in highly competitive levels of men's sport. A study of 105 college men (Caron, Halteman, and Stacy 1997) identified that hyper-competitiveness was significantly correlated with reported sexual aggression. The playing levels in the cases discussed in this chapter are characterized by "The Lombardian Ethic" (Twin 1997, 184), rooted in the now colloquial expression of "winning isn't everything; it's the only thing," popularized by former American football coach Vince Lombardi. Male athletes in junior, college/university, and professional sports in Canada are expected to be fully committed to winning at any cost and required to constantly compete with opposing teams for wins and championships, as well as with teammates for playing time and advancement opportunities, including higher playing levels, limited scholarships, and professional contracts. In this context, male athletes are socialized to aspire to masculine identities that exude toughness, strength, power, and dominance. This identity formation is understood as part of the blueprint for assembling competitive athletes and winning teams (Messner 2007). These developing masculinities thus intersect with the competitive, hierarchical relations within the social institution of sport. As Connell and Messerschmidt (2005) identify, accomplishing hegemonic masculinity in any organizational setting is highly competitive and involves continued power struggles. Competitive men's sport in Canada further fuels such power struggles among young men. The sport ethic that they learn and are expected to adopt in these spaces is to be hyper-competitive with and dominant over all others.

This highly competitive sport ethic is largely inescapable within the institution of sport, particularly at elite playing levels, which often have a totalizing nature. Fogel's (2013) study of junior, college/university, and professional football players found that athletes' involvement in sport is commonly all encompassing. There are times when competitive football players have up to three practices in a day in addition to team sessions reviewing plays and strategies in a classroom, watching game footage, eating meals, and weight-lifting. Not unlike in the military, in competitive sport, athletes are organized, regimented, and trained to fulfill a largely singular purpose: winning athletic contests. This environment can be characterized as a *total institution*, a term first popularized by Erving Goffman (1961).

In his study of asylums, Goffman (1961, 6) described the characteristics of a total institution:

> First, all aspects of life are conducted in the same place and under the same single authority. Second, each phase of the member's daily activity is carried on in the immediate company of a large batch of others, all of whom are treated alike and required to do the same thing together. Third, all phases of the day's activities are tightly scheduled, with one activity leading at a prearranged time into the next, the whole system being imposed from above by a system of explicit formal rulings and a body of officials. Finally, the various enforced activities are brought together into a single rational plan purportedly designed to fulfill the official aims of the institution.

Goffman's total institution has many parallels with the totalizing nature of many competitive sport environments. Although competitive sport differs from the total institutions that Goffman visited and researched in the 1950s, in that there are no high walls, fences, or forests that surround sport venues to prevent escape, the walls around sport environments are largely symbolic. Although conceivably an athlete could decide not to follow along with the deeply prescribed training schedule and meeting times, doing so could result in sanctions that would affect the athlete's career, such as a suspension or removal from the team, which could impact future employment and financial security. In this sense, within competitive sport environments, there is often significant coercive control over athletes' behaviour and decision making.

Goffman (1961) argued that total institutions resocialize the individuals within them, stripping people of their individual identities, values, and beliefs, while socializing individuals into new behaviours, attitudes, and identities. This concept is analogous to Michel Foucault's (1995, 231) notion of the modern prison as a "complete and austere institution." Foucault argued that prisons make the incarcerated person's body and mind "docile" (135) and therefore malleable. In a similar way, the total institution of competitive sport strips athletes of their individual identities and socializes them to be tough, strong, and more likely to win in their athletic endeavours. When a competitive team enters the field, rink, or court, they move in unison like marching military troops. They warm up in concert, choreographed as tightly as an elite dance troupe. And, when the whistle blows to start the game, they are expected to fight in unity to punish and outscore their opponents. In this context, athletes are no longer seen as individuals but as a group of "docile bodies" (Foucault 1995, 135) to be used in athletic conquests.

Although total institutions can be effective in creating conformity and commitment to a shared goal, when combined with other organizational factors discussed later in this chapter, they can also be breeding grounds for violent and destructive behaviours and foster cultures that normalize and trivialize sexual assaults and other forms of interpersonal violence. Approximately 26,000 people in the American military experienced unwanted sexual contact in 2012 alone (Burris 2014). A recent survey revealed that more than a quarter of women in the Canadian military have been sexually assaulted in their workplace (Honderich 2021). In 2008, an estimated 216,600 sexual assaults occurred in American prisons (Kaiser and Stannow 2011). Prisons and the military are clear institutional hot spots for sexual assault where violent attitudes, beliefs, and behaviours are often tolerated and promoted. As the cases discussed in this chapter and elsewhere in this book suggest, so too is competitive men's sport.

The highly competitive, totalizing institution of men's sport in Canada creates a system of what Messner (1992, 33) terms "conditional self-worth" for young male athletes. An athlete might have a poor performance on the field of play, receive condemnation from the crowd and coaches, and be shunned by teammates, even though a few days earlier the athlete hit a game-winning shot and was celebrated as a hero by coaches, teammates, and fans. Likewise, injuries can take athletes out of athletic competitions and instantly end their athletic careers. This notion was expressed well by one junior Canadian football player: "We are all aware of the potential that your career could be over [with] the next snap because some guy rolls up on you from behind and you blow every ligament in your knee" (quoted in Fogel 2013, 39). Hegemonic dominance in competitive men's sport rests largely on performing and winning at the highest possible level, simultaneously cooperating with teammates to achieve shared goals while competing with them for recognition, opportunities, and advancement. As Messner (1992, 88) identifies, "the structure of athletic careers is such that individuals on teams are constantly competing against each other – first for a place on the team, then for playing time, recognition, and 'star' status, and eventually just to stay on the team."

An athlete's worth and masculine status are thus highly unstable. Reflecting this sentiment, Kimmel (1994, 122) writes that "masculinity must be proved, and no sooner is it proved than it is again questioned and must be proved again – constant, relentless, unachievable." Other scholars have used various terms to capture this idea: Michael Kaufman (1987, 7) refers to "the fragility of masculinity," Martin Heesacker and Steven Snowden (2013, 121) identify "precarious manhood," and Curtis Fogel (2017, 139) discusses "precarious masculinity." Each term similarly points to the instability of performances of masculinity. In the context of competitive men's sport, young male athletes develop their masculine identities in a highly competitive environment in which worth is constantly measured and can fluctuate wildly from one practice, game, or season to the next. All the while, the masculine identities of athletes are constantly scrutinized in "the policing of masculinity" (Reigeluth and Addis 2016, 74).

As some scholars have argued, sexual assault against women is one method that some male athletes use to stabilize a sense of power, control, and dominance in a highly competitive male space and to reduce anxieties about and fears of being perceived as unmasculine. According to Kaufman (1999, 17), sexual assault is a *"compensatory mechanism ...* a way of re-establishing the masculine equilibrium, of asserting to oneself and to others one's masculine credentials." Likewise, "sexual harassment and sexual assault are particularly likely to occur in tightly knit competitive male groups (e.g. military units, gangs, college fraternities, sport) that bind men emotionally to one another and contributes to their seeing sex relations from a position of power and status" (Volkwein-Caplan and Sankaran 2002, 11). Picking up on a similar idea, Cossins (2000, 115) asserts that "masculine sexual practices can be said to reinforce and maintain relations of power, not only between women and men, but also between men, since certain sexual practices and the social construction of desire are ways of attaining status among men." Similarly, "men who rape or hit women are not isolated individuals, deviating from some normal form of masculinity. Rather, men's violence against women [can be] understood as *overconformity* with a culturally honored definition of masculinity that reward[s] the successful use of violence to achieve domination over others" (Messner, Greenberg, and Peretz 2015, 11). Within the competitive space of men's sport, in which masculine status is largely precarious and fragile, the sexual conquest of women, with or without consent, can contribute to the stabilization of masculine status.

Interestingly, many of the athletes accused of sexual assault discussed in this chapter were at a stage in their athletic careers where they were new to their current playing level or about to move to a higher playing level. Athletes in these stages of transition can move from being the star or a significant member of their team at a lower level, where they might have achieved a dominant masculine status, to a new level where they might be younger and less accomplished than their new teammates. In these circumstances, an athlete's dominant masculine status on a new team can be thrown into question. Many of the athletes in the cases described above were drafted to play at a higher level but had not yet made the team at the time of the reported sexual assault. Lance Galbraith had just been cut from a professional team and demoted to the junior hockey rank when the alleged sexual assault occurred. Other athletes were battling through injuries at the time that their reported sexual assaults took place. Injuries, demotions, and precarious positions on competitive teams create the conditions for precarious, fragile masculinities in competitive sport. Compounding these gendered dynamics, teams might find newer or injured players more expendable since they have not yet established their worth or have diminished value. This can result in teams being less likely to support the player publicly by excusing or minimizing the reported assault and/or to support the silencing of the sexual assault allegation privately through nondisclosure agreements.[20]

This precarity of masculine status in elite men's sport has dangerous implications. Some male athletes might engage in sexually violent behaviour to stabilize their masculine dominance. Drawing from interview data with thirty former elite-level male athletes, Messner (1992, 97) identified that the "use of women as objects of sexual conquest is important for gaining status in the male peer group." Lori Heise (1997, 425) expanded on this by arguing that "it is partly men's insecurity about their masculinity that promotes abusive behaviour towards women." The precarity of masculine status in competitive men's sport can thus fuel the normalization of sexual aggression toward and sexual assault of women and girls.

Sex as Competition, Women as Trophies
In elite men's sport, sexual intercourse can become a competition between men in which women are often treated as trophies. One athlete interviewed

by Messner (1992, 101) described this as follows: "We were like wolves hunting down prey ... If a girl doesn't give it up in 60 seconds, drop her!" In one of the many sexual assaults perpetrated by current and former male athletes described in a study of campus sexual assaults (Krakauer 2015), a young male athlete stole the pants and underwear of a young woman after he sexually assaulted her. He later explained to police that he stole these items because they were proof for his friends that he had engaged in sexual intercourse with the young woman. Echoing this idea, Canadian journalist Laura Robinson (1998, 118) describes a male athlete's approach to sex as masculine identity confirmation and competition: "His actions have nothing to do with providing sexual pleasure and respect for a woman and everything to do with being seen as a man in his world."

This understanding of masculinity and sex was made clear by an unnamed former junior hockey player who was quoted in a media article describing the pervasive and unhealthy attitudes of his peers toward women: "Everyone wanted to be the biggest badass on the team ... It was a hyper-masculine, hyper-competitive environment and that attitude was also true to the way we approached women ... We looked at women like they were *trophies*. They were 'sluts' and 'puck bunnies' not women. Looking back, I'm ashamed" (quoted in Curtis 2015, paras. 17–19; emphasis added). For some athletes, competition does not stop at the confines of the playing field. They continue to establish and reaffirm their dominant masculine status on the team with competitions off the field, often involving the sexual conquest of women.

Sex competitions in men's sport can be literal in some cases. Some teams engage in formal competitions in which athletes are assigned points for accomplishing sexual acts with women. Laura Bates (2012, para. 9) describes the LAD Point System as one example of a competition in which athletes are awarded points for sexual acts with women, for example three points to "slip a finger in on the dance floor" or receive a "BJ [fellatio] in public," or four points to "photobomb with your balls out," with point deductions for preventing others from engaging in sexual acts, such as "minus two points for every time you cock block." Likewise, Lisa Leff (2012) describes "Fantasy Slut Leagues" as another sex competition in sports. In such "leagues," female students are drafted, largely unknown to them, by male athletes. The draft determines a ranking of the women. Points are then awarded to the male athletes "for documented engagement in sexual activities with female students" (para. 4). Other sex competitions among athletes are discussed in the analysis of group sexual assaults in Chapter 3, in which the element of competition in sexual assault in sport becomes even clearer.

Whether sex competitions are formalized with specific rules or integrated into the norms and cultures of particular sports teams, sexual intercourse with women can be a way that male athletes develop, perform, and stabilize masculine dominance among their peers. In a context in which masculinity is highly unstable, sex is used to maintain and assert dominance and control, not only over women but also among male athletes. Women are thus used as objects within a competition of masculinities.

Within the hierarchical structures of competitive men's sport, and hierarchies of masculinities embedded within it, are deeply entrenched misogynistic and sexist attitudes. Women can become the objects of young men's sex competitions and strivings for masculine dominance within their cultural spaces. Nancy Theberge (1981, 342) contends that competitive men's sport is "a fundamentally sexist institution that is male dominated and masculine in orientation." Expanding on this, Mariah Burton Nelson (1994, 88) writes that "nowhere are masculinity and misogyny so entwined as on the rugby field. At the post-game parties that are an integral part of the rugby culture, drunken men sing songs that depict women as loathsome creatures with insatiable sexual appetites and dangerous sexual organs. Men sing of raping other men's girlfriends and mothers. Rape is also depicted as a joke." Underpinning rape culture in competitive men's sport in Canada are misogynistic notions of women as objects without agency who are fundamentally inferior to men.

Competitive men's sport has been described as a "hierarchical male-dominant gender regime" that celebrates sexism, misogyny, homophobia, and violence against women: "Violence and interpersonal domination are valorized. The interactional 'glue' that bonds men in such groups flows from the tradition of eroticized misogyny and homophobia that polices the boundaries of narrow (and often violent) conceptions of masculinity, while putting at risk women" (Messner, Greenberg, and Peretz 2015, 174). The hatred of women and all things coded as feminine in competitive men's sport fuels male athlete—perpetrated violence against women and girls.

In the context of men's junior hockey, many of the misogynistic values and norms that sustain high rates of sexual assault have been codified in what is termed the Junior Hockey Bible (Top Shelf Hockey 2020). This "bible," which in 2020 was publicly accessible online, explicitly describes methods that athletes can use to sexually violate and degrade women. It features misogynistic, homophobic, ableist, and other oppressive and hateful language, and it clearly reflects the normalization, promotion, and celebration of violence against women in Canadian junior men's hockey.

Women with larger bodies are degradingly referred to as "swamp donkeys" or "swampers" within instructions stating that "swampers must be avoided before the consumption of at least 13 beers, and after that precede [sic] with caution and only poke her if you can degrade her in some way in front of the boys, preferably on video camera" (1). Swamp donkeys are later differentiated from "sea donkeys," or simply "donkeys," defined as women who are highly intoxicated and conventionally unattractive. Instructions for encounters with so-called sea donkeys include the following:

> These beasts of the sea are masters at boozing and once intoxicated, are looking to get some hockey cock. They enjoy being told they are fat when you are waxing their fat asses, so don't be afraid to do it. These Donkeys have been known to cost some of the boys an arm and a leg in Kangaroo Court the next day. Once again, only approach after 25 beers and all other options have failed, including the retarded girl with no legs. (Top Shelf Hockey 2020, 2)

"Kangaroo Court" refers to the "law of the dressing room," where players compare their sexual conquests of women and applaud or criticize one another; accordingly, "credit can be given for pretty much anything that degrades the broad in any way. Extra points for anything filmed on camera" (Top Shelf Hockey 2020, 2). When women are not referred to as "donkeys," "swampers," "sluts," "dirties," "broads," "puck sluts," or "ho trains," they are referenced as "victims." For example, the document offers instructions on how to perform what is termed "the tea bag":

> Tends to work best on unsuspecting sluts, but take what you can get. First, simply remove your pants and Gitch [underwear] and carefully survey the scene. At this point, you want to insure [sic] your safety by carefully establishing a platform from which you will lower the goods. Once this is established, make sure a camera is in place to catch you dropping your doggy nuts onto the *victim's* forehead. If possible, deposit nuts in a slut's mouth, but if not, the forehead will suffice. (Top Shelf Hockey 2020, 5; emphasis added)

By clearly inciting violence against women, the writing and dissemination of this "bible" could be considered a hate crime under Canadian criminal law. Although it is not known how widely the Junior Hockey Bible has been and continues to be read within junior hockey in Canada, its very existence

reflects and promotes a dangerous celebration of sexual violence and socializes athletes to disregard and devalue sexual consent. More broadly, the
Junior Hockey Bible is suggestive of serious unaddressed problems of misogyny in men's junior hockey. A recent poll of more than 400 former junior
hockey players, coaches, managers, and referees found that the majority perceived the treatment of women and girls by young male hockey players as
misogynistic (Hernandez 2021). Similarly, an independent panel hired by the
Canadian Hockey League to assess the effectiveness of its well-being programs recently found that there was a "systemic 'culture of embedded behaviours,' where off-ice misconduct is perpetuated, condoned or ill-addressed"
(Turnpenney 2022, 8). In this context where sexual assault is so explicitly celebrated, the high rates of reported sexual assault in competitive men's sport,
and in junior men's hockey specifically, are not surprising.

Confused Conceptions of Consent and Bodily Autonomy

The Junior Hockey Bible is not the only mechanism through which some athletes learn to devalue the consent and bodily autonomy of others. In the total
institution of men's competitive sport, athletes are trained, often in implicit
ways, to understand consent as largely irrelevant (Fogel 2013). If a coach tells a
competitive athlete to tackle an opposing player with as much force as possible, then the athlete is expected to do so. Refusing to do so can result in the
athlete sitting on the bench for the game or being cut from the team. Likewise,
a competitive hockey player cannot say to a player on the opposing team that
he does not consent to be body-checked in a game. When athletes enter competitions, they are expected to move and use their bodies according to their
coaches' orders, regardless of whether their sense of bodily autonomy is violated in the process. Athletes inflict bodily pain and injury on each other
whether or not they consent to such violence. During play, it is commonly
assumed by leagues and legal officials, without foundation, that athletes consent to the violence that they inflict on others and have inflicted on them (Fogel
2013). This understanding of consent in competitive sport is particularly problematic in a context in which sexual activity becomes a competition.

Nearly all of the male athletes reported for the sexual assaults discussed
in this chapter compete in sports that involve physical, aggressive, and often
violent contact with athletes on opposing teams, including football, hockey,
boxing, soccer, and basketball. Although never an excuse for sexual violence,
athletes in high-contact sports can easily lose sight of the value of consent
and the importance of bodily autonomy. As Messner (1992, 151) writes, "the
fact that winning was premised on physical power, strength, discipline, and

willingness to take, ignore, or deaden pain inclined men to experience their own bodies as machines, as instruments of power and domination – and to see other people's bodies as objects of their power and domination." He further suggests that, through participation in competitive contact sports, male athletes can become estranged from their bodies, which become disconnected from their selves. Messner (1992, 121) argues that male athletes commonly develop "an instrumental relationship toward one's body as a 'tool' or even a 'weapon' to be developed and utilized in athletic competition. The ironic result is that athletes often become alienated from their bodies." High-contact sports train athletes to understand their bodies as tools or weapons that can inflict harm and be harmed regardless of consent. This training can have serious repercussions off the field of play. These misconceptions of consent and understandings of bodies as tools or weapons become particularly dangerous in a highly competitive environment in which sex with women becomes part of the competition to climb the masculine hierarchy.

Furthermore, elite male athletes' lived experiences of spending much of their time with teammates, showering communally and sharing hotel room beds on road trips, can confuse conceptions of consent and bodily autonomy. According to a twenty-one-year-old hockey player interviewed by Samantha Samson (2015, paras. 15–16),

> these guys are naked in front of you all the time. The intimacy of sexuality is just gone. You're really comfortable with your sexuality and your behavior, so no one cares. Some guys think it is the same with women. If you see a guy walk up and smack a girl's ass, it's because that's what he does with his buddies and no one cares.

Many competitive male athletes are not socialized to understand their actions as violent, and in fact they are trained to see nonconsensual physical contact as a necessary act for recognition and dominance within the context of their sport. Although this in no way justifies the violence that some male athletes perpetrate against women, it does provide a crucial context for understanding it.

Institutional Tolerance of Sexual Assault in Competitive Men's Sport

As the analyzed cases illustrate, sexual assault perpetrated by male competitive athletes is often met with tolerance both within and outside sport contexts. Within male-dominated total institutions, sexual assaults, and the attitudes, values, and beliefs that support gender-based violence, are tolerated. In his study of societal responses to various potentially deviant behaviours, Robert Stebbins (1996, xi) introduced the concept of "tolerable deviance." For Stebbins, deviance is defined in relation to the moral norms of the community, a conception similar to the one proposed by Émile Durkheim (1968) and also by Kai Erikson (1966). For Durkheim (1968, 80), when the "collective conscience" is morally offended, a community unites, a crime is socially defined, and the society seeks retribution through the punishment of the offender. Through this process, moral boundaries are defined, clarified, and redefined within the community (Erikson 1966). Building upon this notion, Stebbins (1996) explains that tolerable deviance occurs when individuals engage in disdainful and potentially criminal activity but the surrounding community does not deem it offensive or serious enough to appear morally offended. In the context of competitive men's sport, it can be argued that sexual assaults are routinely tolerated by coaches, university administrators, the sports community, and legal officials. Although the act of sexual assault is deemed criminal in law, it is often tolerated, especially when it is perpetrated by white male athletes.

For example, after Mark Yetman was charged with three brutally violent sexual assaults, he was permitted to continue playing hockey, and he helped his team to win a league championship. Over forty community members wrote letters to the sentencing judge encouraging a noncustodial sentence and stating that they knew Yetman to be of great character. Matthew Alan Meyer was recruited to play for the University of Saskatchewan while he awaited trial for sexually assaulting a woman. When CFL player Bernard Williams was arrested for sexual assault, the team president wrote the cheque securing his bail so that he could rejoin his team. Most white-presenting male athletes accused of sexual assault faced little or no repercussions from their teams or leagues, and most of those who did were able to move on to other teams and leagues and continue their playing careers.

The Canadian criminal legal system has also shown significant tolerance of sexual assaults against women. As Melissa Breger (2018) notes, laws and legal systems often reflect the patriarchal cultures within which they are embedded, and this has led to the ongoing legal tolerance of violence against women. Rates of conviction for sexual assault in Canada are lower than for any other form of assault (Rotenberg 2017). These discrepancies have been the subject of decades of critical scholarship on criminal legal responses to sexual assault. Feminist scholars have long argued that deeply held rape myths – such as the myths that "real rapes" are committed by strangers, against sexually chaste women, and involve significant physical injuries – have shaped how police, prosecutors, defence lawyers, and judges respond to reports of sexual assault (Clark and Lewis 1977; E. Craig 2018; Estrich 1986; Gavey 2005; H. Johnson 2012). As Elaine Craig (2018, 1) writes, "imagine a society – one that purports to be a rule of law society – in which one segment of the population [men] regularly engages in harmful acts of sexual violation against another segment of the community [women] with almost complete legal immunity. Canada is such a society." This tolerance of sexual assault appears as likely, if not heightened, when male athletes are on trial, particularly if they are white. For example, in the case of Chance Macdonald, the judge was transparent in his reluctance to give Macdonald a significant prison sentence because of the effect that it could have on his career prospects. The judge, a former hockey player himself, allowed Macdonald to delay serving his sentence until after he completed an internship. Likewise, in the case of *R v DVV*, a high school basketball player who sexually assaulted a seven-year-old sleeping child was given an absolute discharge with no criminal record because the judge believed that he had good character.

The concern that these judges expressed for the athletes' prospects and the confidence that they asserted in the athletes' character are interesting when put alongside their relative disregard for the victims' prospects and well-being. Kate Manne (2020, 5) uses the term *himpathy* to describe "the way powerful and privileged boys and men who commit acts of sexual violence or engage in other misogynistic behavior often receive sympathy and concern over their female victims." Although many of the young men discussed in this chapter arguably occupy subordinate positions in the hierarchy of competitive men's sport, with continuous public valuation of their worth and minimal opportunities to consent to physical harm, they simultaneously occupy a celebrated, privileged social position. Many of these athletes, particularly white male athletes, carry societal privilege that encourages both the criminal legal system and sport organizations to ignore, excuse, and minimize the violence that they are accused of inflicting on girls and women.

As decades of research have shown, the criminal legal system rarely delivers the justice that it promises to sexual assault victims (H. Johnson and Dawson 2011; Martin 2005; Parnis and Du Mont 1999; A. Quinlan 2017). The cases in this chapter suggest that this is particularly true in sexual assault cases involving competitive male athletes, especially those with racial and class privilege, who are commonly celebrated as "sport heroes" in their communities. Decades of legal reforms have not altered these trends (H. Johnson 2012; Osborne 1984; Page 2010; Sheehy 1999). History suggests that the solution to the tolerance of sexual assaults by male athletes is not further legal reforms or tougher criminal laws and punishments, all of which have proven to be largely ineffective in addressing gender-based violence (Goodmark 2018; Whynacht 2021). Indeed, even in the few cases discussed in this chapter in which athletes were in fact convicted and incarcerated for sexual assaults, for many of them, reports of their violence continued after they were released. Conviction and incarceration of a few individuals clearly do little to disrupt patterns of sexual aggression and violence, not only for those individuals but also within competitive men's sport more broadly.

Relying on the criminal legal system – which both reflects and promotes the racism, sexism, and other forms of inequality and discrimination found in Canadian society – to solve the problem of sexual violence is untenable. Sexual assault in sport is a multifaceted problem fuelled by many unique and complex social dynamics and institutional factors that demands a multifaceted solution that extends beyond both sport organizations and the criminal justice system, a subject that we take up in the concluding chapter of this book.

Tolerance of sexual assaults perpetrated by male athletes in competitive men's sport is a central component of rape culture in sport. In a context in which sexual assault can be used as a tool for accomplishing masculinity and gaining masculine status, sexual assault in competitive men's sport seemingly can become normalized. Compounding this problem, young men in competitive sport accused of sexual assaults are often encircled by what Kimmel (2018, 6) refers to as "a culture of silence and a culture of support." As we have shown in this chapter, accusations of sexual assault are often silenced or minimized by coaches, teams, leagues, and in many cases the Canadian criminal legal system.

Not all competitive male athletes in Canada are perpetrators of sexual assaults. However, various factors in competitive sport coalesce to create a high-risk environment for the perpetration and tolerance of sexual assault. This environment is characterized by intersections of developing, violent masculinities with a highly competitive and structurally misogynistic hierarchy that places value on sexually aggressive definitions of manhood and the tolerance and promotion of violence, including sexual violence.

Sexual assault in sport is supported and promoted by a rape culture that is intricately woven into the fabric of sport institutions. This rape culture is reflected in and maintained by not only sexual assaults by individual male athletes but also, as we explore in the following chapters, other forms of sexual assault in sport.

3

Group Sexual Assault
A Theatre for Performing Violent Masculinities

On March 7, 2015, ten players from the Cobourg Cougars, a junior hockey team in Ontario, attended a house party dubbed the "Cobourg Cougars Classic" (Quigley 2015). The party was later featured on social media, with a photo of a large trophy and a statement that read "whoever hooked up with the most broads last night gets the cup #consentisoverrated" (Longwell 2015, para. 7). In the days that followed, four young women reported that they were sexually assaulted at the party (QMI Agency 2015). One young woman who attended the party disclosed that she saw a hockey player with "a large zip-lock bag one-quarter filled with white pills" who was laughing and saying that "tonight's going to be a good night," and another said that there was going to be a "rape fest" (quoted in Robinson 2016, para. 10).

The young woman reported that her memory of some of the events at the party was foggy even though she consumed only two drinks while there, which suggested to her that she had been drugged. She was able to describe her memory of being alone in a room with two hockey players who pushed a dresser in front of a door to barricade her in and then kissed her, touched her, and took off her clothes without her consent. In an interview later, she stated that "I was saying 'no' the whole time – I know it – and after they moved the dresser, I was freaking. They're so much taller than me" (quoted in Robinson 2016, para. 12). She recalled eventually escaping from the room and calling her mother but was unable to fully remember what the players did to her. She did report, however, that none of it was consensual.

At the time of the report, the Cobourg Cougars were in the second round of playoffs. With multiple players facing police investigations of the sexual assault allegations arising from the party, the team continued playing without suspending any of the players. No names of the players accused of sexual assault have been publicly released, and the team has continued to refute that the original social media post was written by members of the team. After a police investigation of the sexual assault reports and subsequent social media post, the Crown Attorney's Office determined that there was insufficient evidence to lead to any conviction and did not criminally charge any of the hockey players involved in the alleged sexual assaults (McEwan 2015).

Although specific details of what occurred at the Cobourg Cougars hockey team party are scarce in public reports, the few reported details – including sex competitions, stated intentions to ignore consent, use of date rape drugs, sexual assaults, forcible confinement of an intoxicated woman, and gang rape – are disturbing. The Cobourg Cougars party was not an isolated incident. There have been many similar reports and criminal cases involving groups of Canadian male athletes accused of sexual assault, the vast majority of whom were male hockey and football players. Of the hundred athletes involved in reported cases of sexual assault against women and girls examined in this book, at least seventy reportedly committed sexual assaults with other athletes in what is commonly termed a *gang rape* or *group sexual assault*.

In this chapter, we examine group sexual assaults by male athletes against women and girls. We look specifically at twenty-two cases of multiple-athlete sexual assault between 1990 and 2020 involving at least seventy male athletes. Like sexual assault cases involving individual male athletes, these cases of group sexual assault reveal how the Canadian criminal legal system and sport organizations commonly minimize, excuse, and tolerate this form of violence in sport. We use these twenty-two cases to provide a foundation for a broader discussion on not only why group sexual assault occurs but also why it appears to be so common in competitive men's sport in Canada.

Group Sexual Assault and Canadian Law

Group sexual assault involves multiple sexually violent perpetrators in a single incident. Although the term *gang rape* has been used by some scholars (Ullman 1999), we have opted not to use it because it fails to capture the diverse forms of sexual aggression that can occur in groups. The term *gang rape* also no longer aligns with terminology used in Canadian law. In Canadian law, rape historically denoted vaginal penetration; however, since the sexual assault law reforms in Canada in 1983, rape is no longer a distinct offence included in the Criminal Code of Canada. The term *gang* was also removed from the Criminal Code in 2001 and replaced with the term *criminal organization* to describe an offence involving three or more people whose main purpose is to commit serious criminal offences resulting in material or financial benefits to persons in the group. The term *group sexual assault* is more inclusive. As we have discussed, in Canadian law, the term *sexual assault* refers to "an assault committed in circumstances of a sexual nature such that the sexual integrity of the victim is violated."[1] This broad definition includes all nonconsensual fondling, kissing, sexual grabbing or touching, or rape. Although *group* is not a legal term in Canada, it commonly denotes two or more individuals assembled with a unifying relationship.

Although the term *group sexual assault* has no specific relevance to substantive law in Canada, sexual assaults involving multiple accused are treated differently from individual sexual assaults in Canadian procedural law. In cases of group sexual assault, the accused can be tried together by the prosecution and a single judge; however, each of the accused is typically represented by a defence lawyer. Although a single trial can save the victim from testifying in separate court hearings, as well as reduce the strain on court resources by minimizing the number of trials, it creates a clear power differential between the victim and multiple accused perpetrators. In these cases, there is often more testimonial evidence in favour of the defendants, which can increase the likelihood of an unsuccessful prosecution in the absence of other corroborating evidence. This trend is apparent in the cases explored in this chapter. Of the seventy Canadian athletes reported for group sexual assaults, only one led to a conviction, which was overturned on appeal, resulting in a conviction rate of 0 percent in the cases analyzed.[2]

Existing research on group sexual assaults outside sport suggests that, though these acts are less frequent, they are commonly more physically violent than a sexual assault involving a single perpetrator (Gidycz and Koss 1990; Holmstrom and Burgess 1980). Reflecting this trend, previous research suggests that group sexual assaults increase the likelihood that a victim will require crisis and suicide prevention services after the attack (Gidycz and Koss 1990). Group sexual assaults also appear to be far less common than individual sexual assaults. An early study of campus sexual violence (O'Sullivan 1991) reported that between 1 and 2 percent of sexual assaults on university campuses involved multiple perpetrators, with the majority perpetrated by male fraternity members or student athletes.

To date, no comprehensive study of group sexual assault in sport has been done in Canada or internationally. Existing statistics on male athlete–perpetrated sexual violence described in the previous chapter likely include some group sexual assaults; however, available statistics do not differentiate between individual and group sexual assaults. Although group and individual forms of sexual assault share obvious similarities, there are also important distinctions between them. The lack of existing research on this unique form of sexual assault in sport has limited broader discussions and understandings of sexual assault in Canadian sport. A detailed examination of group sexual assaults in Canadian sport, and how sport organizations and the criminal legal system have responded, is thus needed. By revealing how and why group sexual assaults occur in the context of sport, and how institutions have responded to this form of violence, a deeper understanding of the root causes of sexual assault in sport becomes possible.

Reports of Athlete-Perpetrated Group Sexual Assault

The twenty-two reports of male athlete–perpetrated group sexual assault in Canada examined in this chapter appeared in Canadian news media and/or legal case files between 1990 and 2020. What follows is by no means an exhaustive summary of all group sexual assaults that have been reported in Canadian sport. We focus in this chapter on cases of group sexual assault perpetrated by athletes against individuals who were not team members. In the twenty-two cases analyzed, all of the reported victims were identified as women and girls, and all of the alleged perpetrators as male athletes in hockey or football. Although hockey and football are not our intended focus in this chapter, they were the only sports that appeared in cases matching our study inclusion criteria.[3] In Chapter 4, we build upon this analysis by examining cases of hazing, another common form of group sexual assault in Canadian sport, involving male athletes who sexually assault their male teammates during sexually violent hazing rituals.

These cases illustrate common themes of athlete performances of aggressive and violent masculinities, league and legal tolerance of group sexual violence, and the significant role played by drugs and alcohol in group sexual assaults. The cases also demonstrate notable trends of reported sexual assault across playing levels of men's sport. Whereas individual athlete–perpetrated sexual assaults against women and girls have similar reporting rates across junior, university, and professional playing levels, as shown in the previous chapter, group sexual assaults involving younger athletes at junior and university levels are more frequently reported.

Junior Sport

In 1989, Brian Sakic and Wade Smith, who played for the Swift Current Broncos in the Western Hockey League, were charged with sexual assault. According to reports, they invited a young woman who had a diagnosed learning disability to one of their houses to watch television, and there they sexually assaulted her (Robinson 2000). Reports suggested that the physical trauma of the sexual acts caused the woman to bleed for two and a half days (S. White 2018). The young woman detailed the encounter to her friend, disclosing that the sexual acts were nonconsensual and that she was contemplating suicide because of the trauma she endured (S. White 2018). Her friend encouraged her to report the sexual assaults to the police. Sakic and Smith admitted to the sexual acts that the young woman described but claimed that they were consensual. The police charged the young woman with public mischief for allegedly falsely reporting a sexual assault (Robinson 2005). Criminal charges against Sakic and Smith were stayed and then dropped. The judge in the public mischief trial found the young woman not guilty and described the actions of Sakic and Smith, though they were never convicted, as "degrading and disgusting" and that "they ravaged her body for their own sexual gratification" (quoted in Robinson 2000, para. 4). After the reported assault, the two athletes were traded to another team, where their hockey careers continued successfully. No disciplinary measures or repercussions for either player for their reported sexual misconduct have been publicly documented.

On March 13, 1992, players from the Guelph Storm hockey team organized a house party at a billeted player's house to celebrate the end of the junior hockey season. A sixteen-year-old young woman later reported to police that she was sexually assaulted by a number of the players on the team (*Province* 1992). Two players, Michael Cote and Kevin Reid, were taken into custody and charged with sexual assault. Drawing from first-person accounts, Robinson (1998, 101–2) provided a detailed description of the reported sexual assault against the young woman, who fell asleep at the party:

> She woke up when she felt someone undoing her pants, told whoever it was to stop, and pushed an arm away. By this time the lights were off and she couldn't see who it was, but someone told her to go back to sleep. As she did her pants up, she felt someone trying to undo them again. Her eyes were getting used to the dark, and she could see there was a player on either side of her and a third was at the foot of the bed. Her clothes were removed, and

sexual intercourse occurred between [her] and the three players. Sometimes there were two of them trying to put their genitals in her mouth while
she was being penetrated vaginally. When it was over, [she] says she gath-
ered her clothes, got dressed, and rolled over and lay crying on the sofa-
bed. After this, someone went upstairs and returned with a can of whipped
cream. [Her] pants were down again, one player penetrated her, and another
sprayed his genitals with whipped cream and pushed them in her face ...
[She] maintains that none of the sex was consensual, and that she struggled
and cried and told them to stop.

Like Sakic and Smith, the accused athletes agreed that the reported events
took place at the party, but they claimed that the sex with the sleeping
woman was consensual, even though it is not possible to provide consent
while sleeping. However, before the trial was about to commence, charges
were dropped against both players (*Province* 1992). No team or league disciplinary measures against the two players for their involvement in an alleged
group sexual assault have been reported. The team's general manager at the
time, Mike Kelly, chalked the events at the house party up to "hormones"
and publicly stated that "skates and skirts don't mix" (quoted in Robinson
1998, 107), as if to suggest that sexual assault is purely the result of male
biology – a claim that has been thoroughly critiqued and debunked – and
that women do not play hockey.

In 1994 in Quebec, three hockey players, André Dumais, Joel Roy, and
Benoit Huet, were on trial for an alleged sexual assault of a young woman in
her teens. Although details of the group sexual assault have not been made
public (Baker 1994), reports suggest that the full trial was heard, including
the admission of evidence and testimonies. However, at the conclusion of
the proceedings, the trial judge, Raymonde Verreault, declined to render
a verdict because of an ongoing controversy over a previous decision.[4] In
a previous sexual assault trial, Verreault gave what many perceived as a
lenient sentence to a man found guilty of sexually assaulting his stepdaugh-
ter. In that case, Verreault stated that the mitigating factor for the leniency
was that the accused "spared the girl's virginity" (cited in Baker 1994). Amid
the controversy that followed this statement, Verreault voluntarily stopped
rendering decisions and sentences in sexual assault trials, including those
that were in progress or had been concluded, which included the trial of the
three hockey players.[5] As a result, a new trial for the athletes was ordered.
The woman informed the prosecution that she could not go through with
another trial, particularly so soon after the first one. Charges against the

players were then dropped (Baker 1994). No disciplinary measures against the three hockey players for their involvement in the alleged group sexual assault against the young woman have been reported.

Also in 1994, Ed Jovanovski was selected by the Florida Panthers with the number one overall pick in the NHL draft (*Spokesman-Review* 1995b). The following February, while finishing up his junior playing career with the Windsor Spitfires, Jovanovski and teammates Bill Bowler and Corey Evans were charged with sexual assault against a twenty-four-year-old woman (Murray 1995b). The players met the woman at a Windsor bar and went back to her apartment, where reportedly they sexually assaulted her. The players insisted that the sexual activity was consensual. At the hearing to schedule the trial, charges were unexpectedly dropped (Murray 1995c). The prosecuting attorney concluded that there was not enough evidence to secure a conviction (*Spokesman-Review* 1995a). No disciplinary measures against the players related to the alleged group sexual assault were reported. While the investigation was under way, Jovanovski signed a $5.7 million contract with the Panthers, which included unique provisions to accommodate a possible delayed start in case he was found guilty at trial and incarcerated. After the charges were dropped, the Panthers team president stated that "Ed said all along he was innocent and the facts have proven that out" (quoted in Murray 1995b, para. 10). Being innocent and having charges dropped because of insufficient evidence are not, of course, synonymous. This fact was obscured, however, in the team's public communications about the reported group sexual assault.

In 1995 in Saskatchewan, a fifteen-year-old young Indigenous woman at a Saskatoon high school reported that five unnamed players from the Saskatoon Blades junior hockey team sexually assaulted her (Robinson 2011a). The reported assault occurred at a house party where the victim reportedly became intoxicated and passed out on a floor. While in and out of consciousness, she recalled five players sexually assaulting her (Robinson 1998). The Saskatoon police, two of whom were assistant coaches on the Blades team, were reportedly dismissive of the victim (Robinson 2011b). A victim advocate from the Saskatoon Sexual Assault Centre who accompanied the young woman to the police station to report the group sexual assault explained, "they wouldn't let me be there with her, but we could hear what the staff sergeant was saying. He kept telling her, 'You're lying, you're lying. Tell the truth. Your story doesn't match the hockey players' stories.' He was abusive to her" (quoted in Robinson 1998, 139). No charges were ever filed against the five unnamed players. Reports indicate that the young woman transferred high schools before eventually leaving Saskatoon because of the public ridicule she received for accusing the players of sexual assault (Robinson 1998). The players were not disciplined for their reported involvement in the alleged group sexual assault. When asked about the case by members of the media, league commissioner Ed Chynoweth was quoted as saying that "certainly if the reports I'm getting [are true], this wasn't her first time in the kip" (quoted in Dambrofsky 1995, G2), a comment that clearly invoked racist stereotypes of Indigenous women as promiscuous and misogynist assumptions that sexually active women are to blame for the sexual assaults that they experience.[6]

Two members of the Antigonish Bulldogs junior hockey team in Nova Scotia, Michael Stalk and Graham MacIsaac, were accused of sexually assaulting a woman on two separate occasions in 1999 (*National Post* 1999). Minimal details of the case have been publicly released. Although they were initially charged, the charges were dropped against both hockey players before their trials were set to commence (*Charlottetown Guardian* 2000). No disciplinary action by their team or league in the aftermath of the incidents was reported.

In 2000, three junior hockey players for the Barrie Colts – Michael D'Alessandro, Aaron Power, and Nicholas Robinson – were charged with sexually assaulting a sixteen-year-old young woman at a Barrie residence (McLaughlin 2000). After they were charged, they continued to play for the Colts, seemingly without any negative repercussions or disciplinary actions for their reported involvement in the alleged group sexual assault. Justifying the league's lack of response to the charges, the Ontario Hockey League (OHL) commissioner, David Branch, said that "it would be inappropriate for the league to consider any action at this point against the three players" (quoted in Koshan 2000, para. 8). In public statements, the team appeared to be most concerned about how the charges of sexual assault would affect the athletes' capacity to perform on the ice. The managing director of the Colts, James Massie, expressed concerns that the charges were stressful to the players, negatively affected their play, and could lower their rankings in the NHL draft. He stated that "there is no question about it. Aaron's play went downward since the charges were laid and he should have been a high draft choice. How do you reverse that damage?" (quoted in McLaughlin 2000, para. 18). After pretrial hearings were set to begin, charges against all three players were dropped by the prosecution (*CBC Sports* 2000). As in previous cases, team officials and their lawyers were quick to proclaim the athletes' innocence. A detective with the Barrie Police, Bryan Shultz, uncharacteristically

made a public statement expressing disappointment and surprise at the prosecutor's decision to drop the charges: "We believed there was sufficient evidence to lay charges. We can't say why the Crown attorney's office has chosen
not to proceed" (quoted in McLaughlin 2000, para. 20).

In contrast to many of the cases discussed thus far, a report in 2006 of
a sexual assault by junior hockey players in Ontario did lead to a criminal
trial. Two players, Justin Richardson and Nathan Murray, on an unnamed
junior hockey team, were accused of sexually violating an intoxicated
woman at a party after a hockey game. The woman reported that she was
sexually violated with a beer bottle without her consent by Richardson and
that Murray committed other nonconsensual sexual acts on her.[7] Richardson was charged with sexual assault and sexual assault with a weapon,
whereas Murray was not charged with any offence. At the trial, Murray
testified as a witness, reporting that after the incident their coach called a
team meeting and instructed the players to lie to police about the use of a
beer bottle. Other players testified that they did not see a beer bottle and
that their coach did not instruct them to lie about it.[8] As a result of the
contradictions among the testimony of the teammates, the accused, and
the complainant, Richardson was found not guilty. Providing his rationale,
the judge stated that, "in the end, I could not conclude that I was certain
that Justin Richardson had committed the offence. A wise old judge once
told me that if at the end of the day you go home and say to yourself 'I don't
know' – that is what is called a reasonable doubt."[9] There are no reports of
the two players being disciplined by their team or league for their alleged
involvement in a group sexual assault.

In mid-October 2006, a female student at the University of Victoria
reported that she was sexually assaulted by hockey players on the Victoria
Salmon Kings, a junior hockey team (Epp 2006). The woman met one of the
players at a local bar before going back to his hotel room. Other members
of the team reportedly threw her clothing outside and barricaded the door
so that she could not escape (Robinson 2006). No details have been released
on what occurred in the hotel room, nor has the exact number of players involved been reported. After an investigation, prosecutors in British
Columbia decided that no charges would be laid against any of the unnamed
hockey players since it was assumed that there was a limited chance the case
would result in convictions (*Ottawa Citizen* 2007). Victoria police suggested
that the case was difficult to investigate since "the witnesses are all members
of the hockey team" (cited in Robinson 2006). The unnamed players involved
in the investigation continued to play, and at no point were any disciplinary

actions by team or league officials reported. The team president, Dave Dakers, stated that, "if we were scratching somebody because of this, I think we would be telling people. In the event that some player becomes ineligible to play because of their actions as individuals, we're not going to try to hide it" (quoted in Shaw 2006).

Also in 2006, four players for the Joliette L'Action hockey team were arrested following two women's reports of sexual assault (*National Post* 2006). The arrests stemmed from a hockey party, believed to be part of a "rookie night" for new players, at which video evidence revealed "highly degrading sexual acts, binge drinking, and the use of feces" (*CBC News* 2006, para. 3). Reportedly, while one of the hockey players had sex with a young woman, other players video-recorded the act without her knowledge or consent and later distributed the video in their dressing room. Another seventeen-year-old young woman who attended the party also reported that she was sexually assaulted (Block 2006). Two of the unnamed players were charged with voyeurism, and a third was charged with sexual assault (Marowits 2006). There are no public reports of the players going to trial or entering plea deals, which suggests that the charges were likely dropped. There are also no reports of the players being disciplined for their reported involvement in a hazing party, secretly recording a young woman having sex without her consent, or reportedly perpetrating a sexual assault.

In the days before the Sault Ste Marie Greyhounds junior hockey team was about to open the 2012 training camp, three players – Nick Cousins, Andrew Fritsch, and Mark Petaccio – were charged with sexually assaulting a woman at a party at a player's house (Ruicci 2012). The team's general manager at the time, who is now president of hockey operations for the Pittsburgh Penguins, Kyle Dubas, responded to the charges against the three players by stating that "this is so far beyond a hockey situation ... We'll continue to perform our duty and support these players" (quoted in Ruicci 2012, para. 4). The team provided wellness counselling services to the players to help them deal with the presumed stress of the sexual assault charges and to better prepare them for spectators' responses at games in different cities (Smiley 2013). Describing the support that he received from the team and Dubas in particular, one of the criminally charged players, Andrew Fritsch, stated that "I honestly can't thank them enough for what they did for me ... It was just amazing what they did, especially Kyle Dubas. He took me into his home and helped me through it. I can't say enough about him and the organization" (quoted in Smiley 2013, paras. 8–9). There are no reports of any support services that the team provided to the reported victim of the group sexual assault. Charges against all three players were eventually dropped in exchange for the players meeting specific conditions, which included not communicating with the woman who reported the sexual assault or coming within 500 metres of her home, place of work, or school (Isaac 2013). Within less than an hour of the decision, one of the players, Nick Cousins, was contacted by an NHL team, the Philadelphia Flyers, with an offer to sign him to play for its American Hockey League (AHL) affiliate team, the Adirondack Phantoms (*Belleville Intelligencer* 2013). None of the players received disciplinary actions for their reported involvement in a group sexual assault.

In 2014, police in Quebec conducted investigations of two separate reports of sexual misconduct by multiple members of the Gatineau Olympiques junior hockey team. The first report, in February, detailed an incident in which at least six unidentified players from the team barricaded themselves in a Boston Pizza bathroom with an intoxicated woman. A waiter at the restaurant noticed a player outside the bathroom watching the door and ordered him to move and the players and woman to leave the bathroom (Seymour 2015). While exiting the bathroom, at least two of the hockey players were seen pulling up their pants (Muir 2015). While police were investigating the Boston Pizza incident, police in Quebec City received another report of sexual misconduct by players on the Gatineau Olympiques team from an incident in January. A woman reported that she was sexually assaulted by team players at a Quebec City hotel (Hempstead 2015a). In both incidents, police declined to press charges against any of the players, a move that they refused to explain publicly. A police investigator stated to the media that "we won't comment as to why we won't lay charges" (quoted in Hempstead 2015b, para. 9). No disciplinary action by the team or league for either incident has been reported. Media reports indicate that at least some of unnamed players involved continued to play during the investigations.

In 2015, as discussed at the opening of this chapter, members of the Cobourg Cougars junior hockey team were involved in a reported incident of sexual misconduct at a house party involving at least ten members of the team. Minimal details of the party have been released publicly. However, what is known is that after the party, four women reported sexual assaults to police (Larocque 2015). One of the victims provided some details to the media of what occurred, indicating that she believed she was drugged, forcibly confined, and sexually assaulted by two unnamed hockey players (Robinson 2016). At the time of the allegations, the Cougars were in the second round of playoffs and continued to play without any suspension of or disciplinary action against any of the players reportedly involved. After police investigated the reported sexual assault, the Office of the Crown Attorney determined that there was insufficient evidence to lead to a likely conviction and therefore declined to criminally charge any of the hockey players involved in the alleged sexual assaults (McEwan 2015).

In 2016, a youth football team in Manitoba, the Interlake Thunder Football Club, filed a formal complaint with Football Manitoba after two female players on the team were reportedly sexually harassed and assaulted by boys on an opposing team, the Falcons Football Club, after a game (Caruk 2016).[10] One of the female players also filed a police report of sexual assault with the Royal Canadian Mounted Police (RCMP), which initiated a criminal investigation (Crabb 2016). Media reports suggest that the game between the two teams was heated, with sexist and racist banter and multiple penalties because of rough play, which resulted in one player being taken away by ambulance (Caruk 2016). After the game, while one of the young female players was putting away equipment in the team's storage facility, a group of male players from the Falcons reportedly cornered and sexually harassed her. When a female teammate tried to intervene, reports suggest that the harassment escalated, and the male players began grabbing and groping the young woman (Prest 2016). Male players from the Interlake team overheard the commotion and chased away the players from the Falcons. The alleged assailants still had their football uniforms on, so the young women were able to identify them by their jersey numbers. The coaches of both teams were suspended for failing to control their players during the game, and two players were suspended for rough play (Crabb 2016). None of the suspensions, however, appeared to be connected to the reports of sexual harassment and sexual assault that arose from acts after the game. According to one report, Football Manitoba did not initially investigate the complaint because it believed that the RCMP were handling it (Prest 2016). Three weeks after the incident, the two teams played again. Public records suggest that the only step that the team took in response to the reported sexual harassment and sexual assault was to limit the playing time of the two young women, presumably to reduce the likelihood that they would face further abuse by players for the Falcons (Caruk 2016). The RCMP did not charge any of the male players involved in the incident. Likewise, no players were suspended or disciplined by Football Manitoba for their actions after the game. However, in a relatively rare move for a sport organization, several months after the formal complaint, Football Manitoba issued letters of apology to the two young women. The apology acknowledged what happened, stated that the organization did not condone such behaviour, and admitted that it failed to respond appropriately to their complaints (Canadian Press 2017b).

Also in 2016, four unnamed Niagara Region high school football players were charged with sexually assaulting a teenaged young woman following an alcohol-fuelled house party in St. Catharines (Grillo 2018). The accused were sixteen and seventeen at the time of their arrests and as such have not been named under provisions of the Youth Criminal Justice Act.[11] According to reports, at the end of the party, the victim entered a car with three football players in the back seat and two football players in the front seat, and she requested a ride to her boyfriend's house. She testified that she was intoxicated and passed in and out of consciousness in the back seat of the car.[12] She reported that, during the ride and while stopped in a school parking lot, the football players sexually assaulted her. The players did not deny engaging in sexual acts with the young woman but argued that she had consented. The fourteen-day trial revolved around the issue of consent and whether the young woman could give consent while intoxicated. The complainant's testimony lasted four days. Describing the testimony, the presiding judge stated that "I do not believe the complainant has anything for which to blame herself. She has her recollection of how things played out, and her memory may well be the true narrative. She came forward with courage and ran the gauntlet of a criminal trial with dignity" (quoted in Sawchuk 2018, para. 6). Ultimately, however, the judge rendered a not guilty verdict indicating that the Crown failed to prove its case beyond a reasonable doubt. The judge stated that "the standard of proof I must apply, as a judge in a criminal trial, is an extremely exacting one. Any belief I, or anyone else, have may very well be true, or may very well be likely, or even highly likely – but that is not the test" (quoted in Sawchuk 2018, para. 7). No disciplinary actions by the team or high school football league have been reported.

These reported cases of group sexual assaults involving junior-level athletes illustrate how sport organizations commonly ignore reports of sexual assault and how the criminal legal system routinely dismisses them. Most cases did not result in criminal charges, and of those that did, the majority were subsequently dropped on the belief that there was insufficient evidence for convictions. Of the few cases that resulted in criminal trials, all concluded with acquittals after the accused argued that the sexual activity was consensual. Although some might suggest that these outcomes simply reflect the athletes' innocence, the regularity with which reports of group sexual assault by male athletes are dismissed by police, prosecutors, and sport organizations across three decades in Canada, as evident in the cases described, suggests that something else is at play.

Similar to the cases involving individual male athletes discussed in the previous chapter, all of the athletes publicly named in the cases discussed in this chapter present as white.[13] As white-presenting young men, the accused were already statistically less likely to be convicted and incarcerated than Black people, Indigenous people, or people of colour in Canada for any crime of which they were accused (Department of Justice 2019a; Neugebauer 2000; Owusu-Bempah et al. 2021; Owusu-Bempah and Wortley 2013).[14] Compounding these effects, some of the athletes benefited directly from the explicit forms of institutional discrimination and racism that the young women whom they were accused of victimizing experienced, such as the young Indigenous woman who reported being sexually assaulted by junior hockey players on the Saskatoon Blades and who was doubted by police and labelled as sexually promiscuous by the league commissioner. Existing research shows that police are more likely to dismiss and doubt reports of sexual assault compared with any other crime (Crew 2012), particularly when a sexual assault complainant is Indigenous, a woman of colour, disabled, poor, and/or from any other marginalized group (Du Mont, Miller, and Myhr 2003; A. Quinlan 2016; Tasca et al. 2012), as was the case in some of the reports discussed in this chapter.[15] In addition to racial privilege, the accused also carried a degree of privilege as athletes, as demonstrated by the level of support that many of them received from their leagues and team managers. These cases also reflect broader trends in the criminal legal system. Sexual assault charges, compared with other violent crimes, are more likely to be dropped before a case proceeds to trial and less likely to result in a conviction (Rotenberg 2017). Given these trends alongside athletes' relative privilege, it is not surprising that so many of these cases resulted in dropped charges and acquittals.

The criminal legal system (non)response was in many cases mirrored by sport leagues and team managers who invoked no disciplinary measures, mandatory education programs, or forms of accountability for the athletes accused of violence, except in the case of Football Manitoba, which issued a rare apology to the victims. And, like the junior-level athletes discussed in the previous chapter, many of the athletes in these cases enjoyed significant mobility across teams and leagues following reports, charges, and trials of sexual assault. Taken together, these cases suggest that reports of group sexual assault by junior-level athletes are often quickly forgotten. These trends are visible at other playing levels as well.

University Sport

Compared with junior hockey and football, there were far fewer publicly documented reports of group sexual assault perpetrated by male university athletes against young women. Not only were there fewer cases overall, but also the cases that do exist on the public record seemingly involved fewer male athletes; whereas the cases with junior-level athletes involved up to ten per case, cases with university athletes involved only two to three per case. Similar to cases at the junior playing level, no criminal convictions were rendered in reported cases involving university athletes. However, marking a distinct difference from all others in this chapter, the athletes in one case were formally disciplined by their university, a single exception that does little to counter the broader trend of institutional tolerance of group sexual assault in sport.

In the summer of 1991, Brian Wiseman of the University of Michigan Wolverines hockey team, along with a friend, Cory Beausejour, with whom he had played youth hockey, were accused of sexually assaulting a fifteen-year-old young woman at a house party (Hirsley 1996). Canadian courts placed a publication ban[16] on details of the alleged sexual assault (Nash 1994), Wiseman and Beausejour faced a trial by jury, and after several hours of jury deliberations they were found not guilty (Currie 1996). On hearing the verdict, reports indicate that the victim fell to the floor crying. She filed a $1 million lawsuit against the two young men; no details of the outcome of this lawsuit have been publicly reported (Currie 1996). Before the criminal trial commenced, a University of Michigan spokesperson released a statement that the university "ha[s] confidence in Brian" (Nash 1994, para. 7). Wiseman went on to play professionally in multiple leagues, returned to coach at the University of Michigan, and was an assistant coach of the Edmonton Oilers in the NHL at the time of this writing. No team or league disciplinary actions have been reported against either of the men for their reported involvement in the group sexual assault.

On September 10, 2011, an eighteen-year-old Concordia University student reported that several members of the McGill University Redmen football team drugged, confined, and sexually assaulted her. Reports suggest that the young woman and her friend met the football players at a Montreal bar and went back to the residence of the players, where she was offered an open beer, which she reported was drugged. She recalled waking up on a bed while several of the players were sexually assaulting her. She also remembered waking up in the morning, when the players threw her clothes at her and told her to leave because they had a practice to attend (Fazioli 2014). After an investigation by Montreal police, three players were charged with sexual assault, and two of the players were charged with forcible confinement (Shields 2013). Despite these charges, the athletes remained enrolled at McGill University and continued playing for the football team. Julie Michaud, of the Centre for Gender Advocacy at Concordia University, later lamented this decision by McGill University: "This incident happened a long time ago, McGill has known about it for a long time, and there was absolutely no consequence to the people who have been accused of a really serious crime" (quoted in Shields 2013, para. 2). In the fall of 2013, over two years after the alleged sexual assault, the three accused players voluntarily quit the team. In the fall of 2014, all charges against them were dropped just before their trial was scheduled to begin (Montgomery 2014). According to one of the player's lawyers, the charges were dropped because of insufficient evidence (Bachelder 2014). The victim of the football players' alleged group assault has reported that she remains traumatized by her experiences that night as well as by the pre-empted trial (Fazioli 2014).

In 2014, two players from the University of Ottawa Gee-Gees men's hockey team, Guillaume Donovan and David Foucher, were charged with sexual assault of a Thunder Bay woman with whom they connected through an online dating app, though reports suggest that more players were involved. According to the university, "at least three University of Ottawa men's hockey players had sex with a woman in Thunder Bay, Ont., while some other team members 'in various states of undress' and drunkenness heard it, watched or sometimes took part" (*CBC News* 2016b, para. 2). The Gee-Gees coach, Real Paiement, was reportedly aware of the incident and chose not to report it to university officials or the police.[17] The coach was fired, and the Gee-Gees hockey team was suspended indefinitely (Andrew-Gee and Armstrong 2014). These disciplinary sanctions against the players, team, and coach were the first such sanctions reported in Canada for a sexual assault of a female victim by a group of athletes. The suspension was met with much public criticism, and players from the team filed a $6 million lawsuit against the university for damage to their reputations (Pringle 2020). The university settled the class-action lawsuit with the players for $350,000 (*CBC News* 2020). After a ten-day trial, in which the accused players, teammates, and dismissed coach gave their versions of events, Donovan and Foucher were found not guilty, having argued that the sexual activity was consensual. According to the judge, "Donovan and Foucher were by no means gentlemen the night of the alleged assault and … there was a high level of intoxication, but [there is] no reason to question their testimony during which they said the woman consented" (paraphrased in Diaczuk 2018, para. 5).

In November 2017, two players with the St. Francis Xavier X-Men's football team, Jonah Williams and Tyler Ball, were charged with sexually assaulting a first-year student who played on the women's soccer team (Beswick 2019b). The athletes attended a university-sponsored wine mixer at which they dressed in formal attire and consumed wine (Lowthers 2019b). At one point during the party, the first-year student went to Williams's dorm room and reportedly engaged in consensual sexual activity.[18] Williams testified that during the consensual sexual encounter he asked her if she wanted to have a threesome, and according to him she responded in the affirmative. The young woman testified that he never asked for her consent to the threesome, and therefore she never gave it. She reported that Williams, along with Ball, whom she had never met before, sexually assaulted her. She testified that she said "no" and "you're hurting me," and that she physically resisted. The complainant recalled feeling "excruciating pain," and "being frozen in fear," but could not recall how long the sexual assault lasted.[19] She did remember that it ended when her roommate, another member of the women's soccer team, banged on the door, prompting Williams and Ball to stop and get dressed. Two days later she was examined by a sexual assault nurse, who documented bruising on both of her hips. Williams testified that he was responsible for the bruising but that it occurred during consensual sex.[20] Jonah Williams and Tyler Ball were found not guilty. Their names were, however, removed, from the X-Men's online football roster, and both left the university (Beswick 2019a). It was not publicly reported whether this was a disciplinary measure or whether the student athletes left the team and university voluntarily.

Reported cases of group sexual assault involving male university athletes and reported cases involving junior-level athletes reflect similar trends in criminal legal system outcomes. In most of these cases, charges were dropped before trials, or nonguilty verdicts were rendered at trials. Again, many of the athletes involved in these cases present as white, and these outcomes are thus shaped by particular racialized dynamics in the legal response. Interestingly, however, the case involving athletes at the University of Ottawa in 2015 featured a distinctly different response from the team's administration. Instead of publicly ignoring the sexual assault reports, as many other sport organizations and team administrations have done, several University of Ottawa administrators publicly condemned the athletes' reported acts of sexual violence and the broader rape culture in sport.

Although it is not known whether the move was disciplinary, removal of the male athletes accused of sexual assault from the St. Francis Xavier X-Men's football team roster in 2017 was also a marked difference in the team administration's response. Both cases occurred amid heightened news media and public dialogue about the high rates of sexual assault on university and college campuses, sparked in Canada in 2013 when orientation chants about nonconsensual sex with underaged girls at Saint Mary's University and the University of British Columbia were made public (see E. Quinlan 2017 for further discussion). Universities across Canada were quickly drafting sexual assault policies and speaking publicly about their zero-tolerance approach to sexual assault on campus. This context undoubtedly placed greater pressure on the University of Ottawa and perhaps St. Francis Xavier University to respond to the allegations of sexual assault differently.

Professional Sport
There have been few publicly documented reports of professional athletes in Canada perpetrating group sexual assaults, particularly when compared to younger playing levels. The lack of media reports and legal cases of group sexual assaults involving professional athletes does not mean that they do not occur but rather that they are less likely to be reported. As discussed in Chapter 1, 95 percent of sexual assaults are not reported to police in Canada (Department of Justice 2019b), are not documented in legal cases, and are less likely to be reported by the media. The cases that we analyzed likely represent a fraction of the total number of cases at this level. As seen at the other levels of play, no league or legal consequences followed the reported group sexual assaults, though both cases occurred in the 1990s, when sport organizations' disciplinary actions for athlete-perpetrated sexual assaults were largely nonexistent.

In the days before the 1990 CFL Grey Cup in Vancouver, local police received a report of a sexual assault involving five men, at least one of whom was identified as a player on the Edmonton football team (*Vancouver Sun* 1990). The young woman who reported the sexual assault was seventeen years old. On the night of the reported group sexual assault, the young woman and the unnamed Edmonton player met at a nightclub before going to a downtown hotel. She reported that, while they were in the hotel room, four other men entered the room and sexually assaulted her. The Vancouver police investigated the incident, declined to lay any charges, and did not release the names of the men whom she reported, indicating only that at least one played for the Edmonton team. Team management indicated that they saw reports in the media but were not contacted directly by the police and therefore saw no need to take disciplinary action against any of the team's players (*Vancouver Sun* 1990).

In 1995, Canadian hockey player Todd Harvey helped to lead the junior national team to a world championship. The next summer, the first after his rookie season in the NHL with the Dallas Stars, Harvey, along with another Stars player, Grant Marshall, and two other men, Robert Bulchak and Patrick Barton, were charged with sexual assault (*Seattle Times* 1996). The four men reportedly sexually assaulted a twenty-year-old woman at a Winnipeg house party that the players were attending while training in Canada (*AP News* 1996a). Before a trial commenced, all charges were dropped with no reason provided (Dowbiggin 2005). No disciplinary action has been reported against the athletes for their reported involvement in the group sexual assault.

These two reports of group sexual assault occurred after a wave of legal reforms in Canada, which many hoped would improve how police, prosecutors, and judges handled cases of sexual assault. In the 1990s, reforms to Canadian sexual assault laws of the 1980s coupled with the introduction of forensic DNA analysis in sexual assault cases were seen by some victim advocates and legal officials as changes that would increase conviction rates and make it more difficult for police, prosecutors, and judges to continue to disproportionately dismiss sexual assault reports (A. Quinlan 2017). However, the wealth of scholarly research tracking the history of the handling of sexual assault reports by the criminal legal system in Canada suggests that this did not occur. Instead, the pattern of police dropping sexual assault investigations, deeming reports of sexual assault unfounded, and dropping charges of sexual assault has continued (Crew 2012; DuBois 2012; Du Mont, Miller, and Myhr 2003; Russell 2010; A. Quinlan 2017). The two cases discussed here reflect that broader trend.

Making Sense of Athlete-Perpetrated Group Sexual Assaults

Existing research has revealed that the vast majority of reported sexual assaults involve a single perpetrator and a single victim (Franklin 2004; O'Sullivan 1991). This statistical trend does not appear to be consistent with patterns of sexual assault perpetrated by male athletes in Canadian hockey and football. If the sexually violent hazing rituals discussed in Chapter 4 are also understood to be group sexual assaults, as we will argue, then the disproportionately high rates of reported group sexual assault in men's hockey and football in Canada become even more clear. Exploring why this is the case provides a glimpse of the unique aspects of sexual assault in Canadian sport and the continuing institutional tolerance of this form of violence in sport organizations and the criminal legal system.

Group Sexual Assault and Criminal (In)justice

As the cases in this chapter illustrate, group sexual assaults perpetrated by male athletes are routinely dismissed by police, prosecutors, and judges in the Canadian criminal legal system. Of the seventy male athletes reported to have been involved in the group sexual assaults just discussed, none were criminally convicted. Although some might argue that the reports were false accusations and therefore no convictions were warranted, it is difficult to believe that is the case for all of the reports, particularly in light of existing research, which has demonstrated that false accusations of sexual assault are rare (Heenan and Murray 2006; Lisak et al. 2010).

Only one of the cases described in this chapter involved police alleging that the report was false. The young woman was charged with obstructing justice, though she was found not guilty at trial, and the judge concluded that the actions of the accused, Brian Sakic and Wade Smith, were "degrading and disgusting" and that "they ravaged her body for their own sexual gratification" (quoted in Robinson 2000, para. 4). The absence of convictions in the cases discussed cannot be taken as an indication that the sexual assaults did not occur. Rather, more likely it reflects a criminal legal system that often fails to recognize and take seriously athlete-perpetrated group sexual assaults against women and girls.

Feminist scholars have argued that law and the criminal legal system have long been shaped by sexism and misogyny in addition to other forms of prejudice and discrimination (MacKinnon 2005; Smart 1989). Misogyny, according to Manne (2020, 7), is the legal system's "branch of patriarchy – a system that functions to police and enforce gendered norms and expectations, and involves girls and women facing disproportionately or distinctly hostile treatment because of their gender." Competitive men's sport and institutions of law enforcement are what Manne (2018, 61) terms "misogynist social environment[s]" that reflect gendered, as well as racialized and classed, social hierarchies and enforce norms along these markers of social difference. As the analyzed cases illustrate, the Canadian criminal legal system continues to fail victims who turn to the police after experiencing sexual assaults by male hockey and football players.

Prosecuting any sexual assault can be challenging, particularly when it involves victims over the age of sexual consent. These cases demand a high burden of proof with a low prospect of conviction (H. Johnson 2012). Compounding these challenges, in a context in which a victim's word of what happened is set against a team of players who testify about their teammate's actions, the likelihood of a conviction is lowered even further. As a police officer in British Columbia stated in the Victoria Salmon Kings case, "the witnesses are all members of the hockey team" (cited in Robinson 2006). When teammates also face sexual assault allegations, the victim's testimony is more likely to be further silenced and discredited.

The low conviction rates for group sexual assaults by male athletes suggests that legal consequences are unlikely for this form of violence. Legal reform has done little to alter the enduring pattern of sexual assault victims being doubted and dismissed by the police and prosecutors (Crew 2012; DuBois 2012; Du Mont, Miller, and Myhr 2003; Russell 2010; A. Quinlan 2017). For all these reasons, the criminal legal system is not structured to be a viable solution to the problem of sexual assault in Canadian sport. Sport organizations have also proved to be ill equipped to handle reports of sexual assault with compassion and accountability. And, in cases like the alleged Saskatoon Blades group sexual assault against a young Indigenous woman, in which the team coaches were also police investigators, there can be minimal separation between sport and the criminal legal system. Addressing sexual assault in sport thus requires moving beyond both the criminal legal system and sport organizations to find new and more effective paths toward sexual assault prevention and safety in sport.

Sport Organizations and the Institutional Tolerance of Group Sexual Assault

As the analyzed cases suggest, when male athletes are accused of group sexual assaults, teams and leagues commonly provide them with support and encouragement, and they rarely acknowledge the harms that the sexual assault victims faced. Some teams have framed this form of support as a duty to their athletes. For example, when three Sault Ste Marie Greyhounds were charged with sexual assault, the team general manager, Kyle Dubas (now GM and president of hockey operations with the Pittsburgh Penguins in the NHL), stated that "we'll continue to perform our duty and support these players" (quoted in Ruicci 2012, para. 4/7). The accused players praised Dubas and the organization for supporting them throughout the criminal investigation. In most cases discussed in this chapter, the athletes continued to play for their teams, even after being charged, arrested, investigated, and prosecuted; only four of seventy reported athletes did not continue playing for their teams after being reported for sexual assaults. Many athletes climbed the playing hierarchy in their sports while facing sexual assault charges. For example, Ed Jovanovski signed a $5.7 million NHL contract with the Florida Panthers, which included unique provisions to accommodate a possible delayed start because of the potential that he would be found guilty at trial and incarcerated. In the case of Brian Wiseman, after he was accused of being involved in a group sexual assault as a player, his team later hired him as a coach before he went on to become an NHL coach with the Edmonton Oilers.

When charges are dropped or athletes are found not guilty, they are commonly proclaimed to be innocent by team management and in media headlines. As discussed, dropped charges and not guilty verdicts do not necessarily mean that a person is innocent. These outcomes can be a result of a legal technicality or insufficient evidence. This important nuance is often missed in sport organizations' press releases and media commentary on criminal trial outcomes in these cases.

Some athletes might engage in group sexual assaults simply because, seemingly, they can without much consequence. When the victim has the courage to come forward and speak out against them, the athletes can have confidence that their teams and broader communities will likely support them. The victim, in contrast, is more likely to be doubted, accused of lying, and publicly shamed. In the case involving the Saskatoon Blades, the young woman who reported the sexual assault had to move to a new city and change her name for her own protection, even though victim identities in sexual assault cases are typically protected under Canadian law (Robinson 2011b). A mother of another player on the Saskatoon Blades who was not among those accused spoke publicly about the young Indigenous woman who reported that she was sexually assaulted. The mother said, "if it was one of my girls, I'd break her neck ... The boys are nice and polite to everybody. They are not going to tell a kid to take a hike. She stayed because she wanted to. She crashed [the party]; she wasn't invited. She just wants to make a quick buck when the boys turn pro" (quoted in Robinson 1998, 104). Although most junior hockey players in Canada will never play in the NHL, they are often celebrated as though they will. Whereas athletes' testimonies are commonly treated as factual and as corroborative evidence for their teammates' accounts, victims' reports are often seen as inherently distrustful, particularly if the woman making the report is marginalized, as in the Saskatoon Blades case. This hostile climate for victims likely reduces the number of reports of group sexual assault perpetrated by male athletes. In this context of high institutional tolerance of sexual violence, group sexual assault becomes normalized and less visible.

Of the seventy athletes accused of the group sexual assaults discussed in this chapter, twelve are football players and fifty-eight are hockey players. We found no public reports of group sexual assaults against women and girls involving athletes in other sports between 1990 and 2020. One factor contributing to the high prevalence of reports involving hockey and football athletes might be that both sports value aggression and dominance and are physically punishing to the individuals involved. As discussed in Chapter 2, consent and bodily autonomy are often less meaningful in the context of these more violent sports. Laura Finley (2018) refers to such sports as "power and performance" sports and has identified higher rates of abusive behaviour toward women and girls by athletes involved in such sports. Reflecting this trend, a sport manager interviewed by Deb Waterhouse-Watson (2013, 92) explained that, "when we want players on the field, we want them to be aggressive ... So we attract an aggressive, young, risk taking male ... We give him a shower, put a suit on him and then say now we want you to go out there and not have any problems ... It's very difficult to do that." Although hockey and football might attract aggressive young men, these sports also socialize them to be violent and aggressive (Fogel 2013). Athletes in these sports are not given opportunities to provide free and informed consent to the violence and injury inflicted on their bodies in the field of play; instead, this consent is assumed by the leagues governing the sports and by the legal system in those rare occasions when a case of violence during play goes to criminal trial (Fogel 2013). In this context, many athletes are less likely to understand consent and bodily autonomy.

The high prevalence of reported cases of sexual assault involving Canadian hockey and football players might also be connected to the social reverence given to these sports in Canada. Although hockey is not officially Canada's national sport, nor is it the most popular sport based upon participation rates and TV viewership ratings, it has long been held up as the "national" sport based upon a long history of participation, success in international competitions, and folklore around local hockey legends (Wilson 2006). Many rural towns across Canada have stories of at least one NHL player who was born there or billeted there while playing for the local team. An intricate system of amateur and junior hockey has been established to develop and channel elite players to the professional ranks. In their teen years, hockey players who show potential are drafted to junior teams, and their player rights become owned by the clubs that drafted them, and they often move to new cities where they are billeted with minimal parental supervision. The system creates a celebratory culture surrounding the male athlete, whose worth is determined by his performance on the ice and who can be bought, sold, and traded to other teams that generate profits from his labour. As Robinson (1998, 40) writes, "the world of junior hockey is a place where teenage boys learn they are the young gods of a national religion, where their strength, aggression, and physical prowess are coveted skills that older men willingly buy, sell, and trade." Many of the junior-level players described in the cases are commodified celebrities in small-town Canadian communities who are owned by their sport organizations. Others are athlete celebrities on their university campuses. In both contexts, celebrating and privileging athletes in these ways can enhance their feelings of being immune to the law and disciplinary action as well as underpinning a mistaken assumption that admiration of them from young female fans is a form of sexual consent. Some male athletes might feel, as Manne (2020, 11) identifies, *entitled* to sex with women. When their actions become violent and sexually aggressive, they might feel and be seen by others as "entitled not just to be deemed innocent until proven guilty, but to be deemed innocent, period, regardless of their misdeeds" (Manne 2020, 12). These conditions set the stage for increased levels of sexual assault.

Compared with hockey, football is not as revered or popular in Canada. However, the system of football is similarly organized, where athletes move from a youth league to junior and professional ranks. As with Canadian hockey, many young, elite football players in Canada strive to be drafted to a junior football team and eventually play in the Canadian Football League. Although the likelihood that young athletes will play in the professional league is small, in many communities, many are still celebrated as if they will. It is often through this lens that reported sexual assaults are seen, as was the case for the hockey mom who stated that "she [the victim] just wants to make a quick buck when the boys turn pro" (quoted in Robinson 1998, 104). It is interesting that the two sports featured in publicly available reports of group sexual assault by athletes are also the only two sports that have long-established professional levels in Canada: men's hockey and men's football. The cultural celebration of these sports in Canada fuels the tolerance, normalization, and minimization of sexual assaults within them.

A Theatre for Performing Violent Masculinities
Of the seventy hockey and football players accused of the group sexual assaults described in this chapter, all were teenaged or young adult men, and of those who were publicly named, all read as white. No women or people who

identify as nonbinary or gender queer appeared as alleged perpetrators in the media reports and legal case files analyzed. As we discussed in the previous chapter, there is a clear relationship between participation in competitive men's sports, the formation and maintenance of violent masculinities, and the perpetration of sexual assaults.

Many gender studies scholars have described gender as a performance (Butler 1990; C. West and Zimmerman 1987). In the context of sport, the construction and maintenance of dominant masculinities require an ongoing performance in front of teammates, coaches, trainers, and fans. The performative nature of masculinities becomes even more apparent in relation to group sexual assaults. In contrast to sexual assaults involving individual athletes, in group sexual assaults, violent masculinities characterized by dominance, power, and sexual prowess are literally performed in front of and with other athletes. Women's bodies, as several scholars have argued, become props in this group performance of masculinities. As Karen Franklin (2004, 26) writes, "young men ritualistically enact an exaggerated version of the gender-role norms expected of men in hypermasculine social environments. Their victims serve as almost interchangeable dramatic props in this performance art." Describing this further, Robinson (2016, paras. 6–7) writes that

> [sex] becomes a means to demonstrate aggressive, violent masculinity; and as such, it is frequently performed in a group so the teammates can witness one another's performance. But instead of performing on an ice rink, they use the female body. The sexual relationship is between the players; the female body is a conduit. There is no intimacy, love or understanding of female pleasure; only contempt as girls are called "dirties" and "puck bunnies." Teammates cheer each other on as they perform on the female, sometimes entering her body at the same time, and when they have all "scored" they are done.

In this way, group sexual assault in sport serves as a theatre for performing violent masculinities. It allows young men to engage in what Kathryn Ann Farr (1988, 259) terms "dominance bonding," which she describes as "a process of collective alliance in which members affirm and reaffirm their superiority."

As we discussed in Chapter 2, masculine identities formed in and through sport are highly precarious as an athlete's worth is conditional and can shift dramatically from one athletic performance to another or from one playing level to the next. One way that a male athlete can demonstrate his power and dominance in front of teammates off the ice or playing field is by participating in group sexual assaults, the ultimate performance of dominance. The victim becomes an object that athletes use to perform and re-establish their power, dominance, and control in the eyes of their teammates. Group sexual assaults can also be used to develop a group sense of shared dominance among team members. Robinson (1998, 118) writes that

> a player who engages in group sex, who long ago shut down the voice inside him that questions if the [woman] has really consented, does so because he needs to meet his own standards of masculinity and gain approval of his teammates, who will judge him not as a compassionate human being but as a hockey player. His actions have nothing to do with providing sexual pleasure and respect for a woman and everything to do with being seen as a man in his world.

Although several of the cases involved male athletes who argued that the sexual activity was consensual, none featured an athlete who testified that the woman enjoyed the sexual activity. In fact, Jonah Williams, a football player at St. Francis Xavier University, indicated that he was aware that he was physically hurting the woman and admitted to causing bruises on her body, but he argued that she consented to it. In a quest to reassert masculine identities that might have been undermined on the field of play, some male athletes use women's bodies in their performance of violent masculinities to reify their masculine identities and related self-worth in a context in which they are continually questioned.

Of the seventy male athletes accused of participating in the group sexual assaults described in this chapter, only four were professional athletes, whereas sixty-six were junior, high school, or university athletes. While there is an obvious relationship to age, there is also a connection between participation in group sexual assaults and lower playing levels, in which athletes' skills, dominance, and accomplishments are less established. Athletes at junior levels are simultaneously celebrated as having elite skills, but they are also in a constant battle to move to higher levels in their sport and be paid to play. It is at these sport levels, in the space between amateur and professional, and in sports in which playing professionally is possible, where the conditions for group sexual assaults are most clearly set.

The performance of violent masculinities in group sexual assaults is also shaped by the competitive nature of the levels of play. As we discussed in

Chapter 2, sex can become part of the competition among athletes. Illustrating this, some victims reported that, after the assaults, the athletes asked them who had the best sexual performance. Group sexual assaults can thus become competitions of sexual prowess among the perpetrators.

Nick Pappas's (2012) study of male athletes' sexual behaviours offers an illustrative and disturbing example of the competitive nature of group sexual assaults. Pappas interviewed an athlete who described a game that male athletes play referred to as "rodeo" (264), which includes elements of a group sexual assault. In the game, a male athlete encourages a woman to go back to his room and have sex with him, while his teammates hide in the closet to listen and watch without the woman's knowledge or consent. The teammates then jump out and surprise the woman. According to the "rules" of the game, the athlete having sex must maintain penetration as the woman struggles to get away. The athlete is said to have "succeeded" in the game if his penis stayed within the woman's vagina for eight seconds, which is meant to be akin to a rider staying on a bucking bull at a rodeo (Pappas 2012). When sex becomes an explicit competition performed in front of teammates, and the prize is masculine status, high rates of sexual assault are likely.

Part of performing masculine domination of a woman in front of teammates means that male athletes watch one another engage in sexual activity and may engage in sexual activities with one another. To give one example, in the Guelph Storm case of 1992, two hockey players reportedly inserted their penises into the mouth of the victim while another player was penetrating her vaginally. The players reportedly agreed that the acts described by the victim occurred but argued that she consented to them. Some researchers have problematically suggested that in group sexual assaults, male perpetrators gain some sexual gratification from one another by participating in group sexual acts and that the woman is used to provide an illusion that they are not engaged in sexual activity with one another. Peggy Sanday (cited in Robinson 1998, 148–49) takes this line of argument: "The sex should not be mistaken for heterosexual sex ... Her body services their need to perform for each other. Her presence allows them to come as close as they can to an intimate relationship with each other while at the same time presenting visible 'proof' of their masculinity." From this perspective, group sexual assaults can be interpreted as opportunities for male athletes to have sex with one another in a way tolerated by and accepted in their sports. However, there are obvious limitations to and problems with this line of argument.

An explanation of group sexual assault that rests on homosexual gratification assumes that the violent act is about sexual gratification. There is minimal evidence that players' motivation for engaging in group sexual assault is purely for sexual arousal, just as sexual gratification is not typically understood to be the primary and singular motivation of sexual offenders. Sexual assault is a crime of power and control. As Lyn Yonack (2017, para. 1) writes, "although the touch may be sexual, the words seductive or intimidating, and the violation physical, when someone rapes, assaults, or harasses, the motivation stems from the perpetrator's need for dominance and control. In heterosexual and same-sex encounters, sex is the tool used to gain power over another person." Sexual attraction to teammates is not a requirement for male athletes to participate in a group sexual assault. One young hockey player interviewed by Robinson (1998, 122) detailed another player's experience in a group sexual assault of a woman:

> [He] told me ... they had to have sex with this one girl in a hotel room ... She told them to stop it. They were hurting her. [He] knew she didn't want it. There were eight guys altogether. He didn't want to do it, because he knew he was about to rape a girl, and he knew he wasn't a rapist. But he knew what the team would do to him if he didn't rape her, so he did. He feels so terrible about it ... But the girls are seen as the fresh meat, and these guys are the wolves.

In this description, sexual gratification is clearly absent, whereas forms of power and control over the victim and among the athletes are at play. In the context of sport, the power sought is not merely over the victim but also over other men in the highly competitive, hierarchical, misogynistic world of competitive men's sport.

Most importantly, a theory that attributes the sexually violent behaviour of male athletes to homosexuality runs the risk of further marginalizing gay athletes by suggesting that perverse and violent sexual behaviour is the domain of people who identify as gay or queer. As Helen Jefferson Lenskyj (2012, 8) has identified, "sport remains one of the last bastions of heterosexism and homophobia." There is no research to indicate that gay men are more likely than any other group to engage in group sexual assaults. Clearly, any explanation of group sexual assaults in sport that hinges on sexual gratification misses the complexity of social forces that support and maintain sexual assault in sport.

Drugs, Alcohol, and Sexual Assault

In nearly all of the analyzed reports of group sexual assault in Canadian men's hockey and football, alcohol was used by the athletes. In most cases, the alcohol consumption occurred at house parties or in university dorms where there was minimal parental or adult supervision. In one case, one of the accused, Jonah Williams, reportedly consumed cocaine in addition to consuming alcohol at an event organized by St. Francis Xavier University.[21] In other cases, such as the Cobourg Cougars #consentisoverated party, references were made to the use of date rape drugs. In several cases, the victims reported being so intoxicated that they passed in and out of consciousness while the athletes sexually assaulted them.

Janine Benedet (2010b) has estimated that 50,000 women are sexually assaulted each year in Canada while incapacitated by alcohol or drugs. Reflecting a similar trend, a large American study found that approximately 3 million American women have been victimized by drug-facilitated rape in their lifetimes (Kilpatrick et al. 2007). Alcohol and other drugs do appear to be a catalyst for sexual violence, potentially heightening a victim's vulnerability while lowering potential perpetrators' inhibitions. Existing research has consistently shown that alcohol and drug use is rampant in men's sports, particularly those that prioritize rough physical contact, such as hockey and football (Kwan et al. 2014; Roy and Camire 2017). The consumption of alcohol can also be linked to the performance and maintenance of dominant masculinities in some contexts. As Messerschmidt (1997) notes, in sport subcultures, drinking alcohol is commonly associated with masculinity, and drinking copious amounts of alcohol is one way to increase masculine status. Alcohol consumption and intoxicated behaviour among men are often accepted and promoted since they are understood to affirm masculinity and promote bonding and solidarity among men in certain social contexts, such as competitive men's sport (Connell and Messerschmidt 2005; Dunning, Murphy, and Williams 1988). When alcohol and other drugs are added to a sport context with pre-existing elements of precarious masculinities, misogynist ideologies that foster contempt for women and all that is defined as feminine, and a competitive drive to use women to bolster masculine status, the conditions are apt for high rates of sexual assault.

In Canadian law, sexual consent cannot be obtained from a person incapable of providing it. Canadian courts, in many cases, have found complainants incapable of consent because of intoxication,[22] including those involving self-induced states of intoxication.[23] In many of the cases described in this chapter, the victims were reportedly intoxicated to the point of being unconscious. In the Saskatoon Blades case in 1995, the victim was reportedly passed out on a floor. In the Guelph Storm case in 1992, the victim reported that she awoke to players removing her clothing. In the McGill University Redmen football case in 2001, the young Concordia University student reported that she was drugged and that her first memory after consuming a drink was awakening to being sexually violated by three football players. In the Niagara football case in 2016, the young woman reported passing in and out of consciousness in the back seat of a car while four football players reportedly sexually assaulted her. In each case, the athletes were found not guilty, or the charges were dropped, despite the precedent in Canadian law on the negation of sexual consent with intoxication. This not only illustrates a high legal threshold for establishing nonconsent because of intoxication but also is further evidence of the tolerance granted by Canadian courts to reported sexual violence by competitive male athletes.

High numbers of publicly documented reports of group sexual assault appear to be relatively unique to the contexts of competitive men's hockey and football in Canada and seem less common in other sport contexts as well as outside sport. Group sexual assaults appear to be particularly prevalent at junior and university men's playing levels, at which athletes strive to move up in the competitive hierarchy of sport and have much to prove to the young men around them. As with sexual assaults perpetrated by individual athletes, institutions of sport and the law have failed to address, respond to, and prevent group sexual assaults. None of the seventy male athletes reported to have been involved in the group sexual assaults discussed in this chapter was criminally convicted. Likewise, in most cases, sport organizations stood behind their young white-presenting male athletes, providing them with support and care, after they were accused of violent sexual acts against women and girls, and offered no support or care to victims, who were blamed and publicly shamed.

Group sexual assaults against women and girls are not the only form of group sexual violence in sport. Building upon the analysis in this chapter, in Chapter 4 we examine a different form of group sexual assault perpetrated by competitive male athletes: sexually violent hazing rituals targeting younger male teammates. Despite being a different form of sexual assault, similar themes emerge, such as intersections of precarious, violent masculinities in a hierarchical sport system, with limited bodily autonomy and opportunities to provide consent for physical violence and harm, alongside entitlements that lead to the social, legal, and institutional tolerance of sexual assault in sport and the criminal legal system.

4

Sexually Violent Hazing
Power, Humiliation, and Group Dominance Bonding

Sexually violent hazing in sport has long lived in the shadows of both academic literature and public discourse in Canada. Limited scholarly and public attention has been given to the clear connections among sexual assaults, hazing rituals, and sport cultures. The lack of attention to the sexually violent nature of some hazing rituals in sport has left the wide-sweeping harms and impacts of sexually violent hazing largely unseen and unquestioned.

Although some existing research on hazing has touched briefly on the topic of nonconsensual sexual acts during hazing rituals, much of this work has avoided labelling these acts as sexual assaults. For example, some scholars have classified rookie athletes being forced to put their penises into their teammates' mouths as an example of "small act[s] of same-sex sexual activities" (E. Anderson, McCormack, and Lee 2012, 427). In both law and existing scholarly research on sexual assaults, forced oral sex is considered sexual assault. Not acknowledging the sexually violent nature of some hazing acts has been a significant limitation in existing hazing research. Marisalva Favero et al.'s (2018, 1835) work is an exception to this trend, describing sexual hazing as "acts of violence in which the aggressor abuses their power to obtain sexual gratification, without consent." Although this definition acknowledges the violent nature of sexual hazing, its narrow focus on sexual gratification does not align with legal understandings of sexual assault in Canadian law or scholarly literature on sexual violence, as we describe later in this chapter.

Apart from a few select cases of hazing in sport that have generated news headlines over the past decade, sexually violent hazing has been largely ignored by both Canadian media and sport institutions. As Scott Mathers and Jackie Chavez (2018) have identified in an American context, media portrayals of hazing typically downplay its criminal aspects, which distorts public understandings of hazing. Likewise, Hank Nuwer (2004b, 118) writes that sportswriters in North America tend to report hazing in such a way that it appears "fun, traditional, and welcome," even though hazing is illegal in most American states.

A detailed, scholarly investigation of sexually violent hazing committed by athletes against other athletes in Canadian sport is thus long overdue. Taking up this challenge, we begin this chapter by examining definitions of hazing, and sexually violent hazing in particular, and we explore the prevalence and harmful consequences of such hazing. We describe twelve reported incidents of sexually violent hazing in Canadian sport that collectively illustrate some of the diversity of hazing acts, sport cultures, victims, perpetrators, and geographical locations of such hazing in Canada. Crucially, these cases expose how sport organizations and the criminal legal system have responded to these incidents inconsistently, at times ignoring, minimizing, and tolerating the violence, while at other times purporting to address them seriously. Unlike sexual assaults against women and girls, sport organizations often publicly profess zero tolerance of hazing, which creates a unique context in which sexually violent hazing occurs. We use these twelve cases to explore the role of violent masculinities in such hazing as well as the links between sexually violent hazing and athlete-perpetrated sexual violence against women and girls, as discussed in Chapters 2 and 3.

Defining Hazing

Brian Trota and jay johnson (2004, x) define hazing as "a rite of passage wherein youths, neophytes, or rookies are taken through traditional practices by more senior members in order to initiate them into the next stage of their cultural, religious, academic, or athletic lives." Other researchers have found hazing to be a common practice in a wide variety of organizations and institutions, including the military, high schools, fraternities, sororities, police and fire departments, student clubs, and workplaces (Guynn and Aquila 2004; j. johnson and Miller 2004; Malszecki 2004; Nuwer 2000, 2001, 2004a; Sweet 1999). In these contexts, hazing is used to initiate new members into an established group. Although acts of hazing often mirror bullying, there are important distinctions. While hazing and bullying might be similar in nature as well as in result, the purported aims are different: bullying aims to exclude and alienate, whereas hazing aims to integrate and include (Jeckell, Copenhaver, and Diamond 2018). Hazing also commonly takes harmful, degrading, and abusive forms, particularly in the context of sport (Crow and Macintosh 2009). Despite what its intention might be, hazing in sport has been shown to often result in athletes feeling alienated rather than included, which can sometimes lead them to leave their teams or even their sports (Hoover and Pollard 2000; Sussberg 2002; Thompson, Johnstone, and Banks 2018).

To further define hazing, existing research has relied on continuums of hazing behaviour. Nadine Hoover (1999) classifies hazing into four categories: (1) acceptable behaviour, (2) questionable behaviour, (3) alcohol-related behaviour, and (4) unacceptable behaviour. Although this continuum points importantly to the varying forms of hazing, it runs the risk of significantly oversimplifying both the acts and the athletes' understandings of hazing in sport. First, Hoover's categories of hazing are not mutually exclusive, particularly in regard to alcohol consumption during what might be considered "questionable" and "unacceptable" hazing rituals. Second, the continuum assumes shared understandings of acceptable behaviour among all athletes, which other literature suggests is not the case, particularly research demonstrating athletes' diverse understandings of hazing (Crow and MacIntosh 2009; Fogel 2013). Third, the continuum problematically implies that some hazing activities can be definitively labelled "acceptable," which ignores the possibility that the same hazing activity can be perceived as acceptable by some but as physically, psychologically, and/or emotionally harmful by others.

Addressing some of these limitations, Brian Rahill and Elizabeth Allan (2005) suggest a more complex continuum of hazing that spans a range of abusive behaviours in sport. At the far left of their continuum is what they call "subtle hazing," which can involve an athlete being required to carry heavy team equipment, clean up practice facilities, sing in front of groups of people, or receive unwanted nicknames. "Harassment hazing" falls in the middle of their continuum and involves acts such as an athlete being pressured to wear humiliating attire. At the far right of their continuum is "violent hazing," which can involve sexual abuse, physical beating, forced alcohol consumption, abduction, and exposure to harsh weather conditions without adequate clothing. Although their continuum avoids some of the limitations of Hoover's by acknowledging potential harms, it does not align entirely with athletes' perceptions and self-reports of their behaviour.

In a 2013 study, Fogel asked Canadian football players at various playing levels to describe their understandings of hazing. Most participants in the study indicated that they do not use the term *hazing*, even though they described acts that align primarily with what Rahill and Allan (2005) call "subtle hazing." Instead, players at the junior level commonly mentioned "rookieing" (Fogel 2013, 60), university players referred to "initiations" (59), and professional players said that they committed "pranks" (63) on rookie members of their teams. As the athletes described, each term has a distinct meaning. *Rookieing*, they explained, is a process that lasts an entire season. *Initiations* typically occur at the beginning of the season, or before the season begins, and are often conducted in an evening referred to as a "rookie night" (64). At the professional level, they reported, less emphasis is placed on initiating new players and more on playing *pranks* on them. The labels that athletes ascribe to these acts must be understood in their broader context. In Canada, competitive sport organizations at all levels have zero-tolerance policies on hazing. In this environment, athletes might be less inclined to label their behaviour as hazing and adopt alternative terms to avoid sanctions.

Regardless of the language that athletes use to describe their behaviour, existing research makes clear that acts of initiation on sport teams are pervasive and can take many forms. There is a pressing need to recognize and examine the sexually violent nature of many acts of hazing. Although sexually violent hazing in sport is rarely conceptualized as sexual assault, we argue that framing it as such more accurately captures its harms and broader consequences.

In this chapter, we define hazing as any act of initiation by an existing member of a sport team toward a new member, regardless of the type of act or harm that results. To define sexually violent hazing, we draw from the World Health Organization's (2002, 149) definition of sexual violence: "Any sexual act, attempt to obtain a sexual act, unwanted sexual comments or advances, or acts to traffic, or otherwise directed, against a person's sexuality using coercion, by any person regardless of their relationship to the victim, in any setting, including but not limited to home and work." Building upon this definition, we define *sexually violent hazing* as any initiation ritual that involves verbal aggression, such as sexual harassment and threats, and/ or physical acts, such as forced nudity or sexual touching, that need not be done for the purpose of sexual gratification and is an act of power. Most importantly, sexually violent hazing involves any act among teammates that can compromise the sexual integrity of the victim.

The Prevalence of Hazing

As with the other forms of sexual assault in sport discussed in this book, the prevalence of hazing in sport is difficult to determine since many acts of hazing occur behind closed doors at team parties, on team buses, in hotel suites, or in locker rooms (Fogel 2013). With the development of zero-tolerance policies toward hazing in Canada, hazing has likely been pushed further from public view. When incidents of hazing are publicized, details on what occurred, who was involved, and how many victims were harmed are commonly obscured to maintain the privacy of the individuals involved and the reputation of their sport organization. Compounding these challenges in determining prevalence, reporting rates of hazing are low. In a study of NCAA student athletes, Hoover (1999) found that up to 95 percent of those who have experienced hazing are not willing to report it. Hoover's findings highlight a culture of secrecy around hazing in sport. This secrecy is likely heightened in cases of sexually violent hazing given the low police reporting rates for sexual assault (Statistics Canada 2018).

Quantitative studies of the prevalence of hazing are also challenged by the lack of consensus on the definition of hazing. One study found that, although 79 percent of over 60,000 university athletes surveyed in the United States reported participating in activities that typically would be considered hazing, only 12 percent stated that they had been hazed (Hoover and Pollard 2000). Another study found that athletes commonly identify acts of hazing only if they involve physical force (Allan and Madden 2008). Some athletes might also be reluctant to disclose that they have been hazed as part of the larger culture of silence surrounding hazing (Howard and Kennedy 2006).

Despite definitional limitations and cultural pressures not to report hazing in sport, athletes' self-reports still reveal alarmingly high rates of hazing. Although exact rates of the prevalence of hazing in sport are unknown, estimates range from 43 percent to 92 percent of athletes in various contexts have experienced some form of hazing. A study of high school athletes in the United States found that 47 percent had experienced hazing (Allan and Madden 2009). In another study, 55 percent of over 11,000 students surveyed at fifty-three different college and university campuses across the United States had been involved in hazing, and among the student athletes in the study 74 percent had been hazed (Allan and Madden 2008, 2012). Another study of hazing on university campuses in the United States found that 123 of 288 varsity athletes (42.7 percent) had been involved in at least one hazing incident on their teams (Allan, Kerschner, and Payne 2019). A PhD dissertation (McGlone 2005) examined hazing in women's university sports in the United States and found that 48.5 percent of surveyed athletes had been hazed. Collectively, these studies point to the pervasiveness of hazing in American sports.

Canadian studies of hazing expose similar trends. One study (j. johnson et al. 2018) found that 58 percent[1] of 434 surveyed Canadian university athletes at varsity and club levels had experienced hazing, and another study (Hamilton et al. 2013) found that 92 percent reported having been hazed as first-year athletes. A large study at a Canadian university found that only 9 percent of over 1,800 survey respondents had experienced hazing; however, the study did not identify how many of the participants were student athletes or what percentage of student athletes experienced hazing (Massey and Massey 2017). Although existing research illustrates the commonality of hazing, the literature has not included specific measures on sexually violent hazing, and as a result, rates of the prevalence of sexually violent hazing are unknown.

Harmful Consequences of Hazing

Although hazing is often thought of as a fun, team-building activity, its consequences can be harmful and even catastrophic. At the most extreme, there have been cases in Canada in which athletes have died during hazing rituals. In 2010, Andrew Bartlett, a student at St. Thomas University (STU) in New Brunswick, playing his first season on the volleyball team, was found dead at the bottom of the stairwell in his apartment building the morning after a rookie initiation party (D. Webb 2010). At that party, reports suggest, rookies were forced to dress in costumes, consume large amounts of alcohol, and pay for alcohol for veteran players. After the party, a teammate dropped Bartlett off at his apartment, and he was found dead the following day. Police ruled the death an accident, confirming that blood-alcohol levels indicated that alcohol was a factor in the events that led to his death. The STU men's volleyball team was suspended for a season for the rookie initiation party. The STU incident was not an anomaly. Jorge Srabstein (2008) has identified at least 250 hazing-related deaths reported in English-language newspapers. Nuwer (2017) uncovered over 200 hazing-related deaths in North America, with over 40 of those deaths occurring between 2007 and 2017. Although the deaths are not restricted to sport contexts or Canada, they do point to the tragic consequences that hazing rituals can have.

Hazing can also have significant negative impacts on the emotional and psychological well-being of athletes victimized by hazing. According to one study (Hoover and Pollard 2000), nearly three-quarters of all hazing victims report negative impacts such as sleep deprivation, loss of sense of control, declining grades, post-traumatic stress, and mental instability. Thirteen percent of the athletes surveyed in that study reported that they had quit their teams after the hazing. Some athletes who experience hazing decide independently to leave their sports, whereas others have parents who, after becoming aware of hazing practices, discourage their children's participation in the sports (Holman and j. johnson 2015). Three other studies (L. Mann et al. 2015; Sussberg 2002; Waldron and Kowalski 2009) suggest that hazing can result in athletes withdrawing from sports and experiencing serious mental health challenges. Victims of hazing can also develop increased self-doubt, a poor self-image, and an erosion of trust and feelings of support (Lee-Olukoya 2009).

Sexually violent hazing can result in physical injuries and a range of psychological consequences for victims. In an American medical study, doctors reported a serious physical injury to a rookie athlete resulting from an incident of sexually violent hazing (Jeckell et al. 2018). The rookie athlete had a pool cue inserted into his rectum so far and forcefully that it ruptured his colon and bladder, which required emergency surgery. Beyond the physical impacts, athletes subjected to sexually violent hazing can experience psychological and emotional impacts similar to those documented among victims of sexual assault (Davidson et al. 1996; Paolucci, Genuis, and Violato 2001; Putnam 2003).[2] Although the specific consequences of sexually violent hazing have been understudied, the literature on the impacts of sexual assault points to potential wide-sweeping consequences that coercive sexual acts in hazing rituals can have on athletes.

Beyond consequences for individual athletes, hazing has negative consequences for the sport teams and organizations in which it occurred. While it can be argued that sport organizations have an ethical responsibility to ensure that harms are not inflicted on athletes, scholars have noted several additional reasons that organizations should take hazing seriously. Hazing can lead to negative publicity, particularly when it involves degrading sexual acts and is widely publicized. Hazing has also been shown to reduce, rather than build, team cohesiveness, which leads to poorer team performance (Van Raalte et al. 2007). Organizations can also be held legally liable for the harms caused during hazing rituals, which can impose substantial costs on organizations for legal fees and awarded damages (M. Carroll et al. 2009; Crow and Phillips 2004; Crow and Rosner 2002). To provide one example, a single hazing incident at the University of Vermont on the men's hockey team is estimated to have cost the university US$485,000 in legal fees (Gardiner 2001). In 2020, a group of fourteen former Canadian junior hockey players led by Daniel Carcillo filed a class-action lawsuit against the Canadian Hockey League and its member teams for the sexual and physical abuse that they experienced during hazing rituals (Canadian Press 2020a).

More broadly, acts of hazing can promote continued hazing. Studies have shown that athletes describe hazing as a learned behaviour and suggest that their involvement in it often stems from their experiences of being hazed (Fogel 2013; j. johnson 2001; Lee-Olukoya 2009). The cycle of hazing can be particularly problematic when athletes try to outdo the hazing rituals that they experienced as rookies by increasing the level of risk and potential harm (Abdulrehman 2006). In addition to the psychological and physical consequences of hazing, there is also the potential of criminal sanctions for those involved.

Hazing and Criminal Law in Canada

Athletes who perpetrate hazing can face disciplinary sanctions from their teams and leagues, as well as potential criminal sanctions by the courts, although as the cases that we analyzed suggest, hazing-related sanctions in the courts and in sport are relatively uncommon. Forty-six American states have specific laws pertaining to hazing (Tylock 2021); in Canada, there are no criminal laws pertaining directly to hazing. This does not mean, however, that acts of hazing are legal in Canada. Canadian criminal laws pertaining to physical and sexual assault could apply to some hazing acts, depending on their nature.

As we have discussed in previous chapters, under Section 271 of the Criminal Code sexual assault is defined as an assault that violates the sexual integrity of a complainant without that person's consent. In *R v Ewanchuk*, the intent and purpose of Canada's sexual assault laws were described as protecting "personal integrity, both physical and psychological, of every individual," and "having control over who touches one's body, and how, lies at the core of human dignity and autonomy."[3] In Canadian law, nonconsensual contact with a body part commonly understood to be sexual can be defined as sexual assault, even if that contact is not directly intended to be sexual or leads to sexual arousal.[4] Likewise, nonconsensual physical contact with a body part not commonly understood to be sexual, but in which the act is sexual in nature or intended to lead to a sexual act, can also be considered sexual assault.[5] Sexually violent hazing violates the sexual integrity of a victim. Even in hazing incidents in which there is no contact with a sexualized body part, but there are threats of sexual contact or sexual innuendo, coupled with other physical contact, the act can be considered sexual assault in law if consent is not established.

Despite the apparent alignment between criminal definitions of sexual assault and many acts of sexually violent hazing, they are rarely treated as such in Canadian law. There is a pervasive assumption in sports that hazing, sexual or otherwise, is consensual (Fogel 2013), and that athletes who participate in hazing activities consent to the acts voluntarily and therefore that no crime occurs (Smrke 1998). Voluntary consent, as defined in Canadian law, requires that the individual is in a capable mental state, free from coercion, and has the right of refusal.[6] Precedent in sexual assault law has made clear that consenting to an initial activity does not necessarily imply consent to all subsequent activities (Lyon 2004). Sexual consent must be ongoing and continuous. In the context of sexually violent hazing, there are significant power differentials between veterans and rookies. Refusing to participate in a hazing activity can lead to social exclusion from the team and/or other forms of reprisal (Holman 2004; Robinson 1998). Under these potentially coercive circumstances, free, informed, voluntary consent is difficult, if not impossible, to obtain. In this way, many acts of sexually violent hazing fit squarely within the criminal definition of sexual assault in Canada. Additionally, most hazing rituals in sports involve alcohol (Chin et al. 2019), with athletes under the minimum legal age being required to purchase, possess, and consume alcohol, and as a result often violate liquor laws in Canada.[7] Excessive alcohol consumption can also legally negate an individual's ability to provide consent to sexual activity (Benedet 2010b).

Sexually violent hazing is a clear violation of zero-tolerance hazing policies in sports. In junior and university sports in Canada, many such policies were developed in the mid-2000s following heightened media attention to an incident at McGill University in which some players on the football team reportedly sexually violated rookie athletes with a broomstick (Drolet 2006). Although designed to prevent, prohibit, and punish hazing, zero-tolerance hazing policies in men's competitive sports have been shown to be ineffective, commonly violated, and under-enforced (Fogel 2013). Sexually violent hazing has thus persisted in men's and boys' competitive sports despite the potential for significant sanctions in law and sport. Through an analysis of twelve cases of sexually violent hazing in Canadian sport, we illustrate the coercive nature of such incidents to develop a theoretical understanding of the historical tolerance of these acts within sport organizations and the criminal legal system.

Reports of Sexually Violent Hazing

To provide an empirical foundation for theorizing sexually violent hazing, in this section we examine key details of twelve reported cases of such hazing in Canadian sport. To illustrate trends within and across various playing levels, we discuss the cases according to playing level. Unlike in previous chapters, however, this analysis includes a younger playing level, minor sport, a relevant level of play for both this chapter and the next.

Sexually violent hazing in sports is often concealed and silenced, and as a result it is a challenging topic to study. The normalization of sexual violence in sports (Fogel 2017), as well as athletes' team loyalties and fears of reprisal, heighten athletes' reluctance to disclose their experiences of hazing (Fogel 2013). As such, the twelve cases analyzed in this chapter are likely just a glimpse of the overall occurrence of sexually violent hazing in Canadian sport. Only cases for which there was detailed information that was publicly available are included. When the information provided was too limited, we excluded the cases.[8] Similarly, we also excluded articles that relayed information about teams and unnamed athletes disciplined for engaging in hazing but did not provide details on what occurred during the hazing. Through this process, we identified and analyzed twelve incidents of reported sexually violent hazing between 1990 and 2020 with sufficient information available.

Minor Sport

Minor sport in Canada is a competitive playing level one step below junior sport that involves athletes typically between six and fifteen years old. At the minor level, athletes are considered amateurs and not paid or given scholarships to perform their sports. Athletes in minor sport are not drafted to play for teams that own their playing rights. Typically, minor athletes play for teams, clubs, and organizations in their city or geographic area. Some leagues and organizations have formal rules that require athletes to play for their local team and prevent them from switching between teams within and between seasons. In some sports, such as boys' minor hockey in Canada, players are selected in junior league drafts based upon their performance and athletic potential shown in competitive minor league play. Although minor athletes are children or young teenagers and the level is not as totalizing in terms of time commitment, this level can be highly competitive, driven in large part by some parents and adults who run the leagues and have ambitions for the children to make it to higher playing levels (Gillis 2014; Kanters, Bocarro, and Casper 2008; Robidoux and Bocksnick 2010). Of the twelve cases analyzed in this chapter, four occurred at the minor level.

In 1995, sixteen- and seventeen-year-old boys, minor league hockey players from the 100 Mile House Minor Hockey Association in British Columbia, reportedly hazed a younger team of thirteen- and fourteen-year-old boys within their association (Parton 1995). According to media reports, while some veteran players held down the younger players, others rubbed their genitals on the younger players' faces (*Toronto Star* 1995). Ten of the veteran players received one-game suspensions for the act, with one suspension later lifted on appeal (Parton 1995). No criminal charges were ever reported in the incident.

In 1996, Quebec minister of sports Remy Trudel requested an investigation by the province's hockey federation into a hazing ritual involving unnamed teenage boys on a minor hockey team in Jonquière, Quebec (O'Hara 2000). In the alleged hazing, veteran team members forced rookie players to strip naked, watch pornographic videos, spread molasses and mustard on their genitals, drink beer, and eat bananas wedged into the crotches of other players (Todd 1996). The hazing event reportedly lasted ten hours. Again no disciplinary or criminal charges were ever reported in the incident (Todd 1996).

In the same year, Diving Canada investigated a hazing report that involved older team members reportedly shaving the genitals and buttocks of younger boys, squirting toothpaste "up the buttocks" of the young athletes, and sending an athlete tied naked to a chair up and down a hotel elevator, reportedly with the encouragement of the coach (*Globe and Mail* 2005a). Diving Canada did not take any disciplinary action against the athletes or coach involved in the incident, claiming that it only had evidence of athletes shaving other athletes' chests and squirting toothpaste down their shorts, which Diving Canada argued did not warrant disciplinary action. This response generated some criticism. In an open letter in 1996, a concerned parent wrote that

> board members have repeatedly attempted to cover up the extent and nature of the incidents and continue to neglect responsibility for ensuring [the] safety of young athletes in the care of the organization. The lesson that the victims, and other young people who were exposed, have learned is that if you see wrongdoing, by a coach or other official, you had better remain silent, because if you do not ... your diving career will be significantly damaged. (cited in Pruden 2013)

The coach, Trevor Palmatier, was later criminally convicted of sexual exploitation resulting from a different incident not associated with hazing

(Pruden 2013). No disciplinary action or criminal charges were ever reported for the hazing incident.

Two years later, in 1998, in Calgary, three minor hockey players for the Calgary Buffaloes were suspended for a year, later reduced to five games on appeal, for an act of sexually violent hazing. The reported incident occurred while the team was at a tournament in Abbotsford, British Columbia, and staying at a hotel. In the hotel room, three members of the team reportedly slapped their penises against the faces of rookie teammates (Board 1998). The three players argued in their appeal that they were just horse-playing and that the act was not intended to be a form of hazing, which would have carried a year-long suspension under the hockey league rules. The players successfully appealed their one-year suspension. Again, no criminal charges were ever reported for the incident.

Although this is a small sample, boys' hockey once again appears to be overrepresented in cases that could be seen as athlete-perpetrated group sexual assaults of younger male teammates, with three of the four cases involving young male hockey players. Each of the cases involved some forced sexual touching of younger athletes. Where power differentials on teams are at play, and consent is not expressed, such acts could be legally defined as sexual assaults.

Like many of the cases in previous chapters, these cases illustrate the relative tolerance of sexually violent hazing in sport organizations as well as in the criminal legal system. Despite the potential alignment of these acts with legal definitions of sexual assault, the criminal legal system was absent in all four cases. Two cases did involve game suspensions of some athletes, yet these disciplinary measures were short lived and arguably did little to acknowledge or challenge the sexually violent nature of the acts. Additionally, there were no reports of sport organizations taking steps to recognize and address any potential harms for the victims. The lack of accountability for these harms contributes to maintaining a sport culture in which sexually violent hazing is normalized, silenced, and trivialized.

Junior and High School Sport

Junior sport, junior men's hockey in particular, is overrepresented in sexually violent hazing incidents, as it was in the other group sexual assaults examined in Chapter 3. Six of the twelve cases examined here involved junior or high school young men's sport, with five involving junior men's hockey specifically. At the junior playing level, players are drafted to teams and compete for scholarships and positioning in professional drafts. To get to the junior level, athletes must be strong performers at the minor level since there are far fewer playing opportunities available at the junior level, and the competition and time commitment sharply increase. No longer boys and young teenagers, the athletes discussed in these cases were all young men between sixteen and twenty-four at the time.

In 1994, the Ontario Provincial Police (OPP) made the unprecedented move of laying 135 criminal charges, including charges of sexual assault, against thirteen veteran players and a trainer of the Tilbury Hawks junior hockey team (Robinson 2002). The charges arose from a team party in October 1993 that involved numerous sexually violent hazing acts perpetrated by male veteran players against rookies. A sixteen-year-old goalie on the team recounted a sexually abusive act at the party in which he was ordered to strip naked, after which a bucket was tied to his penis and hockey pucks were flipped into the bucket to see how much pain his penis could sustain (Farrey 2002). According to other reports, a rookie team member was required to eat a marshmallow placed in another player's anus (Robinson 2004). Both the team trainer and team captain pleaded guilty to committing indecent acts. In exchange for their guilty pleas, the team trainer was fined $4,000 and the team captain $2,000. All of the other 135 charges, including charges of sexual assault, were dropped (Hornberger 1995). No league disciplinary action was reported.

In 1996, the OPP investigated a sexually violent hazing incident that occurred on a team bus of the Kingsville Comets junior hockey team (Smrke 1998). Six rookie players on the team were reportedly required to undress in the bus bathroom and walk naked up the bus aisle while being slapped on the buttocks by veteran players. Once at the front of the bus, the players had to shake hands with the team coaches, while still nude, before walking back through the bus aisle, again being hit by veteran players before returning to the bathroom to dress. After a parent contacted the police with the allegation of sexual assault, a two-month investigation was initiated. However, the police concluded that participation in the hazing incident was voluntary and that consent of the players involved was implied (Smrke 1998). No league disciplinary actions or criminal charges were reported in this hazing incident.

A similar story came to light in 2018 when several players from the 2002–03 Sarnia Sting junior hockey team went public with numerous reports of sexually violent hazing to which rookies on the team were subjected (Chidley-Hill 2018). These reports became the basis of a class-action lawsuit in 2020 filed by multiple former junior hockey players. These alleged incidents included veteran players beating rookies with a broken goalie stick, locking rookies in the bathroom on the team bus and spitting on them through vents, and urinating on them in the team showers. Additionally, the rookies were forced to perform naked pushups while their genitals dipped into a menthol-based ointment intended for sore muscles, and they were forced to sit naked in a rolling wash bin of unwashed equipment while other athletes pushed them around in what was called "the rookie rocket" (Campbell 2020, para. 11). As in the other cases, no criminal charges or league disciplinary actions were ever reported in these incidents. The class-action lawsuit was denied in February 2023, not because it was without merit but, as the judge indicated, "it is not conceivable that such a plan could be fashioned to deal in one class action with the evil that has persisted for half a century in amateur hockey."[9]

In 2005, the Ontario Hockey League investigated an in-practice fight that occurred between a rookie and a veteran player, Steve Downie, of the Windsor Spitfires. In the practice, Downie reportedly tapped the rookie on the shoulder and cross-checked him in the face with his stick, knocking out multiple teeth (Maki 2005). Through the investigation of the fight between the two players, Downie's actions were found to be a form of retaliation in response to the rookie's refusal to participate in an act of hazing (Joyce 2017). In the hazing incident, veteran players allegedly required all rookies to strip naked and cram into a small bathroom at the back of the team bus with the heat turned up for trip home from an away game. The veteran players called the act the "hot box" (Maki 2005, para. 9). The rookie player refused to participate, which reportedly prompted the subsequent physical fight between him and Downie. The coach and general manager of the team, Moe Mantha, was suspended for one year for allowing the hazing to occur. Downie was suspended five games. The rookie was suspended for a game and instructed to take anger management classes for his role in the fight with Downie and was booed by hometown fans when he returned to play (Maki 2005). Whereas Downie went on to be drafted in the first round of the NHL draft and had a successful nine-year NHL career, the rookie, a person of colour and a highly ranked NHL prospect, was drafted in the second round of the NHL draft but never had a career in the NHL. Commenting on his experiences thirteen years later, the rookie stated that "I strongly believe the publicity around the hazing incident in Windsor turned my career sideways and to this day I've never been able to reclaim my reputation. I was humiliated as a target of hazing and then physically assaulted and yet somehow people looked at me as a villain and troublemaker" (quoted in Joyce 2017). No criminal charges were ever reported in relation to the incident.

In 2011, a complaint was filed in Manitoba after five male players were hazed on the Neepawa Natives junior hockey team. According to the mom of one of the victims, veteran athletes on the team tied a set of water bottles to her son's genitals and "made him walk around the dressing room three times. The other players did their thing. They threw towels on the bottles for extra weight" (Turner 2011, para. 2). In total, sixteen players, the head coach, and an assistant coach received league suspensions for their involvement in the hazing, and the team received a $5,000 fine (*CBC News* 2011a). Although the incident was investigated by the RCMP, no criminal charges were ever reported.

In 2018, male athletes at St. Michael's College School in Toronto were videotaped on two occasions pinning down other students in a locker room and sexually prodding them with a broomstick (Warren 2018). The videos were circulated on social media sites (Carter 2019). In response to the incident and the significant media attention that it garnered, school officials cancelled the varsity football and basketball seasons. Publication bans restricted reporting of the athletes' names and specific details of the incidents. However, uniquely, criminal charges related to assault and sexual assault were laid by the Toronto police against seven boys under the Youth Criminal Justice Act (Warren 2018). Four of the students charged were expelled from St. Michael's College, and three withdrew voluntarily (Carter 2019). Criminal charges against two of the boys were dropped. Three pleaded guilty to sexual assault offences and were sentenced to two years of probation, during which they were required to complete thirty hours of community service and educational training addressing sexual boundaries and consent (L. Casey 2019). Another pleaded guilty and was given an absolute discharge (L. Casey 2021). In the trial, one of the teenage athletes argued that he was required to hold one of the victims down while the sexual assault took place and that, if he refused, he would have risked being a target of bullying from other teammates (L. Casey 2021). He was found guilty of sexual assault and sexual assault with a weapon and received a probationary sentence of two years with no jail time. A victim of the sexually violent hazing later began civil legal proceedings against the school administrators, football team coaches, and veteran players, claiming long-term emotional, physical, and psychological damages from the incident (Mandel 2019). This case marked a significant departure from the more common trend seen in other cases of the criminal legal system largely ignoring incidents of hazing in sports. The judge presiding over the case stated in the trial that it was a "violent and humiliating sexual assault [that called for] strong denunciation" (quoted in L. Casey 2021, para. 5).

The St. Michael's College case, and those before it, involved significant physical violence during acts that align with the legal definition of sexual assault. In these cases, rookie athletes reportedly had their genitals forcefully hit, weighed down with weights, or covered in substances to cause pain, and weapons, such as a broomstick in the St. Michael's College case, were used for nonconsensual anal penetration. A few of these violent acts were met with league sanctions and criminal investigations, particularly the two that occurred in the 2010s, amid a growing public discourse on sexual assault. Changes in technology and its use in incidents of hazing might also have influenced how sport administrators and the criminal legal system responded to sexually violent hazing. The video evidence circulated on social media in the St. Michael's College case generated significant public attention and reflected a clear breach of the culture of silence around sexually violent hazing in competitive men's sport. Given the history of how sexually violent hazing has often been minimized and ignored in sport and law, it is fair to wonder whether the St. Michael's College incident would have received the level of public condemnation that it did without the publicly available video documenting it.

Men's University Sport

Although most publicly documented reports of sexually violent hazing involve boys and young men in competitive sports, two cases have been publicly reported in men's university sport in Canada. One of the cases, at McGill University, led to sweeping changes in hazing prevention in Canadian university sport and sparked the inauguration of zero-tolerance hazing policies at all universities across the country. Although it is commonly believed that the policies have been effective, it is also possible that they are driving sexually violent hazing rituals further underground by encouraging athletes, coaches, and university administrators to maintain silence when such acts occur. Fogel's (2013) study on hazing in Canadian football was conducted in the aftermath of the reported incident at McGill University and the introduction of zero-tolerance hazing policies. All fifty-nine participants interviewed reported that they were hazed by veteran players despite the existence of zero-tolerance hazing policies (Fogel 2013). Interestingly, many of the cases excluded from this analysis because of a lack of publicly available information were connected to university contexts. It is likely that these two cases are therefore a significant underrepresentation of a problem that persists in men's university sport but has been effectively hidden from public view.

In 1996, veterans of the University of Guelph Gryphons men's hockey team notified team rookies of an upcoming initiation party with instructions that they should "bring condoms, booze, and wear loose-fitting clothes, because they wouldn't be wearing them long" (cited in Robinson 1998, 84). One of the rookie players was reportedly hesitant to participate but went anyway. As he entered the room, he saw some of his fellow first-year team-mates naked on the floor and left immediately to report the incident to his coach, Marlin Muylaert. Upon reporting what he witnessed to the coach, the rookie was suspended from the team for not participating in the haz-ing ritual and for reporting it (MacLeod 1996). In a letter to the players and University of Guelph administration, the coach explained his decision by stating that "the bottom line is there are two kinds of hazing rituals, one is the degrading, damaging type, the other is fun and enjoyable. This was the fun and enjoyable type" (quoted in Bryshun 1997, 41). What the coach considered "fun and enjoyable" hazing acts reportedly involved heavy drink-ing, forced nudity, rookie teammates passing eggs mouth to mouth, and rookies eating marshmallows out of other players' anuses (Bryshun 1997). No criminal charges were ever reported for the incident. After an investiga-tion, the University of Guelph gave the coach a one-game suspension for his conduct. The athlete subsequently sued the University of Guelph, claiming psychological damages and harassment that forced him to leave the school and abandon his hockey career (McCarthy 1997).

In contrast to the University of Guelph's response, in 2005, McGill University took what seemed to be an unprecedented stand against hazing in university sport when it suspended the entire football program for the remainder of the season following a hazing incident (*CBC Sports* 2005). After an investigation, university officials released a statement reporting that the hazing incident involved "nudity, degrading positions and behaviours, gag-ging, touching in inappropriate manners with a broomstick, as well as verbal and physical intimidation of rookies by a large portion of the team" (Drolet 2006). The incident had an unsettling resemblance to the more recent haz-ing case at St. Michael's College previously described. The players who were directly involved in the hazing incident at McGill University were penalized by the university and required to do community service, reportedly to learn more appropriate methods of team building. Despite the marked differ-ence in the university's response in this case, no criminal charges were ever reported for the incident. Although the suspension for the remainder of the season might appear to be a harsh penalty, the university did not announce the suspension until the team achieved only one win in their first six games, which meant that they had little hope of a successful season on the field and could no longer make the playoffs (*CBC Sports* 2005).

Making Sense of Sexually Violent Hazing

Existing literature offers a range of explanations for hazing. Fogel (2013) asked the fifty-nine male Canadian football players he interviewed, all of whom had participated in hazing rituals, why hazing occurs in sport. Some athletes reported that they engage in hazing activities to (1) build team cohesion, (2) continue team traditions, (3) deflate the self-confidence of rookie teammates, (4) teach rookie athletes lessons, (5) have fun, and (6) break the monotony of training camps and the playing season. Echoing these findings, other researchers have found that hazing is commonly used to promote team cohesion, group identity, status, and belonging (Chin and j. johnson 2011; Clayton 2012; Crow and Macintosh 2009; Dias and Sa 2012; j. johnson 2011; Lafferty, Wakefield, and Brown 2017; Sweet 1999; Van Raalte et al. 2007; Waldron and Krane 2011).

Although these explanations might cover some forms of hazing, they are limited in explaining why athletes engage in the sexually aggressive, violent forms of hazing seen in the previous examples. What prompts athletes to sexually assault their new teammates? And why does hazing so commonly include sexually degrading and humiliating acts? The unique nature of sexually violent forms of hazing demands a more nuanced explanation.

Robinson (1998, 92) suggests that the sexual nature of some hazing in sports is a key element of the perceived effectiveness of the hazing ritual: "When players are induced to break sexual taboos, they have crossed a line together and shed inhibitions that would otherwise place limits on what they are willing to do for the sake of the team. In this way they become part of a well-oiled machine without friction of each other's conscience." In sport, participating in sexual acts, coerced or otherwise, is perceived by some as a way to build alliances and team allegiance.

Sandra Kirby and Glen Wintrup (2004, 53) suggest that sexually violent hazing can result, in part, from "sport think," a concept that builds upon the psychological notion of group think. They argue that teams can develop a gang-like mentality in which there is a collective disregard for the well-being of individuals, a heightened belief in the secrecy of group rituals, a shared feeling of invincibility, and a diminished collective moral compass. A sport think mentality, they suggest, provides the foundation for excessive alcohol use and violent, sexually aggressive behaviour. Although group dynamics among athletes provide valuable insights into hazing incidents, they do not offer much insight into why sexually violent hazing often takes similar forms across different groups of athletes and different men's sports and levels. To understand this commonality, it is useful to consider broader dynamics within sport institutions.

As we discussed in Chapter 2, the totalizing nature of competitive sport can fuel potentially dangerous norms and traditions in team cultures that are subjected to minimal outside intervention. Goffman (1961) argued that total institutions resocialize individuals trapped within them. Individuals are stripped of their identities, values, and beliefs while new collective behaviours, attitudes, and identities are built. Just as in Goffman's examples of the prison and the military, so too the rigours of competitive sport aim to strip athletes of their individual identities and produce a collective team identity. Competitive male athletes are socialized to be members of a team of tough and strong players who can collectively dominate others in their athletic endeavours. Although total institutions can arguably be effective in achieving desired results of producing winning athletes and teams, they can also be breeding grounds for violent and destructive acts committed in the name of group solidarity, power, and domination.

The twelve cases of hazing described here make clear that sexually violent hazing is largely tolerated by the Canadian criminal legal system, with only two of the twelve acts of reported sexual assault resulting in criminal convictions. In both cases, the athletes, coaches, and trainers received sentences that were significantly less than would be typical for sexual assault offences in Canada, with none receiving prison time. Although incarceration is not the solution to sexually violent hazing or any other form of sexual assault or violence, as many critical scholars have argued (Goodmark 2018; Gruber 2020; Richie 2012), the outcomes of these cases reveal the relative lack of interest in the Canadian criminal legal system to acknowledge and respond to sexually violent hazing. In all cases before 2005, this general indifference was mirrored by sport leagues and team managers.

In one case, involving the Tilbury Hawks, which did result in a criminal conviction, the league did not take any disciplinary action. A player on the Hawks filed a complaint with a league official after he was sexually violated during a team hazing ritual. The official's response to the complaint, as stated in a CBC *Fifth Estate* documentary titled "Thin Ice," was that "Scott would have to get used to it if he's serious about a future in hockey" (Fruman 1996). In the University of Guelph hockey hazing, the athlete who refused to consent to being sexually violated was suspended, whereas the players reported for attempting to commit the sexually violent acts were not. Such hazing, historically, has thus been not only tolerated but also promoted at times in competitive men's sport in Canada.

Sexually violent hazing, like all forms of sexual assault, is an exercise of power and control. The acts are designed to embarrass, degrade, humiliate, and demasculinize new team members to create and maintain a power hierarchy on the team. As Messner (1992, 13) argues, "sport must be viewed as an institution through which domination is not only imposed, but also contested; an institution within which power is constantly at play." These plays of power in sport must be understood in the context of the unique forms of masculinity within sport.

Such power struggles are clear in the examples described in this chapter. In each case, veteran players targeted and assaulted younger players on the team or in the organization. This power struggle can be aimed in part at lessening the status of a rookie athlete, who may have been a strong player who moved up from a lower playing level. In the case of the Windsor Spitfires, the rookie was seen as an upcoming superstar when he joined the team, and thus he had the potential to overshadow the accomplishments and abilities of team veteran Steve Downie. Tensions between veteran and rookie were reportedly high as they jostled to be the star player, and unlike many rookies, this rookie seemingly felt able to fight back physically.

As discussed, Connell and Messerschmidt (2005) assert that masculinities are part of a complex hierarchy within social institutions, characterized by power struggles between dominant and subordinate forms. Masculinities are thus "multiple" (Carrigan, Connell, and Lee 1985, 551) and generate power relations among men, particularly in the context of male-dominated total institutions. One way that this occurs is the othering and marginalizing of masculinities seen to be subordinate through blatant forms of homophobia and the explicit intolerance of everything coded as feminine. Hazing is largely about "making someone submissive to prove your own masculinity. Whether it is sodomizing them or making them wear women's panties, the notion of forcing younger players to submit to team veterans comes right out of the handbook of anti-gay stereotypes" (Cyd Ziegler, quoted in Waldron, Lynn, and Krane 2011). Acts of sexually violent hazing are done to degrade and humiliate, to undermine rookies' masculine status, to reinforce homophobic attitudes, and to devalue femininity in sports (E. Anderson 2005; Groves, Griggs, and Leflay 2012). As Franklin (2004, 25) writes, young men in certain social environments target those who embody the feminine "other": girls, women, gay men, or people who embody traits read as feminine. In some hazing rituals, veteran players coerce younger players into performing the "feminine other" with the aim of demeaning, disempowering, and humiliating them. Through these rituals, femininity thus becomes tied to weakness, fragility, and shame, setting the stage for other forms of athlete-perpetrated violence, particularly against women and girls.

Competitive male sport is an arena of contested masculinities in which male-identified athletes seek to affirm and reassert their masculinity through power over and dominance of others: "A football team is in many ways a social system with its own set of expectations. A social hierarchy exists within the group where veterans who have been members of the team the longest hold the most power, and rookies hold the least. Players who are in power have risen to that status by proving themselves the most masculine" (Allan and DeAngelis 2004, 73). As many scholars have noted, these types of gendered dynamics fuel sexual violence: "Sexual harassment and sexual assault are particularly likely to occur in tightly knit competitive male groups (e.g. military units, gangs, college fraternities, sport) that bind men emotionally to one another and contribute to their seeing sex relations from a position of power and status" (Volkwein-Caplan and Sankaran 2002, 11). In sports, sexually violent hazing is thus used to maintain positions of power and status.

Messner (2002, 27) argues that the "athletic masculinity" constructed in sports is dangerous. Building upon the work of Kaufman (1987), Messner suggests that athletic masculinities lead to "the triad of violence" (27), in which athletes commit violence against opponents, against themselves in the form of playing through injuries, and against women in the form of sexual and physical violence. Masculinity, he argues, becomes a competition in sports in which these three forms of violence become mechanisms by which male athletes climb the rungs of the hierarchy of masculinities. Building upon this triad, sexually violent hazing perpetrated by veteran members against rookies and other new team members could be seen as a fourth form of violence in which violent masculinities in sports are promoted and maintained. Sexually violent hazing can be a tool that some competitive male athletes use to climb the rungs of the hierarchy of masculinities in their sports. Like the other forms of group sexual assault discussed in Chapter 3, hazing in a team setting provides a theatre for performing violent masculinities and engaging in group dominance bonding.

Masculinities in competitive men's sports are precarious and require continued identity work by the athletes. Violent sexual hazing of rookie athletes is one way of stabilizing masculine identities in these highly competitive, hierarchical contexts. In a media interview, the mother of a Tilbury Hawks hazing victim pointed to the hierarchical power structure on male sport teams as a source of the problem: "The boys do these things, they have power over others. Everything is about power. The power is intoxicating. The greater the humiliation, the greater the power" (quoted in Ulmer 2005, 1). Hazing and sexual aggression establish a hierarchy of control and masculine domination within a totalizing institution of sport that historically has tolerated and at times promoted sexually violent hazing.

All of the cases of hazing analyzed in this chapter involved competitive male athletes. We found no publicly documented cases of sexually violent hazing in Canada in which the participants were identified as women, gender queer, or nonbinary athletes in women's or co-ed sports. This finding is echoed in the existing research. In a quantitative study in the United States involving ninety-six female participants who were former high school athletes, zero reported "engaging in or simulating sexual acts" (Tokar and Stewart 2010, 8). Although the lack of publicly documented Canadian cases of sexually violent hazing involving people who identify as women, gender queer, or nonbinary does not mean that this form of violence does not occur within these groups, it does suggest that male athletes are often at the centre of these incidents.

To suggest that sexually violent hazing is a problem in men's competitive sports is not to say that *all* men in these sports engage in such hazing. Rather, competitive men's sports are fertile soil for some athletes in certain contexts and circumstances to engage in sexually violent hazing. Lenskyj (2004) notes that although progressive men who oppose nonconsensual violence and harassment exist in competitive sports, they can be met with resistance, hostility, ostracization, and retaliation from other men seeking to uphold aggressive, masculine ideals. As a result, sexually violent hazing is often left unquestioned and normalized.

Although sexually violent hazing appears to be a problem largely confined to men's competitive sports, the harms are not restricted to men and men's sports. Hazing rituals that involve the denigration of the feminine contribute to normalizing misogyny, sexism, homophobia, and intolerance and hatred of femininity. These rituals thus reflect and reinforce the marginalization of women, girls, and people who embody traits coded as feminine within and outside sports. Most importantly, these rituals, and the intolerance that they reflect, heighten the risk of athlete-perpetrated sexual assaults against women and girls. Sexually violent hazing in competitive men's sports contributes to a climate in which violence against women and girls is not only seen as normal but also often promoted as part of the culture of competitive men's sports. In this way, such hazing and athlete-perpetrated violence against women and girls are intricately linked.

Although cast as fun and games by some, or as an important part of developing team unity by others, sexually violent hazing in sports can be both damaging and destructive. Although rarely defined as criminal, such acts commonly fit definitions of sexual assault in the Criminal Code. Sexually violent hazing involves acts that violate the sexual integrity of the rookie athlete. In a context in which an athlete cannot become a full member of a team, and can face bullying, exclusion, and even discipline for refusing to participate in a hazing ritual, freely given, uncoerced consent is not possible.

In the previous three chapters, disturbing trends have emerged. Athlete-perpetrated sexual assaults appear to be the domain of competitive male athletes in Canada, with a high concentration in junior hockey and football. These contexts can be considered what some criminologists term *hot spots* (Ariel and Partridge 2017, 809) in which there are significantly disproportionate rates of specific criminal activities. Although many criminologists use that term to describe geographic areas (Ariel and Partridge 2017; Braga and Bond 2008; Gerell 2016), in the context of sports, the hot spots can be said to be certain competitive men's sports and playing levels that feature cultures that tolerate and promote sexual violence.

In the following chapter, we move in a new direction to examine cases of sexual assault against young athletes perpetrated by coaches and other authority figures in a variety of sports across the country. Athlete-perpetrated sexual assaults, sexually violent hazing rituals, and sexual assaults by coaches and authority figures are part of a broader cycle of violence in sports. By illustrating in Chapter 5 how sexual assaults can become normalized by some coaches and authority figures who violate young athletes, and minimized by the sport organizations to which they belong, we complete the picture of that cycle.

5

Sexual Exploitation by Authority Figures
Institutional Tolerance and Betrayal within the Canadian Sport System

In 2019, the Canadian Broadcasting Corporation (CBC) ran a groundbreaking three-part series on sexual exploitation in Canadian sport highlighting that over 200 coaches have been charged with sexual offences against children in the past twenty years in Canada (Heroux and L. Ward 2019; Strashin and L. Ward 2019; L. Ward and Strashin 2019). The series generated significant public attention to the sexual exploitation by coaches of young athletes in Canada as well as to the inadequacy of sport organizations' and government officials' responses to sexual exploitation in sports. Responding to the public pressure that the story generated, Minister of Sport Kirsty Duncan stated that "I want people to know that this work is being acted on right now. It continues. That this doesn't stop. It's been a priority for our government ... My No. 1 priority is ending abuse and protecting athletes of all ages and abilities and protecting our children" (quoted in Chidley-Hill 2019). The news story sparked widespread public discussion about sexual exploitation by coaches in Canadian sport and generated new questions about who perpetrates and is victimized by sexual exploitation in sports, how sport organizations and the legal system have responded to these cases, and why sexual exploitation remains a persistent problem in Canadian sport.

In this chapter, we examine 243 reported cases in Canada involving coaches and other authority figures in sports who have been accused, and in some cases convicted, of sexual assault, sexual exploitation, and/or sexual interference. In the vast majority of these cases, the victims are young athletes. Unlike the other forms of sexual assault in sport discussed in this book, criminal legal system responses to adults accused of sexually exploiting children and teenagers in sports feature significantly more criminal convictions. However, as the sheer number of cases occurring over multiple decades suggests, criminalization has done little to curb sexual assault in sport. Many of the cases in this chapter span generations and involve authority figures who have sexually assaulted young athletes for decades without their violence being formally reported or with reports not being taken seriously by sport organizations or police. In some cases, coaches have been convicted of sexual assaults, served prison time, returned to coaching, and committed subsequent sexual assaults leading to further criminal convictions. Through these cases, we explore not only why adult authority figures perpetrate sexual assaults against children and teenagers but also how and why sport organizations and the criminal legal system have been largely ineffective in addressing this violence.

We use the term *authority figure* to refer to any adult formally involved in a sport organization in a capacity that allows that person to work with or have some influence on athletes. Included in this broad definition are coaches, team doctors or trainers, managers, directors, facility staff, billet hosts, drivers, and/or referees. In many of the cases discussed, accused and convicted perpetrators occupy multiple roles of authority within their sport organizations, such as a coach who also serves as a club director or manager and holds considerable power within an organization and over the lives of young athletes in their care.

Prevalence of Sexual Assault by Authority Figures in Sport

Of all the different forms of sexual assault in sport, coach-perpetrated sexual assaults against athletes have been the most widely researched. Much of this research has been conducted outside Canada, with the exception of some quantitative survey-based Canadian research (e.g., Kirby and Greaves 1997; Kirby, Greaves, and Hankivsky 2000; Parent et al. 2016).

Sandra Kirby and Lorraine Greaves (1997) surveyed 266 male and female national team athletes in Canada about their experiences and perceptions of sexual abuse and harassment. They found that 52 percent of national-level athletes in Canada are directly aware of or have witnessed sexual harassment or abuse in their sport environments. In 72 percent of those incidents, the perpetrator of the abuse was a coach (Kirby, Greaves, and Hankivsky 2000). Fifty-eight of the 266 surveyed athletes (22 percent) indicated that they had had sexual intercourse with an authority figure in their sport. Of those, 26 percent also reported being physically or emotionally abused by the authority figure with whom they had had sexual relations. The fifty-eight athletes did not, however, necessarily view their sexual relations with authority figures as sexual assaults, even though they likely could be legally defined as such given the inherent power imbalance between coaches and athletes. A total of thirteen athletes (5 percent) reported experiencing sexual assaults in their sport environments, twelve of whom were identified as female and one as male (Kirby, Greaves, and Hankivsky 2000). A study of youth sexual behaviour surveyed 6,450 teenagers, not all of whom were athletes, between fourteen and sixteen years old in Quebec (Parent et al. 2016). Thirty-three of them indicated that they had been sexually abused by a coach. It is not known how many athletes were in the sample or if the thirty-three victims abused by coaches were athletes.

Similar prevalence studies have been conducted internationally. In Australia, in a study of 370 athletes at various levels of sport (Leahy et al. 2002), 37 (10 percent) reported experiencing sexual abuse in a sport environment, with higher rates of victimization at elite levels than at club or recreational levels. In a quantitative study in Denmark, a survey of 140 student athletes revealed that 8.5 percent had been kissed by a coach on the mouth, 25 percent had been inappropriately stared at by a coach in a sexual manner, and 2 percent had experienced sexual advances by a coach (Nielsen 2001). In the same study, of the 207 coaches surveyed, 41 indicated that they had engaged in a sexual relationship with an athlete over eighteen, and 6 reported that they had engaged in a sexual relationship with an athlete under eighteen (Nielsen 2001). A survey of 210 female university athletes in the United States (Volkwein-Caplan et al. 1997) found that 2 percent had experienced unwanted sexual advances from coaches. A survey of 4,043 athletes in the Netherlands found that 14 percent indicated that they had been sexually victimized (Vertommen et al. 2016).

Studies focusing on sexual harassment have shown even higher estimates. In a Norwegian study of 553 female athletes, 284 (51 percent) had experienced sexual harassment (Fasting et al. 2000). Similarly, in a retrospective British survey of 6,124 young adults responding to questions on their experiences as children in sports, 171 (3 percent) indicated that they had been sexually abused and 1,784 (29 percent) had been sexually harassed (Alexander et al. 2011). Most significant for this chapter, a study in 2008 (Brackenridge et al.) pointed to the commonality of coach-perpetrated sexual violence. Of the 159 cases of sexual violence in sports examined in that study, 98 percent had been perpetrated by coaches.

Although existing literature has clearly illustrated high rates of sexual assault and harassment perpetrated by coaches, little attention has been given to sexual assaults perpetrated by other authority figures in sports, such as trainers, managers, directors, billet hosts, and others in positions of power. Celia Brackenridge (2001, 26) aptly noted that "exploitation can be perpetrated by anyone in a position of authority over an athlete, including medical staff, administrative staff, janitors and bus drivers or even senior peer athletes ... [Yet] very little specific research has been undertaken into the role of non-coaching personnel in sexual exploitation." More recently, the narrow focus on coaches in the literature has begun to shift, particularly in response to the high-profile case of Larry Nassar, which has inspired a growing body of research on sexual assaults perpetrated by personnel other than coaches (see Doyle 2019; Meadows and Meadows 2019; Mountjoy 2018; Smith and Pegararo 2020).

Since 2015, over 260 female gymnasts have reported that they were sexually assaulted by Nassar, a Michigan State University doctor and professor who also served as the USA Gymnastics team doctor (Buncombe 2018). During treatment sessions with athletes, Nassar sexually violated female athletes as young as six years old (Chavez 2018). FBI agents seized more than 37,000 images and videos of him sexually abusing underage girls; he had covertly recorded the abuse during his sessions with them (Kozlowski 2017). The allegations made international headlines as the disturbing details of the crimes, sheer number of reported victims, and high profiles of many of the athletes on Olympic and national teams became clear. Even though athletes began reporting his abuse in the 1990s, it was not until 2015 that USA Gymnastics finally suspended Nassar (Connor 2016). After pleading guilty to charges of sexual assault, sexual assault of minors, and child pornography, he was sentenced to a prison term of up to 175 years (Hauser and Astor 2018). Michigan State University reached a settlement agreement with the victims in the amount of US$500 million (Hobson and Boren 2018), and USA Gymnastics and the US Olympic Committee reached a US$380 million settlement agreement with his victims (Kaplan 2021). The young women whom Nasser sexually abused are now also suing the FBI in the amount of US$130 million for failing to take action against Nassar sooner, which they argue could have prevented some sexual assaults (Bieler 2022). The Nassar case makes clear that not just coaches are involved in the sexual exploitation of athletes within sport as well as the potential costs to sport organizations and law enforcement agencies for failing to address the problem of sexual exploitation by authority figures.

Canadian and international research points to high rates of sexual assault against athletes by coaches and authority figures in sports. Determining precise rates of prevalence, however, remains a challenge. Athletes included in existing studies are often at different age and competition levels, making the samples difficult to compare. The research has also relied on different survey instruments and terminologies for sexual assaults, making comparison of data and results difficult. Whereas some studies conflate *sexual harassment* and *sexual abuse*, others draw a clear distinction between the two, and still others opt not to use either term and simply refer to specific acts, such as kissing, touching, et cetera. However, studies that have differentiated sexual assault from other forms of sexual abuse, focused on athletes as victims, and identified coaches as perpetrators of sexual violence show that between 2 and 10 percent of athletes report having been victimized by a coach.

Building upon existing quantitative literature on the prevalence of coach-perpetrated sexual assaults, in this chapter we provide an in-depth, qualitative analysis of reported sexual assaults by coaches and other authority figures in Canadian sport. Through an analysis of these legal cases, we identify the common forms and some of the consequences of sexual assaults perpetrated by authority figures as well as how sport organizations and the criminal legal system have responded to this form of violence. This analysis provides the foundation for a broader theoretical discussion of how and why authority figures in sports are often able to commit sexual assaults with relative impunity and limited accountability over significant periods of time.

Harmful Consequences of Sexual Assault by Authority Figures in Sport

Existing research indicates that child sexual abuse can have a range of negative consequences for victims, including severe and long-term depression (Ratican 1992; Scarce 1998; Thomas et al. 2011), substance abuse (Browne and Finkelhor 1986), eating disorders (Ratican 1992), lifelong challenges with intimacy and trust (Feinauer et al. 1996; Maltz 2002; Pearson 1994), problems with anger management (Maltz 2002), low perception of self-worth and self-esteem (Hartman et al. 1987; L. Long et al. 2006), and increased risk of self-harm and suicide attempts (L. Anderson 1981; Colton and Vanstone 1996). Many of these consequences have been reported by athletes who have been sexually assaulted by authority figures in sport. Summarizing these consequences, the judge in the trial of multisport coach Michael McNutt described the victim impact statements of thirty-four men abused as boys:

> they have suffered from childhoods that were severely disrupted. Some have dealt with depression. Some have struggled with substance abuse. Some have had ongoing issues with anger. Some have had a series of broken

relationships. It is a familiar pattern in cases that involve sexual violence against children. For each of those damaged lives there are grandparents, parents, spouses, former spouses, children, aunts, uncles, cousins, friends, and professionals who have picked up the pieces, often without knowing why there were pieces to be picked up.[1]

These experiences were echoed by three victims of hockey coach Graham James who have written autobiographies about their experiences of his sexual abuse and the negative impacts that it had on their lives (Fleury 2009; Gilhooly 2018; Kennedy 2006). Despite their successful careers – Fleury and Kennedy both played in the NHL and Gilhooly is an Ivy League–educated lawyer – they all described their struggles with substance abuse, depression, and suicidal thoughts. Gilhooly also reported that he engaged in a variety of self-harming behaviours. Describing one incident of self-harm, he writes that,

> One day, I was lying on my back on my weight bench, sweating, in the middle of a set of chest flies, arms extended out to the side, a dumbbell in each hand. Why? I put the left dumbbell down on the ground. I set the right dumbbell on my chest. I put both hands on the single dumbbell and extended my arms directly toward the ceiling. Then I let go, dropping the dumbbell onto my chest, ribs, and upper abs. Pain. Intense pain. Nothing but pain. Nothing ... I loved the pain for releasing me from my thoughts. All I could think of was pain. It was perfect. (Gilhooly 2018, 69)

Gilhooly also explained how he would self-harm by digging his nails into his skin until he bled, deliberately cutting himself, and overeating. Echoing these experiences, Theoren Fleury wrote in his victim impact statement that

> I was just a kid. A child. I was completely under Graham James's control. And I was scared. I did not have the emotional skills, the knowledge, or the ability to stop the rapes or change my circumstances. I felt lost, alone, and helpless. And those feelings did not stop after I was able to get away from Mr. James; I continued to feel that way for 20+ years afterwards. I descended into years of drug addiction, alcoholism, and addictions to sex, gambling, rage. My loved ones, including my beloved children, spiraled down with me. The pain was all-encompassing. And no matter how many NHL games I won, or money I made, or fame I gained could dull the pain of having been sexually abused by Graham James. His sickness changed my life, changed the lives of everyone who was close to me, and caused more

pain than can be measured. Finally, after a night in the New Mexico desert with a gun in my mouth and finger on the trigger, I found the courage to get help and start a long process of healing. (Fleury 2012, para. 4)

As these autobiographies make clear, the harms of sexual assaults on young athletes can be immense and lifelong.

The harms that victims of sexual assault in sport experience are compounded when sport organizations fail to meaningfully respond when such assaults occur, often further betraying the trust of victims and their families. The term *institutional betrayal* (see Fitzgerald 2017, 483) has been used to describe the ways that organizations tolerate sexual violence, ignore or deny reports that could damage the reputation of the organization, and fail to respond to the needs of victims. The term *systemic trauma* (see Goldsmith, Martin, and Smith 2014, 117) has been used to describe institutional actions, or inactions, that heighten the impacts of traumatic experiences. The context of sport is characterized by both institutional betrayal and resulting systemic trauma.

Beyond the known consequences to victims, sexual assault by authority figures in sport can have consequences for others. When publicized, this form of violence can erode athletes', parents', and the public's trust in sport organizations to keep children safe. Parents might be less likely to enrol their children in sports, fearing potential sexual abuse. Sport organizations can also face lawsuits when one of their coaches, employees, or volunteers sexually assaults an athlete within the organization. In legal terms, the *doctrine of vicarious liability* means that organizations can be liable for the harmful behaviours of their employees or volunteers (Preston 2006; M. White 2005). Unlike *direct liability*, vicarious liability does not require that the organization or employer directly cause the harm that gives rise to the lawsuit. Instead, it must be shown that the organization or employer failed to take reasonable precautionary measures to prevent the harm. The damages sought in vicarious liability cases involving child victims of sexual assaults in sport organizations can be significant. For example, victims of sexual assaults by a former Ottawa basketball coach, Donald Greenham, have filed an $8 million lawsuit against the Ottawa District School Board for failing to protect them from his sexual abuse (Duffy 2018b). Similarly, multiple victims of sexual assaults by former national alpine ski team coach and director Bertrand Charest have filed a class-action lawsuit against Alpine Canada for allegedly covering up his sexual abuse of young female athletes and failing to appropriately address the problem (Canadian Press 2019).

Child sexual abuse within sport organizations can also lead to criminal charges against sport administrators and other coaches who were aware of the abuse but failed to report it. In the United States, when senior officials at Penn State University became aware that a coach, Jerry Sandusky, was sexually abusing young boys but failed to report the crimes to police, they were found guilty of child endangerment and sentenced to prison terms (Thompson 2017). In Canada, in the case of *R v Kaija*, when Peter Kaija, the director of a youth basketball program in Ontario, was informed by a parent that one of the coaches in the program, Jim Miller, had reportedly sexually assaulted a young male basketball player at an away tournament, he removed Miller as a coach.[2] However, because Kaija did not report the alleged sexual assault to police or a Children's Aid Society, he was later charged with failure to report the abuse under the Child and Family Services Act. As these and other cases in this chapter illustrate, sexual assaults by authority figures have not only a range of harmful impacts on victims but also ripple effects on the lives of many others.

Relevant Laws

Although we focus in this chapter on legal cases involving authority figures in sports from the past thirty years, some of the reported sexually violent offences included in these cases date back to the 1950s. In Canada, there is no statute of limitations on sexual offences, so victims can report sexual assaults to police decades after they occurred. In historical cases, the accused can choose to apply the law as it was when the alleged crimes occurred, or they can opt to apply the current laws when the case is brought to trial. In most of the historical cases in this chapter, the accused chose the laws in place when the reported sexual offences occurred, perhaps because they perceived the historical language for sexually violent offences as less stigmatizing (e.g., indecent assault as opposed to sexual exploitation) or the possible sentences as preferable. Although the maximum sentences for the comparable offences have not changed from the 1970s to today, some mandatory minimum sentences have been added, which might encourage the accused who committed sexually violent acts before the sexual assault law reforms of the 1980s to choose to be tried for historical sexual offences.

Before 1983 in Canada, rape was defined in the Criminal Code as "the act of a man having carnal knowledge of a woman who is not his wife without her consent."[3] In law, only women could be raped, and husbands could legally rape their wives. Proving rape in a criminal court of law required demonstrating that vaginal penetration had occurred. Other sexual offences, such as indecent assault and/or gross indecency, more commonly appear in the legal cases involving coaches accused of sexual assaults before the 1980s. Before 1983, indecent assault referred to any form of sexual indecency that did not involve vaginal rape or anal penetration. Indecent assault was seen as "an assault that is committed in circumstances of indecency, or ... an assault with acts of indecency," and was a precursor to current sexual assault offences in Canada.[4] Like the current crime of sexual assault, indecent assault carried a maximum sentence of ten years in prison.[5] In contrast, gross indecency was not clearly defined in the Criminal Code. Before 1987, this offence was used almost exclusively to prosecute men engaged in same-sex sexual activity in which at least one of the men was under twenty-one years old. As such, gross indecency is now understood as a criminal offence that both reflected and promoted homophobia, as it was used to target and criminalize gay men (A. Mann 2016). Gross indecency carried a maximum five-year prison sentence. Unlike the offences of rape and indecent assault that were repealed in 1983, gross indecency was repealed in 1987.[6]

Several historical cases of sexual assault perpetrated by authority figures featured the criminal charge of buggery. Buggery existed in the Criminal Code from 1892 to 1987 and referred to a perceived "unnatural form of sexual intercourse," which primarily included anal intercourse and bestiality.[7] Like gross indecency, the criminal offence of buggery has been recognized as homophobic, as it was historically used to target nonheterosexual activity (R. Elliott et al. 2016). Although gross indecency and buggery laws have troubled pasts, we have included cases in which these laws were used when the victim was a minor and the accused was an adult in a position of authority.

The most significant changes to Canada's sexual assault laws occurred in 1983 (Benedet 2010a). The reforms to Canada's rape laws were fuelled by growing pressure from the Canadian feminist anti-rape movement and came about following the enactment of the Charter of Rights and Freedoms in 1982, which provided a constitutional guarantee of equality rights under the law, freedom from sex discrimination, and the right to security of the person. Once sexual offences could be challenged constitutionally for their inadequacies, and amid public pressure from feminist advocacy groups, the sexual offence laws were amended to remove rape, indecent assault, gross indecency, and buggery, which were replaced with new sexual assault offences (Backhouse 2008).

As a result of the reforms in 1983, sexual assault was separated into three tiers: (1) sexual assault, which carries a maximum sentence of ten years in prison; (2) sexual assault with a weapon, threat of the use of a weapon, or causing bodily harm, which carries a maximum sentence of fourteen years; and (3) aggravated sexual assault, which carries a maximum sentence of life in prison.[8] Unlike the previous offence of rape, sexual assault in the Criminal Code does not require evidence of vaginal penetration and can be perpetrated by and against all sexes and genders, and husbands can be convicted of sexually assaulting their wives. Most of the cases of sexual assault examined in this chapter have been tried as sexual assaults, often referred to as a "level 1 sexual assault" in crime statistics (O'Grady 2007).

Since 1985, the Criminal Code has provided special protections for young people with child-specific sexual assault offences.[9] The three such offences currently include sexual interference, invitation to sexual touching, and sexual exploitation. Sexual interference refers to the touching of a person under sixteen years old, by someone more than five years older for a sexual purpose, and it carries a maximum sentence of ten years and a minimum sentence of ninety days.[10] Invitation to sexual touching refers to the act of inviting or counselling a person under sixteen years of age to touch the body of any other person for a sexual purpose.[11] This can include the accused inviting a child to touch his or her body for a sexual purpose or the accused counselling a child to touch another child or person while the accused watches. The maximum sentence for invitation to sexual touching is ten years, and the minimum sentence is ninety days. Sexual exploitation is defined as an individual in a position of trust, such as a coach, inviting sexual touching or engaging in sexual contact with a person under eighteen years of age.[12] The maximum sentence for sexual exploitation is fourteen years, and the minimum sentence is ninety days. These child-specific sexual offences differ significantly from broader sexual assault laws because sexual consent cannot be used as a legal defence when the act involves children and youth under the age of eighteen. As a result, and as we demonstrate in this chapter, authority figures who sexually assault athletes are significantly more likely to be convicted of their crimes compared with athletes accused of sexual assaults, who typically argue that the sexual activity was consensual.

Child sexual assault cases, including most of those discussed in this chapter, often revolve around multiple charges. A single sexually violent act between an authority figure and an athlete can result in charges of sexual assault, sexual interference, invitation to sexual touching, and/or sexual exploitation. Prosecutors often proceed on all charges but not necessarily with the aim of convicting the accused on all counts. Rather, this strategy often serves as a protection for the prosecution in case one of the charges becomes difficult to establish beyond a reasonable doubt.[13] If all charges remain viable over the course of the trial, then under the Kienapple Principle the authority figure will not be convicted of all offences.[14]

R v Kienapple established that an individual cannot be convicted of more than one crime arising from a single criminal act. The Kienapple Principle was considered in many cases discussed in this chapter. However, most cases did not revolve around a single act and sometimes involved hundreds of reported sexual assaults by a single authority figure against multiple athletes over a significant period of time. For this reason, many of the cases analyzed here featured multiple convictions.

Reports of Sexual Assault Perpetrated by Authority Figures in Sport

Reports of sexual assault involving authority figures in sport are disproportionately high in number compared with the other forms of sexual assault discussed in this book. In total, we found 243 cases involving over 1,000 victims. Here, we focus on 20 cases of reported sexual assault involving authority figures in sport, 4 from each decade.[15] The 20 cases reflect common themes across the 243 cases of sexual assault perpetrated by coaches and other authority figures.[16]

The identities of sexual assault victims are usually kept confidential under publication bans. As such, it is not always possible to determine who the victims are. However, in at least 187 of the cases, the victims were identified as athletes. In 10 cases, the victims were identified as individuals involved in different roles in sport, typically in positions subordinate to the perpetrator within the hierarchy of the sport organization. Forty-six of the cases did not state whether the victims were athletes.

Unlike the other forms of sexual assault discussed in this book, many contemporary criminal trials of authority figures in sport involve sexual assaults that are historical. In some cases, there is a gap of over twenty years between the date when the sexual assault occurred and the date when the corresponding trial took place. Many of the reported sexual assaults also occurred over many years and even decades and involved multiple children. As such, though we focus on cases that had trials between 1990 and 2020, in many cases the reported sexual assaults occurred in previous decades.

Pre-1980s Reports

Although all of the criminal trials discussed in this chapter occurred within the past thirty years, forty-two cases involved sexual assaults that occurred before the 1980s. All forty-two of the authority figures, thirty-seven of whom were coaches, were publicly identified as male, and the vast majority read as white. In contrast to many of the cases discussed in previous chapters, most of the reported victims from these pre-1980s cases were identified as boys or teenage young men. The high prevalence of male victims in cases from this era was likely shaped, in part, by the socio-historical context of both Canadian sport and law before the 1980s.

During this period, same-sex sexual acts were readily criminalized in the Canadian criminal legal system (Hooper 2019). The age of sexual consent was set at fourteen years old, without specific laws pertaining to power differentials that have since raised the age of sexual consent between an authority figure and a person under their care to eighteen. The criminalization of rape hinged on evidence of forced vaginal penetration. Other sexually violent acts against women were not included in the legal definition of rape. As such, the laws at the time lent themselves to criminalizing sexual violence perpetrated by male coaches against male athletes more so than against female athletes.

Participation rates of women and girls in sport were much lower from the 1950s to the 1980s than today (Hall 2016). At an elite level, female athletes in the 1960s and 1970s made up 16 percent of the Canadian athletes in the Winter Olympics on average and 20 percent of Canadian athletes in the Summer Olympics (Hall and Richardson 1982). While men's sport in Canada became increasingly professionalized in the 1980s, with increases in resources and publicity, women's sport remained under-resourced. The first national championships for Canadian university women's hockey were not held until 1998, which was also the first year that women's hockey was played at the Olympics (Theberge 2000). Women were becoming more involved in sport as athletes and coaches; however, "women, as both athletes and leaders, were often left out of the decision-making processes" (Hall 2016, 216). Opportunities in sport for girls and women in Canada in the 1950s to the 1980s lagged far behind those for men.

These legal and sport contexts led to a heightened number of reported male victims compared with female victims, a trend that has shifted dramatically with legal reforms and increased inclusion of girls and women in sport in Canada. As will become clear, white-presenting men have remained at the centre of most reported sexual assaults by authority figures from the 1950s to the present.

One of the most high-profile and widely reported cases of sexual violence in Canadian sport involved the sexual abuse of boys, many of them aspiring young hockey players, at the old Maple Leaf Gardens in Toronto from the 1960s to the early 1990s (Vine and Challen 2002). Gordon Stuckless was a hockey coach in Toronto who worked at Maple Leaf Gardens as a maintenance man. He, along with three other men – John Paul Roby, an arena usher; Dennis Morin, a security guard; and George Hannah, an equipment manager – reportedly used their positions to coax young aspiring hockey players into the arena. They promised them hockey and concert tickets, arena access, part-time jobs, sports equipment, and memorabilia in exchange for sexual favours. One of the victims reported his experience of sexual abuse at Maple Leaf Gardens to the Toronto police in the 1990s. The victim later died by suicide. However, his report opened the door for many other men with similar experiences of abuse at Maple Leaf Gardens to come forward (Vine and Challen 2002).

In a resulting criminal trial in 1998, Stuckless, already convicted of sexually assaulting eight boys on a hockey team that he coached, pleaded guilty to sexually assaulting twenty-four boys between ten and fifteen years old. Stuckless was originally sentenced to two years less a day in prison, which was increased to six years on appeal by the prosecution. In 2016, he again faced a trial after eighteen more victims came forward. Stuckless was sentenced to an additional six and a half years of house arrest,[17] increased to ten years on appeal (Freeman 2020). The appeal judge described Stuckless's systematic approach to gaining access to victims as follows: "Stuckless groomed his victims, providing them with hockey sticks and sports memorabilia, promising to introduce them to Toronto Maple Leaf players, taking them to movies and hockey games, and so on, all with a view to gaining an opportunity to abuse them."[18] Stuckless died shortly after receiving his last sentence (Aguilar 2020). Some of the other men involved in the abuse were not subjected to the same level of legal scrutiny. George Hannah died in 1984 before ever facing trial (Deacon 1997). Dennis Morin, previously convicted of sexual offences against two boys in 1991 and 1997, was convicted of sexually assaulting two additional boys in 2002 and sentenced to three years in prison (Fowlie 2003; Huffman 2002). John Paul Roby was convicted of sexually assaulting twenty-six boys and one girl and given an indeterminate dangerous offender sentence in 1999. He died in prison in 2001 (Pron 2001). It has been estimated that at least fifty victims have filed lawsuits against Maple Leaf Sport and Entertainment for the sexual abuse that they endured by these men and the organization's inaction in preventing and appropriately responding to the sexual assaults (Westhead 2007). All of the lawsuits have been settled out of court.

Similar forms of sexual abuse were seen in the case of Gary Blair Walker, who admitted in 1992 to sexually assaulting approximately 200 boys, many of whom were hockey players he coached, over a thirty-year span from the late 1960s to the early 1990s (Mascoll 1994). At least four of the victims have since died by suicide. At the time of his trial, Crown prosecutor Tom Fitzgerald dubbed Walker "Canada's worst-ever pedophile" (quoted in Leroux 1999, para. 31). Walker pleaded guilty to various sexual offences in 1992 and received an indeterminate sentence with the label of dangerous offender. He last applied for parole in 2009 and was denied (National Parole Board 2009).

Between 1971 and 1981, an Ottawa basketball coach, Donald Greenham, reportedly sexually assaulted fourteen young men between thirteen and seventeen years old (*CBC News* 2016a). Greenham, a former teacher in Ottawa, coached multiple basketball teams at different ages. During the decade when the assaults reportedly occurred, he was celebrated as a coach for winning three regional championships. According to former players who filed the complaints, Greenham would assign a player to share his bed at away tournaments, where many of the sexual assaults would occur, and he would abuse players in his gym office (Duffy 2018b). One athlete reported the sexual abuse to the Ottawa police but was told that, since he was assaulted in a different city at an away tournament, he needed to file a police report in that city. The young athlete did not do so. One of the schools where Greenham coached held a reunion in 2016, during which former classmates shared memories of their coach. Some disclosed the sexual abuse, leading many others to realize, decades later, that their experiences of abuse by Greenham were not unique (Duffy 2018a). In 2016, he was charged with fifty-five counts of indecent assault and gross indecency (*CBC News* 2016a). Two months before his trial was set to begin, Greenham, now seventy-five, died of a heart attack. After his death, the trial was cancelled, and the charges were withdrawn. Former players reportedly abused by Greenham have filed an $8 million lawsuit against his estate and the Ottawa District School Board for failing to protect them from his sexual abuse (Duffy 2018b).

Michael Patrick McNutt was a teacher from the 1970s to 1990s and coached at least eleven baseball, hockey, and football teams in Nova Scotia during that time. Complaints against McNutt began in the early 1980s, which led him to resign from his full-time teaching position in 1983 (Canadian Press 2020b). In 1985, he resumed teaching part time until a sexual assault complaint was made against him in 1994, which led to a conviction and eventual pardon.[19] In 2016, the Halifax police created a special task force titled Operation Apollo after several men reported that they had been sexually abused by teachers and coaches in the Halifax area in the 1970s and 1980s (Bruce 2019). The investigation led to police identifying and locating thirty-four male victims who reported being sexually abused by McNutt. The trial judge stated that McNutt's *modus operandi,* or common method of committing his crimes, was "generally consistent across all victims."[20] According to the judge, McNutt identified one eleven-year-old boy on his football team in the 1970s as particularly talented and invited him to his house after practice to review some plays. McNutt sexually touched the boy and suggested that in exchange the boy would receive more playing opportunities during games. Many other young athletes whom McNutt coached were invited to his house after games and practices, often given alcohol, and then sexually assaulted in a similar manner, and others were sexually assaulted in his hotel room at away tournaments.[21] McNutt pleaded guilty to ten counts of sexual assault, twenty counts of indecent assault, and five counts of gross indecency (Canadian Press 2020b).

In all of these cases dating before the 1980s, sexual abuse went relatively unchecked for long periods of time. Sport organizations did little to respond and, in many cases, have faced subsequent lawsuits for their inaction. Although criminal convictions have been common in the cases, they have occurred long after the sexual assaults occurred. Similar trends can be identified in subsequent eras.

1980s Reports

Sweeping legal reforms in the early 1980s provided new and broadened definitions of sexual offences in Canada. Other major legal reforms, such as the establishment of the Charter of Rights and Freedoms in 1982, expanded equity rights in Canada, which affected the advancement of women in sport. As a result of these changes, in 1986 a young female hockey player, Justine Blainey, successfully challenged the constitutionality of the Ontario Human Rights Code, which granted sport organizations at the time an exemption from sex discrimination laws.[22] Reforms in the Canadian sport system were also creating more opportunities for girls and women to participate, such as the establishment of the Canadian Association for the Advancement of Women and Sport in 1981 (now Canadian Women and Sport; Safai 2013) and the development of Sport Canada's Policy on Women's Sport in 1986, which stated that, "at all levels of the sport system, equal opportunities must exist for women and men to compete, coach, officiate or administer sport" (Sport Canada 1986, 10). Although the aspirational vision of the policy has never been fully realized, the 1980s were characterized by increased rates of participation of girls and women in competitive sport as well as a rise in the number of men involved in coaching and other leadership positions in women's sport (Hall 2016). Correspondingly, a significantly higher number of girls and young women appear in sexual assault cases in the 1980s, though they are still outnumbered by reported male victims. These cases expose a disturbing trend: as more girls and women entered the traditionally male-dominated terrain of competitive sport in Canada, more experienced sexual assaults by coaches, other authority figures, and (as previous chapters have revealed) male athletes. This finding is consistent with research on gender-based violence more broadly, which has identified that the social advancement of women is often met with more male violence perpetrated against them (Chowdhury 2015).

Before his first arrest in 1997, Graham James had a notable coaching career in Canadian junior hockey. He began coaching in 1979 for the Fort Garry Blues before moving to the Western Hockey League (WHL) in 1983, first as a scout for the Winnipeg Warriors, then as a coach throughout the mid-1980s and 1990s. As a coach for the Swift Current Broncos, he won WHL titles in 1989 and 1993. In 1989, James was named the *Hockey News* "Man of the Year" (Kay 2013). During his time with the Broncos, he was not only the coach but also the general manager of the team (Canadian Press 2015a). This unique positioning within the sport organization gave him the power to draft and trade young athletes as well as the ability to remove players from the team or bench them without any oversight from team management. As became clear in later years, during his run of hockey successes, James was sexually abusing players whom he coached and managed. In 1997, he was convicted of sexual assaults against Sheldon Kennedy and another unnamed player, and he was sentenced to three and a half years in jail. James was granted parole in 2001 after having served eighteen months of the sentence and received a pardon for the offences in 2007 (Banerjee 2016). He returned to coaching and became the assistant coach of Spain's national hockey team. In 2011, he was charged with sexually assaulting two Canadian players he had previously coached, Theoren Fleury and another player, from 1983 to 1994. James returned to Canada and entered guilty pleas for the sexual assault charges laid against him. He was sentenced to two years in prison, later increased to five years following an appeal by the prosecution.[23] Through the criminal trials, it was revealed that James used similar strategies to lure and victimize athletes on his teams. He targeted young men with significant athletic potential who lived away from or had more distant relationships with their parents. He promised the athletes that he would facilitate their advancement to higher playing levels, including the NHL, and threatened to block their hockey careers if they reported the sexual abuse. Describing this power dynamic, the judge in the trial in 2013 stated that,

> because Mr. James was, by all accounts, so revered by the Canadian hockey community, Mr. Fleury and Mr. H___, and their families, were thrilled when Mr. James noticed them and took it on himself to manage their hockey careers. The management of their careers, starting at the young age of 14 in the case of Mr. Fleury, and age 15 in the case of Mr. H___, evolved into management of most aspects of their lives, including schooling, accommodation, travelling and of course, hockey. Mr. Fleury and Mr. H___ were vulnerable and trusted Mr. James. Mr. James abused that trust. He controlled what would happen with their hopes and dreams of playing professional hockey. *He could make or break them. He told them that.* And, he did actually have the power to do so. Mr. Fleury knew it. Mr. H___ knew it. And Mr. James made sure they knew it. That knowledge is what made the sexual assaults possible, and created a situation in which Mr. Fleury and Mr. H___, as teenagers, away from their families, and wanting above all else to play professional hockey, were entirely trapped. If they said anything about the assaults, they believed, and in fact it was so, that Mr. James could have put an end to their hockey aspirations. Mr. James could essentially do what he wanted to do to them, and could rely on their compliance and silence, because he controlled whether they would get the chance at what they really wanted or would have their dreams crushed.[24]

In 2010, James had been charged with sexually assaulting another player, Greg Gilhooly, whom James coached in the 1980s. However, as part of the terms of James pleading guilty to sexually assaulting Fleury and another player, charges resulting from his sexual abuse of Gilhooly were stayed. Gilhooly, now a lawyer, has become an advocate of legal reforms in Canada. In the aftermath of James's pardon in 2007, Gilhooly argued for a reform of the Canadian pardoning system, which had allowed James to return to coaching internationally after he was convicted of sexual assaults against young hockey players in 1997 (Cheedle and Bronskill 2011).

Kevin Michael Hicks, a figure skating coach in Windsor, Ontario, used an approach similar to that of James to sexually abuse the young male athletes whom he was coaching. Hicks, a former national figure skating champion, promised one young male athlete that he "held the keys to his future and was quick to point it out when he wanted sexual favours [in return]" (quoted in McGouran 2015, para. 1). Hicks reportedly sexually assaulted the athlete, who was thirteen years old when the sexual abuse began, in the early 1980s. The abuse reportedly continued for five years. At the time in Canadian law, the age of sexual consent was fourteen, and the crime of sexual exploitation did not yet exist. The judge ruled that the prosecution failed to prove that the sexual activities between the adult coach and the athlete under his care were nonconsensual after the athlete turned fourteen. Hicks was convicted, however, of one count of sexual assault against the athlete when he was thirteen as well as multiple other counts of sexual assault, buggery, and indecent assault involving another young male athlete. Hicks was sentenced to four years in prison in 2015 (Boucher 2015).

As in the Hicks trial, the issue of age and consent was central in the criminal trials of Ontario basketball coach Marvin Sazant. He was an assistant coach of a boys' basketball team in the 1980s. The athlete, who was fourteen when the reported sexual abuse began, testified that Sazant paid more attention to him than the other boys on the team, would give him money and rides from school, and would take him out for lunch. Sazant invited the young athlete to his house, where the sexual abuse reportedly began.[25] Sazant, who was thirty years older than the athlete, did not deny engaging in sexual acts with the athlete under his care but argued that the acts were consensual.[26] The law at the time did not expressly prohibit a forty-four-year-old basketball coach from having sexual relations with a fourteen-year-old athlete. Beyond the testimony of the athlete, the prosecution presented no other evidence that the sexual acts were not consensual. Sazant was found not guilty, a verdict that the prosecution appealed unsuccessfully.[27]

In contrast to Sazant's case, in a criminal case involving Ottawa hockey and baseball coach Kelly Jones, the issue of consent was considered irrelevant. The first player to report sexual assaults by Jones was ten years old when the abuse began in the 1980s, which was under the legal age of consent. At the time of the reported abuse, Jones was the boy's hockey coach. He would reportedly host team movie nights with sleepovers at his house, where he would show pornographic films, give athletes alcohol, and target one to sexually assault. Players reported that Jones threatened those whom he assaulted so they would not say anything about what had occurred. Explaining this, one victim stated that "he had me believing he would kill my mother so I pretty much just kept quiet ... To this day I still shudder at the thought of seeing him. Kelly Jones really did a number on my life" (quoted in *CBC News* 2014c, para. 6). Jones coached hockey in the winter and baseball in the summer. Unlike many other coaches and authority figures mentioned in this chapter, he perpetrated sexual assaults against both young men and women. He pleaded guilty to charges of sexual assault, sexual interference, sexual exploitation, and invitation to sexual touching against ten boys and one girl, some of whom were as young as seven. At his trial in 2014, he told the court that there were more victims not yet identified. Jones was sentenced to eight years in prison (*CBC News* 2014b). Multiple lawsuits with damages ranging from $700,000 to $3.1 million were subsequently filed against Jones, the minor leagues in which he coached, and Hockey Canada for the long-term emotional and psychological damages that victims experienced from the abuse (Spears 2015).

1990s Reports

Legal and sport reforms of the 1980s paved the way for more legal protections for children in the 1990s and increasing numbers of girls and women in competitive sport. In contrast to previous eras, the majority of the legal cases in the 1990s involved victims identified in public reports as female. Despite these numbers, girls and women still participated in sports at lower rates than boys and men and received much less funding and fewer resources (Safai 2013). Internationally, the first World Conference on Women and Sport was held in Brighton in 1994, which led to the Brighton Declaration, the first international declaration on gender equity principles in sport (Hall 1996). Broader discussions about sexual violence in sport also began to emerge in the 1990s as a result of increased media coverage of and academic attention to the issue. Within Canadian sport organizations, however, little attention was given to addressing the persistent problem of the sexual assault by coaches and other authority figures of young athletes.

While some authority figures sexually exploit athletes under their care for years without being reported, others are reported and often continue their involvement in minor sports. Gilbert Dubé is one such example. In 1993, Dubé, a Montreal youth hockey coach, pleaded guilty to charges of sexual exploitation. After serving an unreported sentence for that offence, he continued coaching. In 2002, Dubé's son reportedly found sexually explicit photos of his father with a young athlete, which he reported to police (Montgomery 2011). The report did not lead to any criminal charges, and Dubé continued coaching. In 2004, Dubé's son reportedly raised concerns about his father's past criminal behaviour, specifically his history as a sex offender, as well as the photos that he had found, with the Montreal North Minor Hockey Association, for which Dubé was coaching (*CTV*

News 2011). Reports suggest that although Dubé was open about his criminal record, the association allowed him to continue coaching. In 2011, he faced charges for sexually assaulting four young male hockey players, some as young as eleven, whom he was coaching from 2002 to 2009. According to media reports, Dubé targeted boys from impoverished backgrounds, coerced them with gifts and special treatment, and sexually abused them before and after games at the arenas where they played (Montgomery 2011). He pleaded guilty to charges of sexual interference and invitation to sexual touching and was sentenced to five years in prison. When Dubé spoke with reporters before the sentencing hearing, he indicated that Hockey Quebec was to blame for the children's victimization because he was allowed to coach several hockey teams over two decades despite his history as a sex offender, which he said he had not concealed (*CBC News* 2011b).

Bertrand Charest, who coached and held administrative leadership roles for several alpine skiing teams, including the Canadian national team, also continued coaching when reports and rumours of his abuse were circulating. Although there is no record of police reports against him in the 1990s, a recent lawsuit against Alpine Canada by women Charest sexually exploited suggests that other coaches and administrators were aware of the sexual abuse and did nothing (Klowak 2018). Likewise, at his criminal trial in 2017, a witness testified seeing Charest at an away event in the mid-1990s pin down a young female teammate in front of the ski team and sexually assault her (Valiante 2017). Despite the multiple witnesses of this act of violence, Charest continued coaching. In 2014, one of the former athletes whom he had sexually abused filed a police report for sexual assaults in the 1990s, which inspired eleven other former female athletes to come forward with similar experiences of sexual assault by Charest. Their reports detailed how he was controlling, manipulative, and sexually abusive of the athletes. All reported suffering significant mental and physical health consequences long after the abuse. Charest was convicted of sexual assault and sexual exploitation and sentenced to twelve years in prison (Leavitt 2017). He appealed the sentence, and it was reduced to fifty-seven months. He has since been released on parole after serving one third of his sentence (Cherry 2020). The chair of the board of Alpine Canada, Martha Hall Findlay, and the president, Vania Grandi, have apologized to Charest's victims, indicating that the organization had failed to support them when its leaders learned of his behaviour in 1998 (Canadian Press 2017a; Findlay and Grandi 2018).

In 1996, Bill Weston was accused of sexually assaulting a fourteen-year-old female basketball player when he was thirty years old (Engman 1997b).

Weston, who lived with his grandmother, invited the young athlete to his house one night while his grandmother was away. The young woman reported that he sexually assaulted her. He was charged with sexual assault and sexual exploitation (Engman 1997b). Weston testified that the athlete made sexual advances on him, that they only kissed, and that it was consensual. He also argued that at the time he was promoted to coaching a team at a higher level and was no longer her coach. Weston was found not guilty. Invoking a range of sport metaphors, the judge gave his reasoning for the decision by saying "no harm, no foul. Well, *here there was probably harm, but I don't have proof of a foul.* You understand me? An ethical referee may hear a slap, but doesn't call foul unless he sees it. I've heard the loud slap of skin, the very loud slap of skin, but I didn't see it, so I can't call it" (quoted in Engman 1997a, para. 2; emphasis added). The judge was clearly speaking figuratively, as judges do not see the perpetration of the crimes that they adjudicate unless there is video evidence. Even though there is no legal requirement for corroborative evidence of the sexual assault beyond the victim's testimony for conviction, in this case the testimony of the young athlete appeared to be insufficient to establish guilt beyond a reasonable doubt.

Most sexual assaults perpetrated by authority figures occur away from the playing area, in hotel rooms at away tournaments, in the authority figure's home or car, or in sport facility rooms, such as a locker room or the coach's office. In some cases, particularly in sports in which athletes are trained in physical contact, such as wrestling and martial arts, coaches commit sexual assaults during the performance of the sport. The case of Thomas Lee Innerebner, a taekwondo coach from Alberta, is an example. Between 1998 and 2007, Innerebner sexually assaulted seven female athletes who ranged in age from seven to fifteen.[28] Victims testified that during training sessions, he would grab their breasts and put their hands down their pants. Some of the incidents occurred with other athletes in the room, whereas others occurred during private training sessions. Innerebner was convicted of five counts of sexual assault, and six counts of sexual interference, and sentenced to seven years and eight months in prison.[29]

2000s Reports

Despite some recognition of high rates of sexual exploitation occurring in Canadian sport in the 1990s, the problem persisted into the 2000s, during which reports of sexual assaults by coaches and other authority figures rose. The number of victims identified as girls or young women in the reported cases likewise continued to rise, from fifty-eight reported victims in the

1990s to seventy-five in the 2000s. Perhaps the most significant change in the 2000s was the increased role that new communication technologies, such as the internet and text messaging, began to play in the sexual exploitation of athletes by coaches and other authority figures. Increasingly, authority figures communicated with athletes through new technological mediums while grooming them to participate in sexual activities. As many of the cases described in the next section illustrate, while this trend continued into the 2010s, it has often been missed in considerations of policy changes and proposed strategies to address sexual assault in Canadian sport.

Thierry Massimo was a successful boys' soccer coach in the 2000s who won a provincial championship in Quebec. However, during this time reports suggest that Massimo was using email, text messaging, and internet chat forums to convince the young male players whom he coached, who were between twelve and fourteen years old, to engage in sexual activity with him and other boys (*CBC News* 2009b). The athletes later disclosed that Massimo threatened to withdraw training and playing opportunities from players who did not comply with his sexual requests. Having heard some concerning details from her son, a mother of one of the players logged in to the chat forum and pretended to be her son during an online chat with Massimo. Recalling this, she later testified "the things [Massimo] asked me to do! He wanted us to meet somewhere with other children. I can't even go [there], all the things he asked me" (quoted in *CBC News* 2010a, para. 12). Massimo admitted to investigators that he engaged in sexual contact with four of his players and sent sexual emails and messages to ten other players (*CTV News* 2010). He pleaded guilty to four counts of sexual assault and twenty-two counts of child luring and was sentenced to six years in prison (Block 2010).

Coaches who threaten to withdraw their coaching and end future sport opportunities for athletes, as Massimo did, are common in cases of coach-perpetrated sexual assaults against athletes. André Guilmette used this tactic to lure and control the athletes he targeted. His son, Jonathan, is among Canada's most accomplished speedskaters, having won two Olympic medals in Salt Lake City in 2002 (Banerjee 2003). His son's althetic success helped position Guilmette as a top-tier coach for athletes with Olympic aspirations. As reports later revealed, Guilmette used this status to gain leverage with and sexually exploit young female speedskaters whom he coached. Guilmette sexually assaulted two female athletes, who were fourteen and seventeen at the time, during routine massages. Describing the pressure that she felt to remain quiet, one of the victims said that "he promised to bring me to the Olympics, and said he was my key to the Olympics" (quoted in King 2005, para. 5). Guilmette pleaded guilty to sexually touching the two athletes over thirty times in a two-year period and was sentenced to eight months in prison (Hanes 2005).

The ages of the victims in the sexual assault reports that we analyzed are not always reported in media or legal cases and thus cannot always be identified. However, for cases in which the ages of the victims are specified, the majority appear to have been between nine and seventeen. In a few cases, the victims were younger than nine, as in *R v AGA*, in which the victim was only five when the sexual abuse began.[30] The offender was not named in the legal case file to protect the identity of the victim, who was a foster child of AGA's parents. In this case, the accused coached the victim's soccer team. Over a four-year span, AGA repeatedly sexually abused the young boy and was convicted of sexual assault, sexual interference, and invitation to sexual touching and sentenced to three years in prison. The prosecution successfully appealed the sentencing decision by arguing that the judge had failed to acknowledge AGA's position of trust. As a result, the sentence was increased to five years.

In all of the cases of sexual assault, sexual interference, and sexual exploitation involving authority figures discussed thus far, the accused was identified as male. Departing from this trend was Jillian Maureen Anderson, a soccer coach in Prince Edward Island, the only female-identified authority figure we found in publicly documented reports of sexual exploitation in Canadian sport before 2010. Anderson, twenty-two at the time, coached her sister's under-fourteen girls' soccer team. While coaching, she reportedly developed friendships with players on the team and became particularly close with one player. The athlete's parents were concerned and reported the relationship to the soccer association. The reports were deemed to be unsubstantiated and led to no disciplinary action against Anderson. When the athlete turned fourteen, Anderson stopped coaching her team, and their relationship reportedly became more intimate.[31] Anderson was later charged and convicted of sexual exploitation and invitation to sexual touching and sentenced to five months in prison. She appealed the decision, arguing that, since she was no longer coaching the athlete when the sexual relationship reportedly commenced, she was not in a position of trust with the athlete, and therefore no sexual exploitation occurred. In the appeal hearing, the judge indicated that it is possible for a coach to establish a position of trust with a young athlete, stop coaching the athlete, and maintain a position of trust with the athlete, which would negate consent. The judge concluded that therefore sexual exploitation can occur even after a coach is no longer coaching a young athlete. However, in this case, the judge did not believe that Anderson had used her coaching position to establish a position of trust with the athlete to groom her for later sexual exploitation and overturned the conviction.[32]

2010s Reports

The 2010s saw a public reckoning for many social institutions in how they have responded and continue to respond to sexual violence. The rise of social media use led to a corresponding rise in disclosure and publicity of the prevalence of sexual assault. In 2017, #MeToo became a rallying cry for a new wave of activism on sexual violence. The #MeToo movement, founded by American activist Tarana Burke in 2006, became mainstream in October 2017 when actress Alyssa Milano tweeted "if you've been sexually harassed or assaulted write 'me too' as a reply to this tweet" (Milano 2017). Under #MeToo, victims created a collective narration of the prevalence of sexual violence as millions of victims of sexual assaults around the world disclosed their experiences (Ohlheiser 2017).

In the months that followed, a number of powerful men in entertainment, politics, and news media were named and shamed for their acts of sexual violence, including American celebrities Bill Cosby and Harvey Weinstein. In Canada, news stories such as the *Globe and Mail*'s "Unfounded" investigation, which revealed that one in five police reports of sexual assault are deemed unfounded (Doolittle 2017), put pressure on police organizations to account for their failed responses to sexual assaults. A wave of high-profile cases of sexual assault on Canadian university and college campuses likewise put pressure on institutions of higher education to address sexual violence on campus, and some provinces mandated the creation of sexual assault policies and campus sexual assault support centres and services (E. Quinlan 2017).

The #MeToo movement, however, did not rock the institution of sport in the same way. As the cases in this book reveal, athletes and coaches had long been accused of sexual assaults, but their violent behaviour was often excused, ignored, or accepted by sport administrators. Sport organizations, and larger governing bodies, have remained slow to implement significant changes. While many institutions were shifting under the weight of public pressure in the 2010s, the institution of sport remained relatively untouched.

Although no female coaches were convicted of sexual assaults against young athletes before 2010 in the records that we analyzed, at least three have been convicted since 2010, including Kamloops hockey coach Heidi Ferber. In 2014, thirty-nine-year-old Ferber was convicted of sexually exploiting a fifteen-year-old female hockey player. The athlete reported that, because of Ferber's previous successes as a hockey player, she "trusted her a lot and she [Ferber] took advantage of that" (quoted in *CBC News* 2014a, para. 10). During her time as a coach, Ferber reportedly took the athlete to movies, bought her gifts, provided hockey advice and extra training opportunities, and called or texted her daily. Their relationship became sexual at Ferber's and the athlete's homes and in hotels at away games and tournaments (Layes 2014). Ferber reportedly told the athlete that the relationship should remain a secret. A few years later, when the athlete was struggling through emotional and psychological difficulties resulting from her time with Ferber, she reported her experiences to police. Ferber pleaded guilty to sexual exploitation and sexual interference and was sentenced to one year in prison (*CityNews* 2014).

The few cases of female coaches tried for sexual exploitation of athletes followed a similar pattern: the coach cultivated a relationship with a teen-aged athlete, built a friendship, and then engaged in a sexual relationship. Some cases involving male coaches followed this pattern as well. Alberta basketball coach Dean Matthew Vigon developed a relationship with a fifteen-year-old female basketball player on the school and club teams that he was coaching. He bought her a new cell phone, paid her basketball fees, gave her a summer job at his business, and reportedly positioned himself as her friend and life mentor.[33] Sexualized communication began between the coach and athlete when she was fifteen and turned to repeated and regular sexual touching and sexual intercourse shortly before her sixteenth birthday. She later reported that she felt unsure about the relationship with her coach, but he told her that it was okay but should remain a secret. They exchanged sexually explicit photographs, and he recorded a video of them having sex. This continued for approximately three years until his wife found a sexual photo of the young athlete in his possession and reported him to police. Vigon pleaded guilty to sexual assault, child luring, and child pornography. He was sentenced to 3.5 years in prison, increased to 7.6 years on appeal by the prosecution.[34]

The case of Joseph Emile "Luc" Potvin, a volleyball coach in Nova Scotia, shares similarities with the Vigon case. Potvin, fifty-three years old, cultivated a relationship with a seventeen-year-old female player on his volleyball team using text messaging and webcam chats, which evolved to sharing nude images and eventually sexual intercourse. The athlete's father became suspicious of the relationship, and after accessing her text and online messages with her coach, he handed the material over to police. Potvin pleaded guilty to charges of sexual exploitation, sexual assault, child luring, and producing child pornography, and he was sentenced to four years in prison (Rhodes 2014). At the sentencing hearing, information was disclosed that Potvin had been convicted of sexual assault, sexual exploitation, and invitation to sexual touching involving a twelve-year-old girl, for which he was later pardoned (*Halifax City News* 2011). The school where he coached later admitted that it did not do any background screening before he was given the coaching position (*CTV Atlantic* 2011).

In the #MeToo era, social media has played an important role in highlighting persistent problems of sexual violence. It has also been key to how some coaches and other authority figures groom athletes to engage in sexual relationships. The broader trend of technology-facilitated sexual violence involving online communication, which began in the 2000s, escalated in the 2010s (A. Powell and Henry 2017). The trial of Mississauga gymnastics coach Scott McFarlane is another example of an authority figure accused of using technology-facilitated forms of sexual exploitation of an athlete. A fifteen-year-old female athlete first filed a complaint with her gymnastics club regarding inappropriate conduct by her coach. There is no publicly available evidence that the club responded to the complaint. The club later claimed not to have known the full extent of the alleged sexual abuse (Aguilar 2018). According to the athlete, the sexual abuse occurred over a four-year period and involved inappropriate sexual touching by the coach and sexually explicit online communications, including the coach sending digital images of his genitals over private messaging on social media.[35] McFarlane was charged with sexual assault, sexual interference, and indecent exposure. In 2013, he was fired from a previous coaching position in Ottawa when a twelve-year-old athlete reported him for sending inappropriate text and social media messages, including sexually explicit pictures of himself. He was never criminally charged in that case. After McFarlane was hired by the Mississauga gymnastics club soon after, the Ottawa gymnastics club reportedly notified the Mississauga club about his firing and expressed concerns about his continued social media contact with young athletes at the Ottawa club. Reports suggest that the Mississauga club did nothing, however, to prevent McFarlane from coaching or interacting with young female athletes via social media until he was criminally charged after an athlete reported the incident to police (J. Long 2018). In November 2022, McFarlane was acquitted of all sexual assault–related charges (J. Long 2022).

Making Sense of Sexual Exploitation Perpetrated by Authority Figures

The institution of sport is organized by a hierarchical power structure, typically led by white male coaches and administrators, in an environment that provides ample opportunities for coaches and other authority figures to commit sexual assaults with relative impunity and little to no accountability. Indeed, as Helen Owton and Andrew Sparkes (2017, 742) argue, "the structural conditions and power relationships, embedded in a competitive sporting environment, specifically the power invested in the coach, provide a unique socio-cultural context that offers a number of potentialities for sexual abuse and exploitation to take place." Much of the existing research on sexual offences by adults against youth focuses on offender traits or deficits rooted in bio-psychological perspectives. We depart from individualized understandings of the problem to shed light on the context in which authority figures commit sexual assaults.

Power, Trust, and Structural Opportunities

Most of the coaches and authority figures accused of sexual assaults in the reported cases are white-presenting and male, and most of the victims are young athletes. Tremendous trust is given to coaches and other authority figures in sport environments. In most sports, parents are encouraged to drop their children off at team practices and pick them up when they end, making it difficult for parents to observe and assess the dynamics between coaches and their children. Exacerbating this problem, some organizations enforce rules that practices are closed to parents, and some young athletes receive individualized training sessions with their coach or trainer. On some teams, not all parents are encouraged or able to attend away tournaments, during which their children might be driven by other adults and sleep in accommodations that the coach or manager has arranged. As we have shown in this chapter, some coaches and other adult authority figures exploit this trust to create the conditions for sexually abusing young athletes under their care.

In addition to the broader systems of power and oppression within and outside sport that fuel sexual assault, the physical structures of sport organizations can generate opportunities for sexual exploitation. Positions of authority within sport organizations provide physical access to young athletes. For example, in the case of *R v X*, an arena security guard sexually assaulted a fifteen-year-old female hockey player, the last player left in a dressing room when the security guard was making his rounds.[36] Athletic trainers, like coaches, can have one-on-one training sessions with young athletes with minimal supervision. General managers in Canadian junior hockey can draft players to cities where athletes have no family or support systems, which ensures minimal parental supervision and support while the players live with billet hosts. The hosts have access to young athletes living in their private homes. This level of access grants authority figures in sport opportunities to sexually exploit young athletes behind closed doors.

In the cases of child abuse at the old Maple Leaf Gardens, the men used their facility access and job benefits, such as free hockey tickets and memorabilia, to coax young, aspiring hockey players into the arena to be sexually abused. A victim of the sexual abuse at Maple Leaf Gardens described his experience to journalists as follows:

> At age 13, I was first introduced to Maple Leaf Gardens by meeting the equipment manager at the time, George Hannah, who was at a high level of management. His age was approximately 50+. At 13 I am down there in awe at meeting all the hockey players, ... going to the dressing rooms, ... getting sticks, sitting up in the press box. He made me feel like a 13-year-old king. (quoted in Vine and Challen 2002, 21)

Hannah, an equipment manager for the Toronto Maple Leafs, also promised to secure a tryout for the teenaged boy with a Toronto Maple Leafs' farm team, a possible stepping stone to the NHL. Although equipment manager is not a position that typically would be associated with significant power and authority within a sport organization, Hannah used his role on the team to access, manipulate, and sexually exploit boys.

Silencing Sexual Assault

Not only does the Canadian sport system create opportunities for authority figures to sexually assault young people under their care, but it also creates conditions in which sexually abused athletes are unlikely to report their experiences of abuse. The Canadian sport system, as many scholars have argued, is characterized by the silencing of sexual assault. In sport, what has been termed the "wall of silence" (Fortier, Parent, and Lessard 2020, 6), "dome of silence" (Kirby, Greaves, and Hankivsky 2000, 1), or the "culture of inaction and silence" (Parent 2011, 328) keeps victims from reporting their

experiences and discourages bystanders from intervening when they witness or suspect sexual abuse by sport authority figures.

Reflecting on this silencing effect, Theoren Fleury (2009, 25, 30), recount-
ing his sexual abuse by Graham James, writes that "I thought about telling,
but who could I turn to? Who would believe me over him?" and "Graham
cultivated a relationship with Sheldon [Kennedy] and me by isolating us
from our families." In Canadian junior hockey, which Fleury and Kennedy
played, teams own young athletes' playing rights and players often move to
new cities and live away from their parents in homes with minimal adult
supervision. In fact, when James moved from coaching the Winnipeg Warriors to the Swift Current Broncos, he made a trade to ensure that Kennedy would move with him to his new team. Through this system, athletes
can become isolated from family members and friends. Even competitive
athletes not billeted are expected to spend much of their time dedicated to
their sports. Competitive sports can thus be isolating experiences for athletes. Describing his experience of victimization, Greg Gilhooly (2018, 43)
writes that "he was increasingly becoming the major voice and guiding light
in my life, and I was slowly becoming isolated from the people closest to
me." When a coach becomes an athlete's primary support system, reporting
sexual abuse that they perpetrate becomes far more difficult.

The Grooming Process

Many of the analyzed cases began with authority figures targeting and
grooming victims in ways that reinforced their power and control over
them. In sport,

> grooming is central to the abusive relationship … It involves slowly gaining
> the trust of the potential victim before systematically breaking down inter-
> personal barriers prior to committing actual sexual abuse. This process may
> take weeks, months or years with the perpetrator usually moving steadily so
> that he is able to maintain secrecy and avoid exposure. Grooming is import-
> ant because it brings about the appearance of co-operation from the ath-
> lete, making the act of abuse seem to be consensual. (Brackenridge and
> Fasting 2005, 35)

Grooming can also be seen as a "process by which a person prepares a child,
significant adults and the environment for the abuse of this child. Specific
goals include gaining access to the child, gaining the child's compliance, and
maintaining the child's secrecy to avoid disclosure" (Craven, Brown, and

Gilchrist 2006, 297). In many of the cases analyzed in this chapter, the authority figures formed relationships with the athletes and led them to believe that they would facilitate the athletes' athletic goals. In some cases, the authority figure gave the athlete gifts, extra coaching, rides, and meals and paid for some expenses. Increasingly, as some cases showed, much of this grooming is done through technology such as text messaging and private social media messaging. Once trust and dependence were established, many authority figures initiated physical contact, such as massages or stretching assistance, which escalated to sexual contact.

The sexual assaults perpetrated by authority figures in the cases in this chapter were often against multiple victims and went unreported for many years – in some cases, decades. After the sexual abuse began, many victims reported feeling unable to stop the authority figures or report the abuse without putting their athletic careers at risk. One aspiring Olympic female speedskater sexually exploited by her coach stated that "I felt like I was in a Catch 22. If I quit him, it was over, I would never go to the Olympics" (quoted in Hanes 2005, para. 8). Likewise, Fleury (2009, 24) wrote that "Graham convinced me that, if not for him and his help, I would not be going to the NHL." Gilhooly (2018, 63) wrote of James that "I was trapped. I wanted to run away from him and never see him again. Yet, at the same time, he was the one thing in my life that I needed the most ... In the bizarre world of abuse, I couldn't get away from my abuser because he had positioned himself as my one and only savior." James also threatened the athletes that, if they told anyone about his sexual abuse, they would be labelled as gay, a label that carries stigma within the homophobic culture of Canadian men's hockey (C. MacDonald 2018). In other cases, athletes reported other threats of violence made by coaches, such as one young hockey player who stated that "he had me believing he would kill my mother so I pretty much just kept quiet" (quoted in *CBC News* 2014c, para. 6). Authority figures use threats against athletes' futures, reputations, and family members to manipulate and prevent the athletes from reporting the sexual abuse.

For some young athletes, sexual exploitation by an authority figure in sport is their first sexual contact. Many victims who report the crimes years later indicate that at the time they thought that the contact was not right but that the authority figure convinced them that it was appropriate and must remain a secret. Describing this dynamic, the judge in the case of Dean Vigon stated,

> he persistently voiced his opinion to the complainant about issues in her life. He became involved in decisions regarding how and with whom she spent her time. She believed that he isolated her from her family and

friends. She believed she was doing wrong but had no one to confide in. Vigon kept reassuring her that their relationship was okay.[37]

The athlete in this case reported that she felt uncomfortable, but the coach had isolated her from others, and as a result she thought that she had no one to whom she could disclose the abuse. For some athletes, such as the one in this case, it is only when they are older and no longer under the authority figure's direct control that they feel able to report the abuse.

Although not as common, several cases analyzed in this chapter involved sexually violent contact by authority figures without a process of grooming. For example, taekwondo coach Thomas Lee Innerebner sexually violated athletes under his care during training sessions.[38] In such cases, the physical contact and training regime in the sport increase coaches' access to athletes and ability to pass off sexual assault as inadvertent contact.

Institutional Tolerance and Betrayal

When victims do come forward with complaints of sexual assault, sport organizations often fail to acknowledge and address the reports and the broader problem of sexual assault that they signify. Canadian sport organizations' tendency to tolerate and normalize sexual assaults creates a climate in which authority figures can sexually exploit athletes largely without consequences even when they are reported. Sport organizations in Canada predominantly govern themselves (Kerr, Stirling, and McPherson 2014), and as a result there is minimal accountability for or oversight of how sexual assaults are handled within Canadian sport organizations. Indeed, as Gretchen Kerr, Bruce Kidd, and Peter Donnelly (2020, 69) argue,

> with respect to child protection, sport is the only child-populated domain in Canada that is completely autonomous and self-regulating. Unlike other domains in which children engage, such as day care and educational settings, sport lacks a regulatory body to oversee the health and well-being of children, which ensures [that] persons in positions of authority and trust over young people are sufficiently trained and adhere to scope of practice ... and apply sanctions to those who violate codes of conduct. Instead, sport organizations regulate themselves.

The institution of sport has also been described as "a cultural and political island, defined as separate and free from the rest of society" (Brackenridge and Rhind 2014, 328).

In the cases discussed in this chapter, likely there were opportunities for sport administrations, governing bodies, and other adults to intervene in the ongoing instances of sexual abuse, but they did not do so. Margo Mountjoy et al. (2016, 1020) suggest that "sexual harassment and abuse in sport stem from abuses of power relations facilitated by an organizational culture that ignores, denies, fails to prevent, or even tacitly accepts such problems." Likewise, when athletes are sexually assaulted, viable redress seems to be largely unavailable:

> Structurally, high performance sport is essentially an unregulated work-place where athletes are expected to devote themselves to the goal and demonstrate a strong work ethic. Yet they remain ill-protected by regulations, laws and policies that normally offer workers' rights and avenues of redress. This disempowering structure sets the stage for exploitation and silence. If and when sexual abuse occurs [in sport], the structure does not assist the athlete in speaking out, seeking redress or righting situations. (Kirby et al. 2002, 26)

Many of the sport organizations involved in the cases analyzed here simply ignored the reports of sexual assault perpetrated by their coaches and other authority figures. Even when they received such reports, or when authority figures disclosed criminal records for sexual exploitation, many sport organizations chose to do nothing and allowed the authority figures to continue in their roles or move to other sport organizations.

In addition to ignoring reports, some sport organizations work to silence reported abuse. For example, when one victim reported the sexual abuse that he had experienced by Maple Leaf Gardens employees and team managers, he was offered a small financial settlement in exchange for not disclosing what had happened to him to the police or media (Vine and Challen 2002). Furthermore, reflecting on the Larry Nassar case, Mountjoy (2018, 58) writes that "sexual abuse is fostered in a *sport culture* which denies, ignores, or accepts abuse as the norm; a sport culture where athletes have no power or voice and are commodified in a 'win at all costs' environment." This culture of silence and silenc*ing* allows authority figures to sexually exploit athletes and other victims over long periods of time in Canadian sport.

A Male-Dominated, Patriarchal Sport System
Of the 243 alleged offenders in the cases analyzed in this chapter, 238 (98 percent) were identified in public reports as men and 5 (2 percent) as women.

This finding is consistent with existing research on the topic. A study of 159 media articles on sexual abuse in British sport found that 98 percent of perpetrators of reported sexual violence in youth sport were male coaches (Brackenridge et al. 2008). Similarly, in a Danish study of 160 cases of sexual violence and abuse in sport, all of the identified perpetrators (100 percent) were men (Nielsen 2004), and a study of fifteen sexual assault cases in sport that went to court in Norway found that 100 percent of the perpetrators were male coaches (Fasting et al. 2013).

As with the other forms of sexual assault discussed in this book, we argue that sexual assault by authority figures in sport is often rooted in violent masculinity and masculine struggles for power, authority, and control. Suzanne Sgroi (1982, 82) writes that "child sexual abuse is primarily a disorder of power rather than a sexual aberration." Likewise, Cossins (2000, 126–27, 131) argues that "for some men ... sexual practices such as sexual behaviour with a child may be a key experience through which power is derived and masculinity is accomplished," and "the derivation of power through sexual practices is central to understanding child sex offending." Male authority figures in sport exert, reinforce, and maintain power through sexually coercive acts against younger athletes and other individuals below them in the hierarchical sport system. They use their power and status to sexually exploit victims, which further entrenches their power. Arguably, "men who succeed in sport are deified and granted high status and prestige. This sets the stage for the use of power as a way to control others, the absolute underpinning of interpersonal violence" (Kirby, Greaves, and Hankivsky 2002, 136).

The Canadian sport system is a largely male-dominated social institution, even within girls' and women's sports. Men occupy the majority of coaching positions at all levels (Lavoi 2016; Reade, Rodgers, and Norman 2009) as well as the vast majority of other leadership positions within teams, leagues, and sport governing bodies (Krahn 2019; M. Norman, Donnelly, and Kidd 2021). Coaching "remains a domain where gender equity has declined or stalled, despite increasing female sport participation" (Lavoi 2016, 1). Although it is common for men to coach female athletes, it is rare for women to coach men (Knoppers 1992; Walker and Bopp 2010). Men are significantly more likely to be offered coaching positions with fewer qualifications and less experience than women (L. Larsen and Clayton 2019). Compounding these problems, existing research demonstrates that women are more likely to leave coaching sooner than men because of discrimination and other barriers to their advancement (Cunningham et al. 2019). Research has repeatedly shown that women who aspire to attain leadership roles within sport in Canada, and elsewhere, face systemic discrimination and blocked opportunities for advancement, and they are significantly more likely than men to leave their sport leadership positions early (Burton 2015; Hancock and Hums 2016; J. Hoffman 2010; Sartore and Cunningham 2007). These barriers to coaching and leadership positions in sport are exacerbated for people who identify as 2SLGBTQI+, who face limited opportunities because of "the glass closet" (Bass, Hardin, and Taylor 2015, 1), a metaphor for the systemic discrimination people who identify as 2SLGBTQI+ experience in sport.

Gerda von der Lippe (1997) argues that the institution of sport has established a patriarchal structure through a long history in which men's knowledge, practices, experiences, and behaviours have been privileged over those of women and, we could add, people who identify as trans, nonbinary, and gender queer. This is reflected in the clear gender inequities that exist in most Canadian sport organizations. This context sets the stage for sexual violence. As Elizabeth Ward (1985, 77) argues, the sexual abuse of children is "an integral product of our society, based as it is on male supremacist attitudes and organisation." Sport, as currently organized in Canada, promotes and perpetuates values that fuel sexual violence. Most sports are organized around an instructional system in which a person – commonly white, male, older, and perceived to be more experienced and knowledgeable than the athletes under their care – provides instruction on how to become an accomplished athlete and a winning team. According to Peter Donnelly (1997), the structure of the sport system gives the coach significant power over and influence on the athlete to exert more control and dominance than would commonly be tolerated of a teacher, employer, or anyone else in a position of trust and authority. Would a teacher be permitted to yell at students, demean them in front of their peers, and put them through physical torments while controlling their diet, class schedule, and sleep routine? Likely not. However, this behaviour and power structure are normalized in sport. Capturing this idea, Donnelly (1999, 122) describes the typical coach-athlete relationship as a "controlling relationship." Similarly, the relationship has been described as being "based on a patriarchal, autocratic model of authority" (Tomlinson and Yorganci 1997, 151). This structure gives the coach power, marginalizes the athlete, and creates fertile conditions for sexual exploitation. As Brackenridge (2001, 121) argues, "wherever there is a power imbalance, then, there is the potential for abuses to occur. In a sports culture that thrives on authoritarian leadership the climate is ripe for individual exploitation."

Disempowered Athletes

While authority figures, and white male coaches in particular, within the institution of sport are entrusted with power and authority, athletes are simultaneously stripped of power. Athletes, within the sport system, hold minimal power, authority, or autonomy. They are expected to follow the coach's orders both on and away from the playing area. If they do not, athletes risk losing opportunities in their sports that are offered and controlled by their coaches. A basketball coach can bench an athlete, a hockey coach can limit a player's shifts on the ice, and a gymnastics coach can select a different athlete to compete in an event. In a context in which coaches have the power to control athletes and their chances to succeed in their sports, and in which athletes have little opportunity to resist without risking their athletic futures, consent has little meaning.

Although all athletes are marginalized within a hierarchical sport system, in which they are positioned below coaches, sport administrators, and league officials, some athletes are further marginalized by larger social forces of oppression both within and outside sport. Younger athletes are marginalized because of their age. Nearly all of the victims in the cases analyzed in this chapter were under eighteen at the time of the reported sexual abuse, exploitation, and/or assault. This finding is consistent with the finding that child athletes are more vulnerable to sexual abuse by coaches than adult athletes (Brackenridge and Kirby 1997). Children are not afforded much power and influence inside and outside sport, and thus they are more likely to be targets of sexual exploitation.

Athletes with disabilities and athletes who identify as 2SLGBTQI+ are also at higher risk of being sexually assaulted by their coaches (Kirby, Demers, and Parent 2008; Mountjoy et al. 2016; Vertommen et al. 2015). Known trends in sexual violence also suggest that Black athletes, Indigenous athletes, and athletes of colour are at a heightened risk of sexual violence in sports (C.M. West and K. Johnson 2013). The unobtrusive methodology and use of publicly available data did not allow for the identification of victim's sexuality, disability, and/or race. However, existing research points to how racism, ableism, homophobia, transphobia, cisnormativity, and other forms of oppression fuel sexual assault in sport. Where heightened power differentials between adult authority figures and children exist, the conditions for sexual exploitation are set in place.

Much literature has illustrated the high risk of sexual assaults by coaches that female athletes face (Fasting et al. 2000; Kirby, Greaves, and Hankivsky 2000; Leahy et al. 2002; Parent and Bannon 2011). At first glance, the findings in this chapter suggest different results: within the 243 cases analyzed, there were 793 male victims and 238 female victims. However, as discussed earlier in the chapter, the socio-historical context of these numbers in terms of both sport and the law is significant. If only those cases from 1990 to the present are examined, after the significant Canadian sexual assault legal reforms of the 1980s occurred, when female athletes entered competitive sport in Canada in larger numbers, and when male coaches and authority figures increasingly became involved in women's sport, there were 109 male victims and 173 female victims. Recent numbers in Canadian sport suggest that young women and girls experience high rates of sexual assault by authority figures in sport.

Research has shown that athletes at higher levels of performance and competition, where the power hierarchy between coach and athlete is often more extreme, are at higher risk of sexual exploitation. A comparison of Olympic-level athletes and athletes at lower playing levels (Fasting et al. 2000) found that 20 percent of the elite athletes experienced sexual harassment by an authority figure compared with 8 percent of the lower-level athletes. Those at higher levels of competition spend more time in their sports and with their coaches, creating more opportunities for violence. The elite level of sport is also arguably more totalizing, which isolates athletes from outside contacts and gives coaches and other authority figures increased opportunities for sexual exploitation.

Beyond the athlete's level of performance, many of the cases in this chapter featured coaches and authority figures with high levels of perceived ability, influence, and power in their sports. Coaches who have won championships, coached athletes to higher levels such as playing professionally or making an Olympic team, or were successful athletes themselves can gain more power over and influence on the athletes whom they coach. Coaches seen as accomplished in their sports are most likely to coach at highly competitive levels instead of recreational levels. Many of the same male coaches have also been socialized in the competitive world of men's sport, characterized by rape culture and tolerance of sexual violence, as former male athletes. Some of the authority figures in the cases openly used the power, trust, and influence that their status in their sports afforded them to sexually exploit athletes and others lower in the sport hierarchy. Many created and maintained a power differential in which the athletes were dependent on them for athletic opportunities and career advancement. Some authority figures threatened to withdraw their help if the athlete resisted or reported the abuse. This power dynamic increases the risk of sexual exploitation. As stated by Brackenridge (2001, 36), "the power afforded to the coach in his position of authority offers an effective alibi or camouflage for grooming and abuse."

Furthermore, as Kirby (1995) identifies, many athletes simply have no alternative elite-level team to play for if they reject the sexual advances of a coach or report the coach for sexual abuse. A national-level athlete cannot easily compete for another country. Many organizations and leagues have rules that prevent athletes from switching teams or require them to sit out an entire season if they do. Players under contract must perform for their teams, or they are considered in breach of contract. William Murphy (2019) also notes that in some sports, particularly martial arts and other combative sports, the coach can be physically imposing and able to inflict physical harm to a young athlete, which could heighten an athlete's fear of resisting unwanted sexual advances or reporting an abusive coach. These unique dimensions of power in sport contribute to a climate that enables the sexual exploitation and abuse of athletes.

The Canadian sport system is structured in ways that facilitate authority figures' use of power, authority, and control in the perpetration of sexual assaults. As the cases in this chapter have shown, some authority figures in sport exert, reinforce, and maintain power through sexually coercive acts against young athletes and other individuals below them in the hierarchical Canadian sport system. These dynamics are commonly left unquestioned in sport organizations. The reluctance of many organizations to acknowledge and address sexual assaults by coaches and other authority figures allows those who sexually exploit athletes to continue doing so with little consequence or accountability and to move seamlessly among roles, sports, and sport organizations.

Unlike other forms of sexual assault discussed in this book, many of the cases in this chapter resulted in conviction and incarceration of the accused. Notably, however, increased rates of criminalization have had little influence on reducing the number of reports of sexual assault perpetrated by authority figures in sport over the past three decades. In fact, reports increased over this period. The increase was likely influenced by a variety of factors, including the legal reforms in the 1980s that expanded and clarified criminal offences of sexual assault and the increased public attention to the issue of sexual violence in the 2010s. However, the increase in reports does suggest that policing, prosecution, and incarceration have done little to curb, much less prevent, this form of sexual assault in sport. As much sexual assault research has shown, sexual assault reporting rates remain low relative to other crimes, and as such reports of sexual assault represent a fraction of the total number of sexual assaults in any context (Department of Justice 2019b). An increase in reports of sexual assault by authority figures in sport thus suggests a continuing, pervasive problem of sexual assault in the Canadian sport system.

By examining cases across several decades, it becomes clear that relying on the criminal legal system to solve the problem of sexual assault in sport has been largely ineffective and that efforts within sport to eradicate such assaults have not worked. In the next chapter, we delve further into how and why criminal legal system responses to address the persistent problem of sexual assault in Canadian sport have failed to live up to their promise, and we propose alternative avenues for addressing this complex, multidimensional problem.

Breaking the Cycle of Sexual Assault in Canadian Sport

Sport organizations and the Canadian criminal legal system have routinely failed to respond appropriately to and prevent sexual assaults. Since reports of sexual assault are often minimized, doubted, or dismissed by police, judges, and sport administrators, many athletes accused and convicted of sexual assaults are able to advance their playing careers and move between teams and to higher playing levels, with minimal to no interruption. Coaches and other authority figures are often able to sexually exploit athletes for many years, and sometimes even decades, without consequence or accountability. Within the Canadian sport system, sexual assault is tolerated and even in some cases promoted as part of a competitive, hierarchical culture of masculine violence. By tracing a thirty-year span of sexual assault cases from 1990 to 2020, this book reveals how sport organizations and the legal system have been largely ineffective in responding to the enduring problem of sexual assault in sport.

In recent years, various sport-specific strategies have been developed in Canada to address such assaults. In 2019, the 1-800 Canadian Sport HELPline and Universal Code of Conduct to Prevent and Address Maltreatment in Sport (UCCMS) were implemented after increased media scrutiny drew government attention to the issue of sexual abuse in sport (*CBC Sports* 2019). These developments are a start. However, initiatives focused on addressing and preventing sexual assault in sport have been few and far between and remain limited in scope. Furthermore, even when initiatives such as SafeSport policies[1] are in place, they are often not enforced or effective in preventing sexual abuse (Donnelly et al. 2016). An investigation of the efficacy of the newly established US Center for SafeSport, which was created in 2017 to independently investigate sexual misconduct allegations within the US Olympic and Paralympic Committees' jurisdiction and appears to be a model that Canada is adopting, has revealed many of the issues already plaguing Canadian sport organizations' responses to sexual assaults, including a lack of transparency in the handling of sexual assault reports, financial interference, and a lack of consequences or mechanisms of accountability for coaches who have been found to be sexually assaulting athletes under their care (Coleman 2022).

Historically, most sport organizations in Canada have tried to avoid dealing directly with sexual assaults perpetrated by and against athletes. Instead, they have relied on the Canadian criminal legal system to address the problem and to identify, convict, and incarcerate individual perpetrators of sexual assaults. As critical scholars studying gender-based violence have long argued, the criminal legal system has proven to be ineffective in addressing sexual assault and gender-based violence more generally (Busby 2014; Goodmark 2018; H. Johnson 2012; Whynacht 2021). The low reporting rates of sexual assaults and dramatically lower conviction rates of sexual offenders (H. Johnson 2012; Perreault 2015), coupled with significantly high rates of recidivism (Harris and Hanson 2004) and a high burden of proof that advantages the accused in sexual assault trials (Backhouse 2008; H. Johnson 2012; Sheehy 1999), demonstrate that the criminal legal system cannot be depended on to address sexual assaults. Furthermore, the reliance on police and prisons to solve the problem of sexual assault ignores the harms that the criminal legal system inflicts, particularly on Black people, Indigenous people, people of colour, people with disabilities, and people who identify as 2SLGBTQI+, all of whom face a heightened risk of police violence, criminalization, and incarceration (Maynard 2017; Richie 2012; Whynacht 2021). Indeed, as Critical Resistance and INCITE! Women of Color against Violence (2016, 223) have argued, "as an overall strategy for ending violence, criminalization has not worked."

Depending on the criminal legal system to address sexual assault is a passive, reactive approach to violence and mischaracterizes the problem as an individualized one. If sexual assault in sport is understood as a problem of dangerous individuals, instead of one with deep roots in the cultural and structural organization of the institution of sport in Canada and its broader context, then it cannot be effectively challenged. We have illustrated many of the structural and cultural elements of Canadian sport that promote, facilitate, and normalize sexual assaults by and against athletes. Sexual assault in sport is a multidimensional problem that requires a multidimensional solution.

Developing effective strategies to address sexual assault in sport depends on first understanding its multifaceted, cyclical nature. In this concluding chapter, we explore the commonalities or interconnections between different forms of sexual assault in Canadian sport. We conclude with some strategies aimed at breaking the cycle of sexual assault that has long persisted in Canadian sport.

The Cycle of Sexual Assault in Canadian Sport

Much of the existing research on sexual assault in sport has focused on specific forms of sexual assault, including coach-perpetrated sexual assaults and harassment of athletes (e.g., Brackenridge 2001; Hartill 2017; Morton 2016; Owton 2016; Owton and Sparkes 2017) or athlete-perpetrated sexual assaults against women and girls (e.g., Benedict 1997, 1998, 2001; Crosset, Benedict, and McDonald 1995; Lavigne and Schlabach 2017; Krein 2013; Pappas 2012). As a result, the commonalities and interconnections among different forms of sexual assault in sport have been left largely unexamined. The forms of sexual assault examined in this book reflect and perpetuate hierarchies of power, dominance, and control within the Canadian sport system. Most significantly for this discussion, these forms of sexual assault fuel one another. A significant number of coaches and authority figures sexually assault young athletes. Some teenage male athletes sexually assault one another during hazing rituals. Teenage and young adult male athletes sexually assault women and girls, often in group sexual assaults, at rates significantly disproportionate to those of their non-athlete peers. Some competitive male athletes who commit sexual assaults later become coaches, and the cycle of violence and institutional tolerance of sexual assault continues.

Sexual assault in sport thus has a cyclical nature. However, if the problem is examined at the microlevel of individual athletes, then the connections among types of sexual assault are less clear. Media articles rarely draw connections among athletes who engaged in sexually violent hazing against teammates, sexually assaulted women or children, and sexually assaulted athletes whom they coached. Although these links may exist in some individual cases, a microlevel focus on individual athletes misses the opportunity to understand the broader, structural, and cultural connections among these forms of violence and how they collectively maintain and perpetuate a system that tolerates, minimizes, ignores, and dismisses sexual assault in sport.

Adopting a microlevel analysis, some scholars have referred to this cyclical aspect of individual experiences of sexual assault as the "victim-to-perpetrator cycle" (Paolucci et al. 2001, 27) or the "abused/ abuser hypothesis of child sexual abuse" (Garland and Dougher 1990, 488). These terms are based upon the theory that sexual abuse at a young age can cause sexual maladjustment in which the victim fails to learn what healthy sexual relationships are and is socialized instead to believe that sexually coercive behaviour without consent is normal, including between an adult and a child. Existing research on the victim-to-perpetrator cycle, in which the victimization history of perpetrators of sexual violence is examined, has yielded mixed conclusions on its validity. Research in this field has concluded that the prevalence of childhood sexual victimization among adult perpetrators of sexual assault ranges from 9 percent (Fagan and Wexler 1988) to 70 percent (Graham 1996), with many studies showing percentages in between.

No study of the victim-to-perpetrator hypothesis has been completed in a sport context. This study does not seek to fill this void or to argue that this type of direct connection between victimization and perpetration exists. Under Canadian law, victims of sexual assaults typically have publication bans on their identities, so it is not possible to determine whether any of the perpetrators of sexual assaults discussed in this book were previously victimized. Regardless of the methodological challenges of identifying these links, this form of analysis is problematic.

The suggestion that victims of sexual assaults are inherently more likely to perpetrate sexual assaults runs the risk of reinforcing negative, stigmatizing views of those who experience sexual assault. Many sexual assault victims are already hesitant to report the crimes that have been perpetrated against them. Explanatory theories of sexual assault that rely on individualized explanations are at best unhelpful in capturing the multifaceted nature of sexual assault and at worst harmful and stigmatizing to victims.

A more fruitful form of analysis moves beyond individualized perspectives to examine the cultures and institutional structures that fuel the problem of sexual assault in sport. The relative ease with which many athletes convicted of sexual assaults move between teams and sport organizations and the resulting lack of safety and accountability for victims are significant issues in need of attention. The cases examined in this book provide a plethora of examples. As we described in Chapter 2, Jarrett Reid was accused of sexually assaulting two young women while he was a veteran player on the Sault Ste Marie Greyhounds (Robinson 1998). After his release from prison for violence against women, Reid joined the St. Francis Xavier University men's hockey team. Shortly after, both he and a team-mate, Andrew Power, were accused of sexual assaults. Both Reid and Power then went on to become youth hockey coaches. In a similar case, soon after Lonzel Lowe's university basketball career ended at St. Thomas University, Lowe sexually assaulted an intoxicated woman and was sentenced to ninety days in prison in 2016 (Gill and Donkin 2017). After his release from prison, he began coaching an under-twelve boys' basketball team. Although Reid, Power, and Lowe have not been reported for sexually exploiting athletes under their care, they are now responsible for socializing young athletes. When sport organizations ignore sexual assaults, attitudes and beliefs tolerant and supportive of sexual assault are left to circulate and pass from one generation of athletes to the next. In this cycle of violence, the cultural tolerance and celebration of sexual assault are reproduced. The result is a system in which sexual assault is silenced, normalized, and at times celebrated in Canadian sport and competitive men's sport in particular.

The cycle of sexual assault in Canadian sport is a cycle of socialization to norms and values that cultivate the conditions for sexual assault. Although there are clear differences among the different forms of sexual assault discussed in this book, such as varying conviction rates for athletes versus coaches accused of sexual assaults, there are commonalities that unite them. In all but 5 of the 307 cases of sexual assault in Canadian sport discussed in this book, the reported perpetrators were identified as men, most of whom present as white. In all cases, the reported victims were identified as women, teenagers, or children. Most cases involved athletes, coaches, and authority figures at highly competitive levels of sport, where sport becomes a total institution in the individuals' lives characterized by a hierarchal structure of autocratic authority and control, in which bodily autonomy and consent have little meaning. In all cases occurring directly within sports, the perpetrator ranked higher within the organizational hierarchy of sport than the victim. And, in many cases, sexual assault by and against athletes was tolerated not just by sport organizations but also by the Canadian legal system.

Understanding these commonalities among forms of sexual assault in sport moves the analysis away from individualized explanations of and solutions to the problem and draws attention to the cultural and structural forces sustaining sexual assault in sport. This shift in analysis opens the possibility of exploring multifaceted, sweeping changes that have the potential to more effectively address the problem of sexual assault in Canadian sport.

Strategies to Break the Cycle of Sexual Assault in Canadian Sport

The Coaching Association of Canada and Canadian Centre for Ethics in Sport have recently consulted with various stakeholders in Canadian sport to develop guidelines for creating healthy and safe sport environments. Their outlined strategy involves (1) background screening for coaches, (2) "a rule of two," which states that at least two certified coaches must always be present with athletes, and (3) respect and ethics training for all coaches (Hachey 2018). Existing research on sexual assault prevention in sport, in Canada and internationally, has outlined similar strategies (Brackenridge 2001; Donnelly 1999; Parent 2010). More recently, the Sport Information Resource Centre has developed the UCCMS, and various national and provincial sport organizations have developed SafeSport policies adhering to it. Although this is valuable work, much more needs to be done to adequately address all forms of sexual assault in sport. Sport organizations have legal and moral obligations to respond appropriately to disclosures of sexual assault, provide resources and support to victims of sexual assault, and foster an environment free from sexual violence. Most sport organizations in Canada have dismally failed to meet these obligations.

Canadian sport organizations have commonly understood and treated sexual assault as a criminal issue to be dealt with by police, criminal courts, and the prison system. This approach has been ineffective in addressing sexual assault. Sport organizations' strategy of depending on the criminal legal system to police and incarcerate perpetrators of sexual assault in sport has done little to prevent sexual assault, as the sheer number of reports of sexual assault over the past three decades in Canadian sport illustrates. Criminal legal system approaches are reactive and aimed at addressing violence after it has already occurred through the punishment of an individual. In contrast, a multidimensional approach to the prevention of sexual assault and gender-based violence aims to understand the problem, identify its prevalence and root causes, engage with knowledgeable community groups, and develop a wide range of intervention strategies (Goodmark 2018). The strategies outlined in this chapter are interconnected and emphasize proactive prevention and compassionate, empathetic, trauma-informed responses.

Based upon a systematic review of the efficacy of gender-based violence prevention programs, Claire Crooks et al. (2020, 1) argue that the most effective approaches "address the problem before it starts." Preventing any form of sexual assault in sport is a complex endeavour. The institutional structures, practices, and cultural attitudes supporting sexual violence, all of which maintain and promote the cycle of sexual assault in sport, present significant challenges for prevention work. Additionally, the unique power dynamics at play within the competitive hierarchies of most sport organizations make prevention, and prevention work, particularly difficult. There is therefore no simple solution to sexual assault in sport. There are some steps, however, that follow from the empirical and theoretical discussions in this book that can be utilized to address the enduring patterns of sexual assault in sport. These strategies are aimed at altering the terrain in Canadian sport so that it is no longer fertile ground for the tolerance, promotion, celebration, and perpetration of sexual assault and at providing better responses to sexual assault disclosures to ensure safety and accountability for victims and others in the sport community.

We have organized these strategies along different dimensions, including government responsibility and leadership, policy initiatives, community engagement, education and training, structural changes to the sport system, alternative legal approaches, and research-informed action. Some of these strategies are already being used by some sport organizations but could be adopted more universally. Others are novel and should be integrated more widely. Importantly, these strategies should not be seen or used in isolation and must be viewed instead as parts of a multidimensional approach to addressing the problem of sexual assault in sport.

Government Responsibility and Leadership

Federal and provincial governments play a central role in the Canadian sport system by providing policy direction and funding to national, provincial, and club-level sport organizations. Yet, until recently, they have allowed sport organizations to handle the persistent problem of sexual assault in sport autonomously, without much oversight or government intervention. In 2022, amid new reports of group sexual assault in Canadian junior hockey and sexual abuse perpetrated by coaches and other authority figures in gymnastics, Sport Canada froze all funding to Hockey Canada and Gymnastics Canada (Brady 2022). This move sparked public statements from both organizations vowing to address sexual assault in sport (Gillespie 2022; Iveson 2022). Withdrawing funding can be a useful instrument for change within Canadian sport organizations. There have been some steps in this direction. For example, in 2023, Minister of Sport Pascale St-Onge announced that federal funding to all National Sport Organizations (NSOs) would be contingent on adhering to SafeSport measures and foundational governance principles developed by a panel of experts (Canadian Heritage, 2023). National and provincial governments should also contribute significant funding and resources to implement initiatives to prevent and respond to sexual assault in sport, such as those outlined in this chapter. Sport organizations, and the community organizations with which they work, need financial support to implement change.

Beyond funding contingencies and support, the federal government can draft bills and pass new laws to prevent and address sexual assault in sport. One law long overdue in Canada is a restriction on the use of nondisclosure agreements in sexual assault cases. As the media scrutiny of Hockey Canada's settlements with sexual assault victims has made clear (Burke 2022), one method by which sexual assault in sport remains silenced is through nondisclosure agreements, in which sport organizations pay victims not to disclose details of their victimization to the media and, in some cases, police. The coerced silencing of victims of sexual assault in sport should not be possible.

The federal government also collects crime statistics through police-generated uniform crime reports and victimization surveys. Currently, these statistics do not record the social contexts, locations, and institutions in which the crimes occurred. Although uniform crime reports and victimization surveys are not perfect measures of the statistical prevalence of sexual assault, they would be more useful if they captured the contexts (e.g., sport, prison, military, university campus) in which sexual assaults occurred.

Federal and provincial governments should also take a central role in bringing sport organizations together to examine best practices, learn from established community leaders and experts on sexual assault in sport, and collaboratively develop more effective approaches to sexual assault prevention, education, and response. In the current structure of the Canadian sport system, governments have a prominent place. They therefore must take on more responsibility for responding to sexual assault in sport.

Policy Initiatives

Although regulatory policies are not a panacea, and have potential to be effective only when fully implemented, backed by required resources, and combined with other strategies, it is clear that the historical absence of sexual assault prevention, education, and response policies and protocols (hereafter called sexual assault policies) in Canadian sport organizations has facilitated the institutional silencing and tolerance of sexual assault. National, provincial, and organizational policies that condemn and expressly prohibit sexual violence in all forms are needed. Although recent SafeSport policies such as the UCCMS and various national and provincial policies adhering to it are a start, specific policies on sexual assault prevention, education, and response are also necessary to cover a broader range of issues (e.g., athlete-perpetrated sexual assaults against nonathletes), more specific terms (e.g., a clear definition of sexual assault), and more nuance, as we discuss in more detail in this section. Furthermore, where policies already exist, more can be done to enforce them. Indeed, existing sport policies to protect athletes often "lack any measure of accountability" (Kerr and Stirling 2008, 311).

As we argue in the next section on community engagement, the development of sexual assault policies should involve people who have experienced sexual assaults, community partners, and experts in sexual assault response and trauma-informed care and must include and centre perspectives of people from diverse communities. In this section, we offer some points of entry into sexual assault policy development and provide some key points that should be considered in the development of all sexual assault policies in sport.

Like many existing anti-hazing policies in Canadian sport, sexual assault policies should indicate that sport organizations have zero tolerance of sexual assaults. Athletes and authority figures implicated in cases of sexual assault should not be hired as coaches or be placed in leadership roles in sport organizations. Research has shown that the rehabilitation of sexual offenders behind bars is rare and that rates of recidivism are high. Rates for child sexual offenders are among the highest of all crimes at 23 percent, which rises to 35 percent for offenders who victimize boys who are not family members (Harris and Hanson 2004). In many of the cases discussed in this book, authority figures had previous criminal records for sexual offences that were either ignored or never checked. The case of Montreal hockey coach Gilbert Dubé provides such an example. In 1993, Dubé pleaded guilty to charges of sexual exploitation. After being released from prison, he continued coaching. Multiple concerns were brought to the attention of Montreal police and the organization for which he was coaching, and Dubé reportedly was open about his past convictions for sexual exploitation, yet he continued coaching. In 2011, he faced charges for sexually abusing four young male hockey players whom he had coached from 2002 to 2009 (*CBC News* 2011b). Sexual assault convictions are reflective of systemic issues in the criminal legal system, including institutionalized discrimination against some victims and accused, as well as the ongoing minimizing and silencing of the harms of sexual violence. Therefore, the presence or absence of a sexual assault conviction cannot be taken as a reliable measure of the safety of a future coach. However, without effective programs for the rehabilitation of those who have been convicted of sexual assaults, and without systems in place in sport organizations to ensure accountability for such assaults, it is currently unsafe for organizations to ignore coaches' and athletes' known histories of sexual violence.

Individuals implicated in sexual assaults should not be involved in sport organizations that provide access to athletes. In 1986, a Quebec hockey coach, Martin Dubuc, was convicted of sexually assaulting two minors and received a lifetime ban on coaching hockey in the Quebec Ice Hockey Federation. Shortly after his release from prison, he became the president of a federation-affiliated minor hockey association in Montreal (King 1995). As we have shown, coaches are not the only authority figures with opportunities to sexually exploit young athletes. Bans should therefore be on all involvement.

Those implicated in enabling sexual assault and exploitation in sport, such as individuals found to have known about sexual abuse but participated in silencing the issue, whom Amos Guiora (2020, 10) calls the "armies of enablers," should not be placed in leadership positions in sport. As Guiora argues, sexual assault perpetrators benefit greatly from the complicity of enablers, and the harm of the betrayal that victims experience through the inaction of institutional enablers is significant. Both perpetrators and enablers of sexual assault in sport therefore must be held accountable.

Sexual assault prevention policies should also prohibit coaches and other authority figures from being alone with athletes. Although this stipulation likely will not prevent all coaches from being alone with athletes, such an inclusion can help to redefine norms and expectations of safer practices in sport. Coaches should be prohibited from driving a single athlete to a game or practice, providing individual training sessions without others around, holding meetings in offices behind closed doors, and sharing a hotel room during away games and tournaments. Coaches should not be permitted to allow athletes to move into their homes, sleep over, or have private individual film or play-learning sessions. There has been much promotion of a two-deep coaching rule or what is sometimes termed the *rule of two*, which stipulates that there should be two certified coaches always present with athletes (Hachey 2018, para. 7). The rule appears to be a variation of the long-standing "two-deep leadership" and "no one-on-one contact" rules of the Boy Scouts of America, which prohibit an adult from being alone with a youth member (Wendell 2018). This rule clearly has been ineffective in preventing sexual assaults in the Boy Scouts, as a recent class-action lawsuit against the Boy Scouts of America revealed that over 12,000 boy scouts reported experiencing sexual abuse between 1944 and 2016 (Dockterman

2019). Beyond its questionable effectiveness, the rule of two does not necessarily translate well to all sports and playing levels. Perhaps a more straightforward policy is that coaches and other adult authority figures are never permitted to be alone in nonpublic spaces with athletes under their care. No closed doors. No private meetings. No driving of individual athletes home. No private training or film sessions.

Sexual assault policies should also stipulate rules on authority figure and athlete telecommunication. As cases discussed in this book and American research (Sanderson and Weathers 2020) have shown, the rapid development of social media, the internet, and text messaging has introduced a new method by which authority figures can groom and sexually exploit athletes. Just as authority figures should be prohibited from being alone with athletes in the physical world, they should also be discouraged from accessing isolated athletes in the online world. Authority figures should be instructed not to send private texts, emails, and messages to young athletes. Instead, any communication via social media, the internet, and text messaging should include other coaches, parents, and/or members of a team.

Sport-specific policies on physical contact with athletes should also be included in all sexual assault prevention policies. Joannie Pépin-Gagné and Sylvie Parent (2016, 165) challenge this view by arguing that "touch is important in coaching" and express concerns about coaches becoming fearful of touching athletes because of potential sexual assault allegations. In most sports, however, physical touch by coaches is unnecessary. They should also be prohibited from providing private massages or physical stretching assistance to athletes, particularly when they have no qualifications to do so. This form of touching was used to initiate sexual contact with athletes in many cases discussed in this book. Graham James reportedly began his contact with athletes by giving them foot massages to aid in their recovery, which eventually shifted to other forms of sexual abuse (Gilhooly 2018). Speedskating coach André Guilmette gave massages to two teenage female athletes whom he was coaching, during which he sexually assaulted them, claiming that it would benefit their athletic performance (King 2005). Track and field coach Glen Haugo also massaged and sexually violated the female athletes whom he was coaching, claiming that it would aid their athletic performance and recovery.[2] Sport organizations can play a larger role in discouraging, if not prohibiting, unnecessary physical contact between athletes and coaches.

Arguably, some physical contact by a coach might be necessary to correct athletes' form and technique in some sports. For example, in gymnastics, a coach might need to provide support to an athlete learning how to do a handspring on a beam. Likewise, a judo coach might need to show an athlete a particular hold. In sports in which some contact is necessary, clear guidelines should be established for coaches to follow on which forms of contact are considered permissible and which forms are not. Or, where possible, demonstrations should be done with another adult. When touching appears to be necessary for instructional or safety reasons, athletes and their parents should have an opportunity before participating in the sport to review the list of potential forms of coach contact, including parts of the body that will be touched, and decide which touching they consent to and which touching they do not. Athletes' right to revoke their consent to coach contact at any time should also be made clear to all involved in the sport.

Sexual assault policies should also stipulate that management positions within sport organizations should be independent from coaching positions and boards of directors. Single individuals should not be able to start and operate a sport organization, appoint themselves to be the managing director of that organization, and name themselves as the head coach. Granting this much power and authority to one individual, who can bypass background checks, and is accountable to no one within the organization, produces a dangerous power structure that provides ample opportunities for sexual exploitation. Governing sport bodies should prohibit this autocratic governance model.

Victims should also have increased access to support and resources for reporting. Sexual assault policies should include steps that victims can follow to disclose a sexual assault, assurances that their identities will remain confidential, as well as information on the existing 1-800 Canadian Sport HELPline and other victim support resources.

Mandatory reporting of suspicions of sexual abuse involving minors should also be stipulated in sexual assault policies. Under Ontario's Child and Family Services Act, "a person who performs professional or official duties with respect to children, has reasonable grounds to suspect [sexual abuse], the person shall forthwith report the suspicion and the information on which it is based to a [Children's Aid] society."[3] When athletes, parents, or others involved in youth sport witness or have reason to suspect sexual abuse of a minor, a Children's Aid Society should be notified. A child protection worker can then investigate the report and provide support to the victim.

Sexual assault policies must also specifically denounce sexual assaults perpetrated by athletes. Although young athletes are commonly the victims of sexual assault in sport, some are also reported as perpetrators. Existing

SafeSport policies typically miss this form of sexual assault. Likewise, hazing policies typically do not specifically define and prohibit sexual assaults in hazing rituals. All members of a sport community – whether coaches, athletes, parents, trainers, drivers, or first aiders – should be protected by the sexual assault policy but must also be required to adhere to it with clear and specific sanctions for any violations.

Sexual assault policies should mandate that educational sessions on consent, human rights, and healthy sexual relationships be provided by experts in these areas, as we discuss in more detail later in this chapter. All stakeholders and members of the sport organization should be required to attend these education sessions and sign an agreement on conduct after completing them.

Federal and provincial funding to sport organizations should be contingent on developing and adhering to adequate sexual assault policies and procedures. This approach would be consistent with recent developments in the Canadian postsecondary education sector, in which most provinces have mandated sexual violence prevention, education, and response policies and protocols, with potential funding withdrawal for noncompliance (E. Quinlan et al. 2017). Sport organizations that show exemplary responses to and strategies for addressing sexual assault could also be recognized and rewarded financially by federal and provincial sport funding bodies, providing additional incentives for organizations to do this much-needed work.

Community Engagement
Sylvie Parent and Karim El Hlimi (2012) suggest that sport organizations can do a much better job of utilizing existing resources and services on child sexual abuse to address sexual assault in sport. They suggest enhancing partnerships with existing organizations that work in child protective services and support. There is a wealth of knowledge on sexual assault prevention and consent education among community-based sexual assault centres and anti-violence activist groups. Rather than sport organizations developing sexual assault policies and procedures on their own, they should draw from existing knowledge and practices of organizations that have established expertise in identifying and responding to sexual assaults. Potential community partners include sexual assault crisis centres, local trauma-informed counselling services, survivor support groups, family healing centres, human rights advocates, and academic researchers who study sexual assault. Sport organizations should also develop partnerships with people who have experienced sexual assault, in sport in particular, since their experiences of and perspectives on sexual assault can inform productive

changes in the sport system. Ensuring that these community partners include Black people, Indigenous people, people of colour, people with disabilities, and people from 2SLGBTQI+ communities will be a crucial step toward developing more inclusive policies, procedures, and supports. Sport organizations have not been and will not be able to deal effectively with sexual assaults on their own. For this reason, community partners should meet regularly with leaders in sport organizations, examine ongoing issues, and develop victim-centred,[4] trauma-informed approaches and practices to respond to sexual assaults. Sport organizations must financially compensate these community partners for the expertise that they provide.

One community partnership between the Sport Dispute Resolution Centre of Canada and the Canadian Centre for Mental Health in Sport has led to the establishment of the Canadian Sport HELPline, drawing from existing community resources and collaborations (Asselin and Van Slingerton 2019). The HELPline is a national, toll-free line supporting victims and witnesses of sexual assault and harassment in sport. Athletes and their parents have long needed clear avenues to confidentially report sexual assaults. Although it is not yet clear how helpful the HELPline will be and whether it will fill this void effectively, it aims to provide anonymous and confidential assistance to athletes and other sport stakeholders when reporting their experiences and concerns (e.g., learning options for reporting and receiving referrals to other supports and resources). However, helplines are only effective if they are used. Should the HELPline prove to be effective, it could be more widely advertised in all sport organizations in Canada. All sexual assault policies could make specific reference to it, and it could be advertised in public places in sport organizations such as team webpages and training facilities.

Community partners outside sport organizations and the broader Canadian sport system should also be employed for investigations of sexual assault allegations against members of sport organizations. Consistent with recommendations in the UCCMS, an independent body external to any sport organization should be established to conduct impartial investigations of sexual assault reports. This body must be truly independent, for most sport organizations have shown themselves to be largely incapable of meaningfully responding to sexual assault complaints. Independent sexual assault investigation and review panels should be available to all sport organizations in Canada, not just at elite or national levels. These investigations should receive government funding independent from sport organizations, including Sport Canada, national sport organizations, and provincial sport organizations.

Although the independent investigation elements outlined in the UCCMS are still under development at the time of this writing, it appears that national sport organizations will be able to hire their own independent investigators to review allegations of sexual abuse of athletes (Robertson and Brady 2022b). This is problematic since it does not allow for enough separation from the sport organization, which can hire or fire investigators to gain the investigative results hoped for. Reflecting on past independent investigations in which she has been involved, Gretchen Kerr (quoted in Robertson and Brady 2022b, para. 22) states that, "if you run up against a situation as an investigator where someone wants something put under the rug, then that case never gets into the public eye, or even people in the organization don't become aware of it ... It's just so riddled with conflicts of interest." Independent investigations must be truly independent.

Anti-Violence Education

Anti-violence education on consent, healthy sexual relationships, diversity and inclusion, anti-oppressive language, human rights, and nonviolent masculinities is an important part of sexual assault prevention work. This training must be provided by recognized experts in sexual assault prevention (e.g., community-based sexual assault centres, anti-violence activists, and advocacy groups) and not by sport organizations, and it should be conducted on a regular basis. Work must be done to ensure that community experts who deliver anti-violence education in sport organizations are from diverse communities and include people who identify as Black, Indigenous, persons of colour, 2SLGBTQI+, and/or as having a disability. Anti-violence advocates and educators have described the world of men's sport as difficult to access for sexual assault prevention work (Messner, Greenberg, and Peretz 2015). Sport organizations must open their doors to people doing anti-violence work and adequately compensate them for it.

Athlete-specific workshops should be provided to all athletes, particularly competitive male athletes in high-contact sports. These anti-violence education initiatives should target men and the underlying cultural norms of sport and violent masculinities that contribute to the normalization and perpetration of sexual assaults. Male athletes must be taught that admiration from fans is not equivalent to sexual consent and does not provide entitlement to sexually violate women and girls. Violent masculinities that promote gender-based violence must be openly confronted with male athletes, with a focus on separating understandings of masculinity from the tolerance and celebration of sexual assault and other forms of gender-based violence. More work needs to be done to train, educate, and socialize young male athletes to value masculinities rooted in appreciating differences, valuing equality and consent, and practising nonviolence.

Beginning at early ages, when they first enter organized sports, young athletes should receive consent and human rights education training. As Jackson Katz (2019, 319), who provides sexual assault prevention training to men and boys, points out, "[children] learn what we teach them." Breger (2014) similarly contends that educating children is central to changing cultures of domination and violation that sustain high rates of sexual assault. Consent and human rights education training for young athletes can lead to increased and earlier reporting of coaches who engage in sexually abusive behaviours and encourage renewed commitments to and better understandings of consent in the world of competitive sport. Parents of young athletes should also be educated on sexual assault in sport and encouraged to communicate with their children about their relationships with their coaches, other adults, and teammates whom they are in contact with in their sports.

Young athletes should also be educated on what hazing is, its potential harms for victims and the team, potential sanctions that perpetrators can face, and strategies to intervene and stop hazing when it takes place. Dedicated hazing workshops with athletes should also address the topics of consent, sexual coercion, sexual harassment, and sexual assault to ensure that athletes understand that, even in jurisdictions in which no direct hazing laws exist, hazing can still be considered sexual assault.

Coaches and other authority figures should receive ongoing consent education and diversity training to challenge misogynist, homophobic, racist, and other oppressive cultures within sports. They should commit to promoting nonviolent attitudes and modelling appropriate behaviours and beliefs for their young players, a process that has been referred to as "re-norming sport for inclusivity" (Breger, Holman, and Guerrero 2019, 274). Coaching could be reconceptualized as a form of community education, in which the curriculum is one of respect, acceptance, and nonviolence. More generally, coaching education in Canada should be reoriented away from winning games and competitions and toward positive, long-term athlete development, which places the health and well-being of athletes as the top priority.

Anti-violence education initiatives for athletes, coaches, other sport leaders, and parents should promote awareness of the issue of sexual assault and the underlying cultures and norms in sport that lead to silencing and institutional tolerance of the issue. Many existing education programs and initiatives to prevent male violence and change toxic subcultural norms already exist and can be adapted for specific sport organizations in cooperation with community partners. For example, Katz (2019) has established the Mentors in Violence Prevention program to discuss issues of gender-based violence with men and work toward solutions. Many other bystander intervention programs have been developed in Canada and the United States that aim to change norms related to consent and sexual assault and promote action to intervene in and prevent gender-based violence in all of its forms (Labhardt et al. 2016). There is some evidence that existing sexual assault awareness and bystander intervention programs have positive impacts on building community capacities to better identify and intervene in gender-based violence as well as a reduction in attitudes and beliefs that support rape cultures (Senn and Forrest 2016; Stewart 2013; Storer, Casey, and Herrenkohl 2016). Such programs can inform new anti-violence education programming in Canadian sport to change the underlying cultures and norms of domination, exploitation, coercion, and tolerance of sexual assault.

Structural and Cultural Changes to the Sport System
Canadian sport organizations need to take a more visible and leading role in addressing sexual assault in sport. As Kirby, Greaves, and Hankivsky (2000, 137) note, "we reject the notion sexual abusers are just 'individuals gone bad' and accept that organized sport has a responsibility to ensure a culture of harassment and abuse [does] not thrive in the sport environment." Although some SafeSport policies and strategies have begun to emerge in sport, much more needs to be done to address those aspects of the Canadian sport system that allow sexual violence to flourish.

The data in this book point to a need for sport organizations to take a hard look at their programs, with an eye to broad structural changes to reduce the totalizing nature of the sport and an overemphasis on winning ahead of the safety and well-being of athletes. The male-dominated, autocratic coaching structure of most sport organizations in Canada needs to be problematized, challenged, and ultimately reorganized. Increasing opportunities for women and people who identify as two-spirit, trans, nonbinary, and gender queer to enter coaching and leadership roles in Canadian sport, at all levels, should be prioritized. The vast majority of reported cases of sexual assault in sport are perpetrated by men, who account for 99 percent of reported offenders in the cases discussed in this book. Furthermore, the male-dominated sport system, as it is currently organized in Canada, promotes a culture that perpetuates gender inequalities and fuels sexual violence within and outside sport.

Likewise, much more work needs to be done to increase the diversity of sport leadership in Canada. The patriarchal and racialized model of authoritarian leadership dominated by white men in Canadian sport needs to be challenged, dismantled, and replaced with a more inclusive sport system that promotes equity and diversity and places the health and well-being of young athletes at its centre. As Breger, Holman, and Guerrero (2019, 275) argue,

> National Sport Organizations, universities and colleges, and community sport all need to take broader responsibility for a culture that allows discrimination to be unchallenged and to be held accountable for transforming this culture. Within such a masculine culture, gender bias and sexual violence against women and girls tends to be ignored or at best ... minimized. Athletes and other vulnerable participants must feel respected and safe to benefit equitably from sport opportunity.

The culture of white male dominance and entitlement in Canadian sport needs to change to make sport a safer place for women, children, people who identify as 2SLGBTQI+, Black people, Indigenous people, and/or people of colour. All coaches should receive training in positive coaching and human rights, which places the emotional and physical well-being of the athlete at the forefront. Furthermore, young athletes' voices should be heard and recognized as significant in decision-making processes within sport organizations. As Mountjoy (2018, 59) writes, "safe sport can only occur if the culture of sport changes so that athletes are respected and empowered to speak and influence change."

New forms of team bonding that do not involve violence and copious amounts of alcohol should also be promoted for players. Teams can organize events for athletes that do not centre on drinking alcohol, such as outdoor and adventure education-based activities. Studies of these team-building activities have shown consistently that they help athletes to develop cooperation and communication skills and an inclusive and egalitarian team dynamic (j. johnson 2007, 2009; j. johnson and Chin 2016a, 2016b; Meyer 2000).

The junior hockey draft system and billet system in Canada is long overdue for a major overhaul. Fifteen-year-old players should not be considered the property of a team that can cut, trade, or force them to move away from their families to live in homes with minimal adult supervision. Like all young people, athletes in junior hockey leagues require a stable support system as they mature physically, emotionally, and psychologically. If the billet system, and the draft system that supports it, were eliminated, young athletes would have greater freedom to choose the teams that they play for, where they live, and with whom. In 2007, the Canadian Hockey League commissioned a report on sexual abuse in its member leagues titled the Players First Report (Kirke 1997). The report defends the CHL draft and billet system and argues that, with other measures of protection in place, these systems do not contribute to the sexual abuse of young athletes. While other measures of protection may contribute to reducing the sexual abuse of athletes, this reduction could be more significant with the removal of the draft and billet systems, which not only leave athletes unsafe but also place them in positions with reduced adult supervision, leading to increased risks of sexually violent hazing and unsupervised parties with drugs and alcohol where many sexual assaults against women and girls have reportedly occurred.

Sport organizations should also have designated safeguarding officers who have undergone advanced training on sexual harassment and abuse, who work to ensure that the organization adheres to sexual assault policies and procedures, and who take a leading role in coordinating and scheduling training workshops for stakeholders within the organization. The International Olympic Committee (2021) recently created an eight-month Safeguarding Officer in Sport Certificate program. Although still in its infancy, if it proves to be effective, this training program could provide a starting point for Canadian sport organizations to have trained safeguarding officers who take leadership roles within the organizations to make sure that sexual assault prevention and education and victim-centred responses remain priorities.

Alternative Legal Approaches

When sexual assault in sport occurs, and victims want to pursue legal action as part of their healing process, the application of criminal law is rarely the most promising avenue. Although it is important to acknowledge that some sexual assault victims can find a sense of justice through the criminal legal system, this outcome is less common than the institutional betrayal and trauma that many more victims experience (E. Craig 2018). Sexual assault convictions are rare. In the few cases that do result in convictions, most commonly in cases considered easier to prosecute because they involve adult perpetrators and child victims under the age of sexual consent, the result is often the temporary incarceration of the offender, who has limited access to meaningful rehabilitation and can easily return to harming others upon release. Other legal avenues might yield more effective results, with greater potential to offer victims a feeling of justice and create systemic change within sport to better prevent future harms.

One approach, which has been used by some victims of sexual assault in sport, is a civil lawsuit against the accused for the harm caused and against the sport organization for failing to prevent the harm. Lawsuits can run parallel to criminal proceedings, so they do not preclude the offender also facing criminal sanctions. They do differ, however, in many ways from criminal proceedings that some suggest are more favourable to victims (Szklarski 2017). In a civil lawsuit, a victim has relatively more control over the process compared with a trial in the criminal legal system and can decide if and when to agree to a settlement, as well as the remedy sought, which is typically financial compensation for physical, mental, and psychological harms.

In contrast, in a criminal trial, the victim is seen as a potential witness to the crime, might get called to testify, does not determine whether a case will move forward, and has no meaningful involvement when plea deals are arranged. Victims can also be required to testify in criminal proceedings against their will (E. Craig 2018). If an accused is convicted, then a victim in a criminal proceeding can submit a victim impact statement describing the harm experienced and its impacts, which the judge can consider when deciding on an appropriate sentence. If the accused is found not guilty, however, then there is no opportunity to provide a victim impact statement. The victim thus has minimal control and agency in the criminal court, and many victims report feeling retraumatized, commonly referred to as a "second assault," by the criminal legal system process (Martin and R.M. Powell 1994, 853; Werner 2021, 573). As one sexual assault victim stated after testifying in a criminal trial, "the bulk of my rape trauma is not the result of the sexual assault itself but of the brutality of the legal system" (Gray 2016, para. 5). Although civil proceedings are not entirely unproblematic and can be expensive and traumatizing for those who experience sexual assault, they have potential to offer victims additional controls over the process that are lacking in criminal courts.

In civil lawsuits, the burden of proof is also relatively lower. Whereas in criminal proceedings it must be shown beyond a reasonable doubt that a sexual assault occurred, in civil lawsuits it must only be shown beyond the balance of probability. As such, the likelihood that the accused is held responsible for a reported sexual assault is higher in civil proceedings, and liability extends more commonly not just to the individual perpetrator but also to the sport organization and its leaders who failed to prevent the sexually violent acts. In so doing, civil lawsuits can help to hold sport organizations accountable for the harms that occur within them and responsible for creating environments free from sexual assault.

Another legal avenue for addressing sexual assaults within institutions is a human rights complaint. Although we are not aware of any victim discussed in this book who has used this approach, there have been successful human rights cases involving sexual assault cases in other contexts in Canada. For example, in 2015, a York University student filed a human rights complaint against the university after she was sexually assaulted by another student and the university reportedly failed to take appropriate actions to provide her with support and care (K. Hoffman 2015). York University agreed to a settlement and although the exact terms were not disclosed, both sides indicated that they included systemic changes on the campus that would benefit the entire campus community (Joy 2016).

Sexual assault is a human rights issue. Under various laws, such as provincial human rights legislation, the federal Charter of Rights and Freedoms, and international declarations such as the Universal Declaration of Human Rights, all humans are granted the right to safety, security of person, and freedom from discrimination. Sexual assault is a violation of those human rights. It violates the sexual integrity of the victim, can have lifelong impacts, and is disproportionately targeted at specific groups, including women and children.

Human rights law is not intended to be used to seek retribution against individuals, nor does it serve as an avenue for holding individuals accountable for the harms that they caused. Instead, human rights complaints offer a legal avenue for seeking systemic change within an organization. Like civil proceedings, the burden of proof in human rights complaints is beyond the balance of probability, which creates more favourable odds for victims. Although an individual perpetrator might not be held personally accountable, organizations can be required by a human rights tribunal to implement systemic remedies for the harms inflicted. Such remedies can include many of the strategies outlined in this chapter, such as mandatory consent training administered by community-based sexual assault centres and the development of and adherence to sexual violence prevention, education, and response policies and protocols.

Although criminal cases bring some short-lived media attention to the problem of sexual assault in sport and can, in some cases, temporarily incapacitate an individual sexual offender through incarceration – which may or may not be what a victim wants – they do little to bring about large-scale, structural changes to the sport system. In contrast, civil lawsuits and human rights complaints can lead to greater systemic changes and lasting impacts on responses to sexual assault in sport.

Research-Informed Action

Increasing the visibility and understanding of the problem of sexual assault in sport is a necessary step in promoting change. More scholarly and journalistic investigation is needed on sexual assault, and sexual violence more broadly, in sport in Canada and internationally. As noted in a literature review of violence in sport, "it is important to grow scientific attention [to] and work about institutional and structural violence toward athletes to better capture the whole picture" (Parent and Fortier 2018, 239). This book is not intended to be an exhaustive, definitive account of all forms of sexual violence in Canadian sport. Instead, it provides a window into the persistent problem of such violence and how sport and legal institutions respond to it, looking at athletes as both victims and perpetrators of sexual assaults. In so doing, it has presented new questions for further exploration.

More needs to be learned about the statistical prevalence and lived experience of sexual assault of athletes and other participants in Canadian sport. Quantitative surveys of Canadian athletes, coaches, and other authority figures on their attitudes, perspectives, and behaviours related to sexual assault are needed. The experiences and demographic characteristics of those who experience sexual assault in sport need more scholarly attention. Future research needs to be directed toward the lived experiences of athletes who identify as 2SLGBTQI+, Black, Indigenous, persons of colour, and/or as having a disability and have experienced sexual assault in sport.

Additionally, qualitative, interview-based research on athletes' and victims' understandings of sexual assaults they witness and perpetrate will shed new light on the problem and offer more depth to existing quantitative research on the topic. Additional links can also be forged through a broader exploration of other forms of sexual violence not examined in detail in this book, such as the production of child pornography by coaches and sexual harassment in sport organizations. Sexual abuse in sport is not restricted to physical sexual assaults and includes exhibitionism, voyeurism, and verbal sexual harassment (Fortier, Parent, and Lessard 2020). More research is needed on different forms of sexual abuse in sport as well as on their interconnections with more commonly recognized forms of sexual assault. Community-based research with victims and organizations that have expertise in sexual assault prevention, which focuses on identifying contributing factors and ways of addressing sexual assaults by and against athletes, is also necessary. Importantly, empirical studies should also be conducted on the efficacy of different sexual assault prevention, education, and response strategies in sport for the purposes of developing and refinding best practices.

Overall, more data can enhance understanding and awareness of the issues, enable and encourage new policy and education programs on sexual assault and consent within and outside sport organizations, and ultimately lead to the development of more research-informed strategies to break the cycle of sexual assault in sport.

Together, these strategies can contribute to fostering an environment that counters the institutional tolerance, silence, and betrayal that currently characterize many cases of sexual assault in sport. Such assault is rooted in oppressive social structures within and outside sport organizations, including sexism, misogyny, racism, homophobia, transphobia, cisnormativity, and ableism, among others (Fogel 2017; Kirby, Demers, and Parent 2008). Without dismantling these larger oppressive structures fuelling sexual violence, it will be impossible to eliminate all forms of sexual assault in sport. However, the strategies outlined in this chapter can play a role in drawing attention to the problem, reducing its prevalence, and leading to better trauma-informed responses when it does occur. By eliminating the widespread tolerance of and silence around sexual assault in sport and increasing efforts to acknowledge and address sexual assaults perpetrated by and against athletes, we can begin to create safer and healthier spaces in sport.

Appendix A: Reports of Athlete-Perpetrated Sexual Assault

Table A.1 Reports of athlete-perpetrated sexual assault by sport, 1990–2020

Sport	# of reports	% of total
Hockey	12	40
Football	8	27
Basketball	3	10
Soccer	2	6
Boxing	1	3
Volleyball	1	3
Baseball	1	3
Wrestling	1	3
Lacrosse	1	3
TOTAL	30	100

Table A.2 Reports of athlete-perpetrated sexual assault by province, 1990–2020

Province	# of reports	% of total
British Columbia	6	20
Alberta	4	13
Saskatchewan	2	7
Manitoba	2	7
Ontario	12	40
Quebec	1	3
Nova Scotia	2	7
Prince Edward Island	1	3
TOTAL	30	100

Table A.3 Reports of athlete-perpetrated sexual assault by playing level, 1990–2020

Playing level	# of reports	% of total
High school	2	7
Junior	8	27
University/college	9	30
Professional	11	37
TOTAL	30	100

Appendix B: Reports of Athlete-Perpetrated Group Sexual Assault

Table B.1 Reports of athlete-perpetrated group sexual assault by sport, 1990–2020

Sport	# of reports	% of total
Hockey	17	77
Football	5	23
TOTAL	22	100

Table B.2 Reports of athlete-perpetrated group sexual assault by province, 1990–2020

Province	# of reports	% of total
British Columbia	1	5
Alberta	1	5
Saskatchewan	2	9
Manitoba	2	9
Ontario	9	41
Quebec	5	23
Nova Scotia	2	9
TOTAL	22	100

Table B.3 Reports of athlete-perpetrated group sexual assault by playing level, 1990–2020

Playing level	# of reports	% of total
High school	2	9
Junior	14	64
University/college	4	18
Professional	2	9
TOTAL	22	100

Appendix C: Reports of Sexually Violent Hazing

Table C.1 Reports of sexually violent hazing by sport, 1990–2020

Sport	# of reports	% of total
Football	2	17
Hockey	9	75
Basketball	1	8
Diving	1	8
TOTAL	13*	100

* Of the twelve cases analyzed, one involved athletes from two sports: basketball and football.

Table C.2 Reports of sexually violent hazing by province, 1990–2020

Province	# of reports	% of total
British Columbia	1	8
Alberta	1	8
Manitoba	1	8
Ontario	7	58
Quebec	2	17
TOTAL	12	100

Table C.3 Reports of sexually violent hazing by playing level, 1990–2020

Playing level	# of reports	% of total
Minor	4	33
High school	1	8
Junior	5	42
University/college	2	17.
Professional	0	0
TOTAL	12	100

Appendix D: Reports of Sexual Assault Involving Authority Figures in Sport

Table D.1 Reports of sexual assault involving authority figures by sport, 1990–2020

Sport	# of reports	% of total
Hockey	80	33
Football	8	3
Basketball	34	14
Soccer	30	12
Boxing	3	1
Volleyball	15	6
Baseball	15	6
Wrestling	3	1
Lacrosse	2	<1
Track and field	11	5
Badminton	1	<1
Fencing	1	<1
Softball	5	2
Swimming	13	5
Figure skating	3	1
Canoe and kayak	1	<1
Cross-country skiing	1	<1
Alpine skiing	2	<1
Biathlon	2	<1

(Continued)

Table D.1 (Continued)

Sport	# of reports	% of total
Speedskating	2	<1
Tennis	2	<1
Gymnastics	9	4
Bowling	2	<1
Cycling	1	<1
Martial arts	7	3
Rugby	2	<1
Tee-ball	1	<1
Golf	1	<1
Cheerleading	1	<1
Weightlifting	1	<1
Sailing	1	<1
Water polo	2	<1
Equestrian	1	<1
Ringette	1	<1
Diving	1	<1
Curling	1	<1
Unspecified	8	3
TOTAL	274*	100

* Of the 243 cases analyzed, 25 involved two or more sports.

Table D.2 Reports of sexual assault involving authority figures in sport by province and territory, 1990–2020

Province	# of reports	% of total
British Columbia	27	11
Alberta	27	11
Saskatchewan	14	6
Manitoba	8	3
Ontario	106	44
Quebec	25	10
New Brunswick	8	3
Nova Scotia	16	7
Prince Edward Island	4	2
Newfoundland	7	3
Yukon	1	<1
Northwest Territories	2	1
Nunavut	1	<1
TOTAL	243	100

Table D.3 Individual versus team sports in reports of sexual assault involving authority figures, 1990–2020

Type of sport	# of reports	% of total
Individual	61	25
Team	174	72
Unspecified	8	3
TOTAL	243	100

Table D.4 Reports of sexual assault involving authority figures by decade and gender of victims

Decade and gender	# of reports	% of total within decade
Pre-1980s male victims	585	98
Pre-1980s female victims	14	2
Pre-1980s unidentified gender	-	-
1980s male victims	99	66
1980s female victims	51	34
1980s unidentified gender	-	-
1990s male victims	36	36
1990s female victims	58	59
1990s unidentified gender	5	5
2000s male victims	49	40
2000s female victims	75	60
2000s unidentified gender	-	-
2010s male victims	24	36
2010s female victims	40	60
2010s unidentified gender	3	4
TOTAL	1,039	-

Table D.5 Reports of sexual assault involving authority figures by decade and gender of accused

Decade and gender	# of reports	% of total within decade
Pre-1980s male accused	41	100
Pre-1980s female accused	0	0
1980s male accused	39	100
1980s female accused	0	0
1990s male accused	45	100

(Continued)

Table D.5 (Continued)

Decade and gender	# of reports	% of total within decade
1990s female accused	0	0
2000s male accused	62	98
2000s female accused	1	2
2010s male accused	51	93
2010s female accused	4	7
Total male accused	238	98
Total female accused	5	2
TOTAL	243	-

Notes

Chapter 1: Sport, Sexual Assault, and the Law

1 *Criminal Code,* RSC 1985, c C-46 [*Criminal Code*].
2 *R v Chase,* 1987 23 SC 2 SCR 293, para. 3.
3 *Criminal Code,* s 271.
4 *Criminal Code,* s 151.
5 *Criminal Code,* s 152.
6 *Criminal Code,* s 153.

Chapter 2: Athlete-Perpetrated Sexual Assault

1 Some cases of male athletes reported for sexually assaulting their male teammates
   have been publicized, and we will discuss them in Chapter 4.
2 *Simpson v University of Colorado,* 500 F (3d) 1170 (10th Cir 2007).
3 *R v Smith,* 2008 SKCA 61.
4 *Criminal Code,* RSC 1985, c C-46, s 273.1.
5 Descriptive statistics on reported perpetration rates by sport and province are provided in Appendix A.
6 Not all playing levels of sports in Canada are included in this analysis (e.g., national-
   level sports, Paralympic sports, etc.). We discuss only those playing levels featured
   in the cases that we located through our search methods (see Chapter 1).
7 *Berg v Canadian Hockey League,* 2017 ONSC 2608.
8 *Berg v Canadian Hockey League,* 2020 ONSC 2608.
9 *R v DVV,* 2005 BCPC 88.
10 *R v DVV,* para. 24.
11 *R v Vandergunst,* 2014 [unreported]. Summary retrieved from Fleming (2015a).

12 *R v Vandergunst.*
13 *R v Johnson,* 2016 ONSC 3947.
14 *R v DVV,* para. 24.
15 For example, a single regular season university men's hockey game played in St. Catharines in 2019 between the Brock University Badgers and the University of Guelph Gryphons sold out the Meridian Centre with a crowd of 4,752 people (Leithwood 2019). That number is comparable to a junior men's hockey playoff game played by the Niagara IceDogs at the Meridian Centre.
16 *R v Smith,* 2008 SKCA 61.
17 *R v Smith.*
18 *R v Smith.* The criminalization of HIV nondisclosure during sexual activity has been widely criticized in Canada. Critics argue that these prosecutions are based upon misunderstandings of the scientific evidence of HIV transmission risk and can unjustly target people diagnosed with HIV, particularly women who are HIV positive (Canadian HIV/AIDS Legal Network 2012; Kaida and Spencer 2019). Although the criminalization of HIV nondisclosure has been touted by some as a crucial step toward protecting women from gender-based violence, research suggests that it has not had this effect and in fact has many detrimental impacts on women, particularly those living with HIV (Greene et al. 2019).
19 See note 18 above for further discussion.
20 Nondisclosure agreements in sexual assault cases involve a confidential agreement in which the victim receives compensation in exchange for not publicly disclosing the sexual assault or pursuing further legal action.

Chapter 3: Group Sexual Assault

1 *Criminal Code,* RSC 1985, c C-46, s 271.
2 In a recent case not included in this analysis, two junior hockey players in Quebec, along with another male, were charged with sexually assaulting a sixteen-year-old young woman. One of the junior hockey players pleaded guilty. As a minor, he cannot be publicly named. The other player, Noah Corson, pleaded not guilty and is awaiting trial at the time of writing (Leclerc 2022).
3 To identify these cases, we used the same search procedures outlined in Chapter 1. The cases included are those that contained publicly available information on the alleged perpetrators of the sexual assaults, the location and playing level of the team that they played for, where the sexual assault occurred, which crime or crimes were reportedly committed, and how both league and legal officials responded to the allegations. No other sports or playing levels were represented in the legal cases. That does not mean that group sexual assaults do not occur in these contexts, only that they were not reported and therefore could not be included in our analysis. Given the low reporting rates of sexual assault, these twenty-two cases likely represent a small fraction of the total number of group sexual assaults that occur in Canadian sport.
4 *Guillemette c Verreault,* 1994 QC CM 1786 [*Guillemette*].
5 *Guillemette.*

6 Victim blaming refers to the tendency to hold victims of a crime responsible for its occurrence: that is, blaming them for their own victimization. Victims of sexual assault are commonly blamed for it, unlike victims of most other crimes, such as robbery, theft, homicide, et cetera (Gravelin, Biernat, and Bucher 2019).

7 *R v Richardson*, 2009 ONSC 80253 [*Richardson*].

8 *Richardson*.

9 *Richardson*, para. 14.

10 The Football Manitoba league is composed of fifteen- to seventeen-year-old athletes. Although the vast majority of the players are young men, there are some female players.

11 *R v NB*, 2018 ONCJ 527.

12 *R v NB*.

13 These cases might have involved other athletes not publicly named in media reports and legal case files who are not white. Here, however, we reflect on the athletes publicly named, all of whom present as white.

14 For further discussion of the impacts of racism on the rates of conviction and incarceration of Black people, Indigenous people, and people of colour in Canada, see Neugebauer (2000), Owusu-Bempah and Wortley (2013), and Owusu-Bempah et al. (2021).

15 As discussed in Chapter 1, demographics on victims of sexual assault are rarely included in legal case files and media reports of sexual assault. We have included these details when available.

16 Publication bans refer to a court order preventing anyone from publishing any identifying information on a person involved in a particular criminal case. Although most information in court cases is open to the public, the names of victims of sexual assaults are typically placed under a publication ban to provide privacy and seemingly to reduce barriers for victims to come forward. Some sexual assault victims choose to have publication bans on their identities lifted, though most do not. When other details of a case can identify a victim, such as who the perpetrator is and the relationship to the victim, those details can also be placed under a publication ban.

17 *Creppin v University of Ottawa*, 2015 ONSC 4449.

18 *R v Williams*, 2019 NSSC 399 [*Williams* 2019b].

19 *R v Williams*, 2019 NSSC 352, para. 53 [*Williams* 2019a].

20 *Williams* 2019a.

21 *Williams* 2019a.

22 See, for example, *R v Cedeno*, 2005 195 CCC (3d) 468 (OCJ); *R v Cornejo*, 2003 68 OR (3d) 117 (CA); *R v GJD*, 1995 PEIJ 173 (SCTD).

23 See *R v Laude*, 1965 51 WWR 175.

Chapter 4: Sexually Violent Hazing

Acknowledgment: A previously published version of this chapter presented similar data (Fogel and Quinlan 2021).

1 The relatively lower figure reported by j. johnson et al. (2018) could be attributed to the survey error they reported, which eliminated ten questions pertaining to different hazing behaviours, including all questions related to sexually violent hazing.

Because of this error, the survey did not capture the total occurrence of hazing experienced by survey participants.

2 See Chapter 2 for more discussion.

3 *R v Ewanchuk*, 1999 1 SCR 330, para. 28.

4 See *R v S (VCA)*, 2001 MBCA 85.

5 See *R v Higginbottom*, 2001 CanLII 3989.

6 *Criminal Code*, RSC 1985, c C-46.

7 The minimum legal drinking age is eighteen in Alberta, Manitoba, and Quebec and nineteen in the rest of the Canadian provinces and territories (Canadian Centre on Substance Abuse 2017).

8 For example, in one media article, an athlete described how a hazing experience nearly led him to end his life. He was required by veteran athletes to strip naked and run outside on a public street, drink large amounts of alcohol, and do the "elephant walk" in which each rookie hunched over and held the genitals of the player in front of him as they walked (MacGregor 2013). No details were publicly reported on who was involved, when it happened, which team, or whether any disciplinary or legal sanctions resulted. We excluded this case and others with a similar lack of publicly available details.

9 *Carcillo v Canadian Hockey League*, 2023 ONSC 886 at 98.

Chapter 5: Sexual Exploitation by Authority Figures

1 *R v McNutt*, 2020 NSSC 219, para. 1.

2 *R v Kaija*, 2006 ONCJ 193.

3 *Criminal Code of Canada*, SC 1892, c 29, s 266.

4 *R v Swietlinski*, 1980 53 SCC 2 SCR 956, 968.

5 *Criminal Code*, RSC 1970, c C-34, s 156.

6 *Criminal Law Amendment Act*, SC 1985, c 19.

7 *R v Triller*, 1980 2850 BCSC, 413. In 1987, buggery was replaced with two distinct crimes of anal intercourse and bestiality; *An Act to Amend the Criminal Code and the Canada Evidence Act*, SC 1987 c 24. Neither offence appeared in the Canadian sport cases analyzed in this book.

8 *Criminal Code*, RSC 1985, c C-46 [*Criminal Code*].

9 *Criminal Law Amendment Act*, SC 1985, c 19.

10 *Criminal Code*, s 151.

11 *Criminal Code*, s 152.

12 *Criminal Code*, s 153.

13 For example, if the exact age of the victim at the time of the alleged sexual acts is questioned in a historical case, then sexual interference and invitation to sexual touching charges might be dropped, but the authority figure can still be convicted of sexual assault.

14 *R v Kienapple*, 1974 1 SCR 729.

15 The cases have been categorized based upon when the reports of sexual assault by the authority figure first began.

16 Descriptive statistics on the 243 cases can be found in Appendix D.

17 *R v Stuckless*, 2016 ONCJ 338.

18 *R v Stuckless,* 2019 ONCA 504, para. 9.
19 *R v McNutt.* A pardon is a government decision to allow a person to be absolved of a criminal record for a prior crime or crimes, making it possible for the person to move more freely between countries or obtain work that requires a clean criminal record.
20 *R v McNutt,* para. 10.
21 *R v McNutt.*
22 *Blainey v OHA,* 1986 7 CHRR 3529.
23 *R v James,* 2013 MBCA 14.
24 *R v James,* 2012 MBPC 31, para. 18; emphasis added.
25 *R v Sazant,* 2004 SCC 77.
26 *R v Sazant,* 2002 OTC 203.
27 *R v Sazant,* 2002 OTC 203; *R v Sazant,* 2004 SCC 77.
28 *R v Innerebner,* 2010 ABQB 188 [*Innerebner*].
29 *Innerebner.*
30 *R v AGA,* 2010 ABCA 61.
31 *R v JMA,* 2009 283 NFLD 179 [*JMA*].
32 *JMA.*
33 *R v Vigon,* 2016 ABCA 75 [*Vigon*].
34 *Vigon.*
35 *R v McFarlane,* 2020 ONSC 5194.
36 *LSJPA – 1954,* 2019 QCCQ 10339.
37 *Vigon,* para. 4.
38 *Innerebner.*

Chapter 6: Breaking the Cycle of Sexual Assault in Canadian Sport

1 SafeSport policies refer to policies and procedures within sport organizations and governing bodies that aim to safeguard athletes and other sport stakeholders from harassment, abuse, and maltreatment.
2 *R v Haugo,* 2006 BCPC 0319.
3 *Child and Family Services Act,* RSO 1990, c C-11, s 72(1). This act has since been repealed and replaced with Ontario's *Child, Youth and Family Services Act,* 2017, SO 2017, c 14.
4 As human rights lawyer Kat Craig (2020) identifies, a victim-centred approach involves ensuring that victims (1) have access to appropriate and high-quality support services, (2) receive detailed information to make informed decisions, (3) have their privacy protected, (4) have opportunities to be involved in solutions, (5) are treated with dignity and respect, and (6) have their rights and needs prioritized.

References

Abdulrehman, Rehman. 2006. "The Cycle of Abuse in Sports Hazing: Is It Simply a Case of Boys Being Boys?" PhD diss., University of Manitoba.

Adams, J.J. 2018. "Lions Release Euclid Cummings after Learning of Criminal Charges." *Province* (Vancouver), March 7. https://theprovince.com/sports/football/cfl/bc-lions/lions-release-euclid-cummings-after-learning-of-criminal-charges.

—. 2020. "Former Whitecaps Striker Anthony Blondell Charged with Sexual Assault from 2018." *Province* (Vancouver), April 10. https://theprovince.com/sports/former-whitecaps-striker-anthony-blondell-charged-with-sexual-assault-from-2018.

Aguilar, Bryann. 2018. "Mississauga Gymnastics Coach Charged with Sexual Assault." *Toronto Star*, January 30. https://www.thestar.com/news/crime/2018/01/30/mississauga-gymnastics-coach-charged-with-sexual-assault.html.

—. 2020. "Maple Leaf Gardens Sex Offender Gordon Stuckless Dies in Hospital." *CTV News*, April 10. https://toronto.ctvnews.ca/maple-leaf-gardens-sex-offender-gordon-stuckless-dies-in-hospital-1.4891286.

Alexander, Kate, Anne Stafford, and Ruth Lewis. 2011. *The Experiences of Children Participating in Organised Sport in the UK*. London: NSPCC.

Allan, Elizabeth, and G. DeAngelis. 2004. "Hazing, Masculinity, and Collision Sports: (Un)becoming Heroes." In *Making the Team: Inside the World of Sport Initiations and Hazing*, edited by jay johnson and Margery Holman, 61–82. Toronto: Canadian Scholars Press.

Allan, Elizabeth, David Kerschner, and Jessica Payne. 2019. "College Student Hazing Experiences, Attitudes, and Perceptions: Implications for Prevention." *Journal of Student Affairs Research and Practice* 56(1): 32–48.

Allan, Elizabeth, and Mary Madden. 2008. *Hazing in View: College Students at Risk*. https://www.stophazing.org/wp-content/uploads/2014/06/hazing_in_view_web1.pdf.

—. 2009. "Hazing in View: High School Students at Risk." Paper presented at the American Educational Research Association Annual Conference, San Diego, CA, April.

—. 2012. "The Nature and Extent of College Student Hazing." *International Journal of Adolescent Medicine and Health* 24: 83–90.

Allard, Sharon. 1997. "Rethinking Battered Woman Syndrome: A Black Feminist Perspective." In *The Legal Response to Violence against Women,* edited by Karen Maschke, 73–90. New York: Garland Publishing.

Alphonso, Caroline, and Laura Robinson. 2008. "Skating Instructor Raises Red Flags for Parents." *Globe and Mail,* November 12. https://www.theglobeandmail.com /sports/skating-instructor-raises-red-flag-for-parents/article17974449/.

Anderson, Eric. 2005. *In the Game: Gay Athletes and the Cult of Masculinity.* Albany: SUNY Press.

Anderson, Eric, Mark McCormack, and Harry Lee. 2012. "Male Team Sport Hazing Initiations in a Culture of Decreasing Homohysteria." *Journal of Adolescent Research* 27(4): 427–48.

Anderson, Luleen. 1981. "Notes on the Linkage between the Sexually Abused Child and the Suicidal Adolescent." *Journal of Adolescence* 4(2): 147–62.

Andrew-Gee, Eric, and Laura Armstrong. 2014. "University of Ottawa Sexual Assault Scandal Highlights Campus Rape Culture." *Toronto Star,* August 22. https://www .thestar.com/news/crime/2014/08/22/university_of_ottawa_sexual_assault_scan-dal_highlights_campus_rape_culture.html.

AP News. 1996a. "Dallas Stars Players Charged with Sexual Assault." August 12. https://apnews.com/9199000ddb3c70f6fd9af1d706302162.

—. 1996b. "Nedved Charged with Sexual Assault." February 7. https://apnews.com/6 c402c63e93a4bbf3e68f48905700684.

Ariel, Barak, and Henry Partridge. 2017. "Predictable Policing: Measuring the Crime Control Benefits of Hotspots Policing at Bus Stops." *Journal of Quantitative Criminology* 33(4): 809–33.

Asselin, Marie-Claude, and Krista Van Slingerton. 2019. "Launch of the Canadian Sport Helpline." Sport Dispute Resolution Centre of Canada and Canadian Centre for Mental Health and Sport. http://www.crdsc-sdrcc.ca/eng/ documents/2019-03-13-Canadian_Sport_Helpline_EN.pdf.

Au, Teresa, Benjamin Dickstein, Jonathan Comer, Kristalyn Salters-Pedneault, and Brett Litz. 2013. "Co-Occurring Posttraumatic Stress and Depression Symptoms after Sexual Assault: A Latent Profile Analysis." *Journal of Affective Disorders* 149: 209–16.

Bachelder, Jill. 2014. "Sexual Assault Charges against Former Redmen Football Players Dropped: Prosecution Cites Insufficient Evidence as Reason for Withdrawal." *McGill Daily,* November 19. http://www.mcgilldaily.com/2014/11/sexual-assault-charges-former-redmen-football-players-dropped/.

Backhouse, Constance. 2008. *Carnal Crimes: Sexual Assault Law in Canada, 1900–1975.* Toronto: Irwin Law.

Baker, Geoff. 1994. "Criticized Judge Faces Inquiry after Trio Escape Rape Charges." *Vancouver Sun,* February 18, A12.

Banerjee, Sidhartha. 2003. "Speed-Skating Coach Charged." *Gazette* [Montreal], October 8, A1.

—. 2016. "Former Hockey Coach Graham James Granted Full Parole." *CTV News,* September 15. https://www.ctvnews.ca/canada/former-hockey-coach-graham-james-granted-full-parole-1.3073370.

Bass, Jordan, Robin Hardin, and Elizabeth Taylor. 2015. "The Glass Closet: Perceptions of Homosexuality in Intercollegiate Sport." *Journal of Applied Sport Management* 7(4): 1–31.

Bates, Laura. 2012. "Sites Like Uni Lad Only Act to Support Our Everyday Rape Culture." *Independent,* November 27. http://www.independent.co.uk/voices /comment/sites-like-uni-lad-only-act-to-support-our-everyday-rape-culture-8360109.html.

Belleville Intelligencer. 2013. "Rape Charges Withdrawn against Ontario Junior Players." April 4. https://www.intelligencer.ca/2013/04/04/rape-charges-withdrawn -against-ontario-junior-players/wcm/960b72ae-b7bb-0d39-acf7-efa4b4bba540.

Benedet, Janine. 2010a. "The Age of Innocence: A Cautious Defence of Raising the Age of Consent in Canadian Sexual Assault Law." *New Criminal Law Review* 13(4): 665–87.

—. 2010b. "The Sexual Assault of Intoxicated Women." *Canadian Journal of Women and the Law* 22(2): 435–61.

Benedict, Jeff. 1997. *Public Heroes, Private Felons: Athletes and Crimes against Women.* Boston: Northeastern University Press.

—. 1998. *Athletes and Acquaintance Rape.* Thousand Oaks, CA: Sage.

—. 2001. *Out of Bounds: Inside the NBA's Culture of Rape, Violence, and Crime.* New York: HarperCollins.

Beswick, Aaron. 2019a. "Accused in St. F.X. Sex Assault Trial Says He Got Consent from Woman." *Chronicle Herald,* October 30. https://www.thechronicleherald .ca/news/provincial/accused-in-st-fx-sex-assault-trial-says-he-got-consent-from-woman-369782/.

—. 2019b. "Trial Begins for Two Former St. F.X. Football Players Charged with Sex Assault." *Journal Pioneer,* October 22. https://www.journalpioneer.com/news /canada/trial-begins-for-two-former-st-fx-football-players-charged-with-sex-assault-366604/.

Bieler, Des. 2022. "Larry Nassar Victims Seek $130 Million from FBI for Mishandling Case." *Washington Post,* April 22. https://www.washingtonpost.com /sports/2022/04/22/larry-nassar-fbi-claims/.

Blais, Tony. 2013. "Ex-Eskimos Lineman Adam Braidwood Sentenced to 4 1/2 Years for Sex Assault." *Toronto Sun,* April 19. https://torontosun.com/2013/04/19/ ex-eskimos-lineman-adam-braidwood-sentenced-to-4-12-years-for-sex-assault.

Block, Irwin. 2006. "Secret Sex Tape Trips Up Junior Hockey Team." *Gazette* [Montreal], December 22. https://www.pressreader.com/canada/montreal-gazette/20061222/281608120948819.

—. 2010. "Coach Given Jail Term." *Gazette* [Montreal], October 2, A13.

Board, Mike. 1998. "Hockey Suspension Reduction Appealed." *Calgary Herald,* June 25.

Boeringer, Scot B. 1996. "Influences of Fraternity Membership, Athletics, and Male Living Arrangements on Sexual Aggression." *Violence against Women* 2(2): 134–47.

—. 1999. "Associations of Rape-Supportive Attitudes with Fraternal and Athletic Participation." *Violence against Women* 5(1): 81–90.

Bolan, Kim. 2009. "One-Time B.C. Lion Charged with Sexual Assault in Vancouver." *Vancouver Sun,* September 9. http://www.vancouversun.com/news/time+Lion+c harged+with+sexual+assault+Vancouver/1980208/story.html.

Boucher, Marianne. 2015. "Former Figure Skating Coach Sentenced to 4 Years in Sex Assault Cases." *CityNews,* May 29. https://toronto.citynews.ca/2015/05/29 /former-figure-skating-coach-sentenced-to-4-years-in-sex-assault-cases/.

Brackenridge, Celia. 2001. *Spoilsports: Understanding and Preventing Sexual Exploitation in Sport.* London: Routledge.

Brackenridge, Celia, Daz Bishop, Sybille Moussali, and James Tapp. 2008. "The Characteristics of Sexual Abuse in Sport: A Multidimensional Scaling Analysis of Events Described in Media Reports." *International Journal of Sport and Exercise Psychology* 6(4): 385–406.

Brackenridge, Celia, and Kari Fasting. 2005. "The Grooming Process in Sport." *Auto/Biography* 13: 33–52.

Brackenridge, Celia, and Sandra Kirby. 1997. "Playing Safe: Assessing the Risk of Sexual Abuse to Young Elite Athletes." *International Review for the Sociology of Sport* 32(4): 407–18.

Brackenridge, Celia, and Daniel Rhind. 2014. "Child Protection in Sport: Reflections on Thirty Years of Science and Activism." *Social Sciences* 3: 326–40.

Brady, Rachel. 2022. "Federal Government Freezes Gymnastics Canada Funding amid Calls for Investigation." *Globe and Mail,* July 22. https://www.theglobeandmail.com/canada/article-federal-government-freezes-gymnastics-canada-funding-amid-calls-for/.

Braga, Anthony, and Brenda Bond. 2008. "Policing Crime and Disorder Hot Spots: A Randomized Controlled Trial." *Criminology* 46(3): 577–608.

Breger, Melissa. 2014. "Transforming Cultural Norms of Sexual Violence against Women." *Journal of Research in Gender Studies* 4(2): 39–51.

–. 2018. "Reforming by Re-Norming: How the Legal System Has the Potential to Change a Toxic Culture of Domestic Violence." *Notre Dame Journal of Legislation* 44: 170–203.

Breger, Melissa, Margery Holman, and Michelle Guerrero. 2019. "Re-Norming Sport for Inclusivity: How the Sport Community Has the Potential to Change a Toxic Culture of Harassment and Abuse." *Journal of Clinical Sport Psychology* 13: 274–89.

Broadley, Laura. 2015. "Vandergunst Convictions a 'Non-Issue' for Radars Executive." *Clinton News Record,* November 9. https://www.clintonnewsrecord.com/2015/11/09/vandergunst-convictions-a-non-issue-for-radars-executive/wcm/21d62a43-85fd-bef7-c7c9-c46a10edea18.

Brooker, Charlie, and Karen Tocque. 2016. "Mental Health Risk Factors in Sexual Assault: What Should Sexual Assault Referral Centre Staff Be Aware Of?" *Journal of Forensic and Legal Medicine* 40: 28–33.

Browne, Angela, and David Finkelhor. 1986. "The Impact of Child Sexual Abuse: A Review of the Research." *Psychological Bulletin* 99(1): 66–77.

Bruce, Steve. 2019. "Halifax Police Announce New Charges in Historical Sexual Abuse Probe." *Chronicle Herald,* December 19. https://www.thechronicleherald.ca/news/local/halifax-police-announce-new-charges-in-historical-sexual-abuse-probe-390229/.

Bryan, Craig, Mary McNaugton-Cassill, Augustine Osman, and Ann Marie Hernandez. 2013. "The Associations of Physical and Sexual Assault with Suicide Risk in Nonclinical Military and Undergraduate Samples." *Suicide and Life-Threatening Behavior* 43: 223–34.

Bryshun, Jamie. 1997. "Hazing in Sport: An Exploratory Study of Veteran/Rookie Relations." MA thesis, University of Calgary.

Buncombe, Andrew. 2018. "Larry Nassar Latest: 265 Young Women Say They Were Abused by Former USA Gymnastic Doctor, Judge Says." *Independent,* January 31.

https://www.independent.co.uk/news/world/americas/larry-nasser-abuse-senten ce-victims-latest-court-judge-michigan-judge-janice-cunningham-a8187926.html.

Burke, Ashley. 2022. "Crisis on Ice: What You Need to Know about the Hockey Canada Scandal." *CBC News,* July 29. https://www.cbc.ca/news/politics/hockey-canada-sexual-assault-crisis-parliamentary-committee-1.6535248.

Burris, Matthew. 2014. "Thinking Slow about Sexual Assault in the Military." *Buffalo Journal of Gender, Law, and Social Policy* 23: 21–72.

Burstyn, Varda. 1999. *The Rites of Men: Manhood, Politics and the Culture of Sport.* Toronto: University of Toronto Press.

Burton, Laura. 2015. "Underrepresentation of Women in Sport Leadership: A Review of Research." *Sport Management Review* 18(2): 155–65.

Burton Nelson, Mariah. 1994. *The Stronger Women Get, the More Men Love Football: Sexism and the American Culture of Sport.* New York: Harcourt Brace.

Busby, Karen. 2014. "Sex Was in the Air: Pernicious Myths and Other Problems with Sexual Violence Prosecutions." In *Locating Law,* 3rd ed., edited by Elizabeth Cormack, 259–93. Halifax: Fernwood.

Butler, Judith. 1990. *Gender Trouble: Feminism and the Subversion of Identity.* New York: Routledge.

Campbell, Ken. 2020. "More Explosive and Shocking Allegations against Junior Hockey in Newly Filed Lawsuit." *Hockey News,* June 18. https://www.si.com/hockey/news/more-explosive-and-shocking-allegations-against-junior-hockey-in-newly-filed-lawsuit.

Canadian Centre on Substance Abuse. 2017. "The Impact and Effectiveness of Minimum Legal Drinking Age Legislation in Canada." https://ccsa.ca/sites/default/files/2019-04/CCSA-Impact-Effectiveness-MLDA-Legislation-2017-en.pdf.

Canadian Heritage. 2023. "Minister St-Onge Announces New Measures to Improve Accountability and Foster a Safe and Sustainable Culture Change in Sport." News release, May 11. https://www.canada.ca/en/canadian-heritage/news/2023/05/minister-st-onge-announces-new-measures-to-improve-accountability-and-foster-a-safe-and-sustainable-culture-change-in-sport.html.

Canadian HIV/AIDS Legal Network. 2012. *Women and the Criminalization of HIV Non-Disclosure.* http://www.hivlegalnetwork.ca/site/wp-content/uploads/2013/04/Women_crim-ENG.pdf.

Canadian Press. 2015a. "A Timeline of Graham James's Legal History." *Global News,* May 25. https://globalnews.ca/news/2016827/a-timeline-of-graham-jam ess-legal-history/.

–. 2015b. "Whitecaps Farm Player Sahil Sandhu Charged with Sex Assault." *Global News,* December 12. https://globalnews.ca/news/2397707/whitecaps-farm-play er-sahil-sandhu-charged-with-sex-assault/.

–. 2017a. "Alpine Canada Apologizes to Victims of Former National Ski Coach Bertrand Charest." *Global News,* December 9. https://globalnews.ca/news/3907179/alpine-canada-apologizes-to-victims-of-former-national-ski-coach-bertand-charest/.

–. 2017b. "Football Manitoba Apologizes to Teen Girls." *CTV News,* March 21. https://www.toronto.com/community-story/7202301-football-manitoba-apolo-gizes-to-teen-girls/.

–. 2019. "Former Skiers Strike Out-of-Court Deal with Alpine Canada in Sex Assault Lawsuit." *Global News,* July 2. https://globalnews.ca/news/5453401/former-skii ers-alpine-canada-deal-sexual-assault-lawsuit/.

—. 2020a. "Former Canadian Hockey League Players Detail Allegations of Abuse, Hazing." *CBC News,* December 9. https://www.cbc.ca/sports/hockey/canadian-hockey-league-class-action-lawsuit-1.5834716.

—. 2020b. "Former N.S. Teacher Pleads Guilty to Sexual Abuse Dating Back Decades." *CTV News,* June 10. https://atlantic.ctvnews.ca/former-n-s-teacher-pleads-guilty-to-sexual-abuse-dating-back-decades-1.4978195.

Caron, Sandra, William Halteman, and Cheri Stacy. 1997. "Athletes and Rape: Is There a Connection?" *Perceptual and Motor Skills* 85(3): 1379–93.

Carrigan, Tim, Raewyn Connell, and John Lee. 1985. "Toward a New Sociology of Masculinity." *Theory and Society* 14(5): 551–604.

Carroll, Luke, and Blair Crawford. 2019. "Former Ravens Basketball Player Eddie Ekiyor Charged with Sexual Assault, Kidnapping." *Ottawa Citizen,* August 17. https://ottawacitizen.com/news/local-news/former-ravens-basketball-player-charged-with-sexual-assault-kidnapping.

Carroll, Michael, Daniel Connaughton, John Spengler, and James Zhang. 2009. "Case Law and Analysis regarding High School and Collegiate Liability for Hazing." *European Sport Management Quarterly* 9(4): 389–410.

Carter, Adam. 2019. "3 Ex-Students Plead Guilty to Sex Assault Offences at St. Michael's College School." *CBC News,* October 3. https://www.cbc.ca/news/canada/toronto/st-michaels-college-school-shared-on-social-media-1.5307426.

Caruk, Holly. 2016. "Female Football Players Allege Catcalling and Assault in Formal Complaint." *CBC News,* October 24. https://www.cbc.ca/news/canada/manitoba/female-football-player-sexually-harassed-1.3810721.

Case, Mary Anne. 2019. "Institutional Responses to #MeToo Claims: #VaticanToo, #KavanaughToo, and the Stumbling Block of Scandal." University of Chicago Legal Forum. https://chicagounbound.uchicago.edu/cgi/viewcontent.cgi?article=1637andcontext=uclf.

Casey, Liam. 2019. "Students in St. Michael's College School Sex Assault Sentenced to 2 Years Probation." *CTV News,* December 19. https://toronto.ctvnews.ca/students-in-st-michael-s-college-school-sex-assault-sentenced-to-2-years-probation-1.4736512.

—. 2021. "Teen Guilty of Sex Assault at St. Mike's Given No Time behind Bars." *Canadian Press,* November 2. https://www.cp24.com/news/teen-guilty-of-sex-assault-at-st-mike-s-given-no-time-behind-bars-1.5648019.

CBC News. 2004. "P.E.I. Baseball Player's Sex Conviction Overturned." April 23. https://www.cbc.ca/news/canada/p-e-i-baseball-player-s-sex-conviction-overturned-1.498730.

—. 2006. "Junior Hockey Players Face Charges over Sex Tape." December 21. https://www.cbc.ca/news/canada/junior-hockey-players-face-charges-over-sex-tape-1.581386.

—. 2009a. "Former Boxing Champ Dave Hilton Jr. Acquitted of New Charges." January 7. https://www.cbc.ca/news/canada/montreal/former-boxing-champ-dave-hilton-jr-acquitted-of-new-charges-1.797011.

—. 2009b. "Montreal Soccer Coach Charged with Sexual Assault." July 15. https://www.cbc.ca/news/canada/montreal/montreal-soccer-coach-charged-with-sexual-assault-1.836269.

—. 2010a. "Coach Sorry for Sexually Assaulting Teens." June 7. https://www.cbc.ca/news/canada/montreal/coach-sorry-for-sexually-assaulting-teens-lawyer-1.910548.

—. 2010b. "Kelowna Rapist Gets 5-Year Prison Term." June 7. https://www.cbc.ca/news/canada/british-columbia/kelowna-rapist-gets-5-year-prison-term-1.916939.

—. 2011a. "Bottles Tied to Genitals in Manitoba Hockey Hazing." October 26. https://www.cbc.ca/news/canada/manitoba/bottles-tied-to-genitals-in-manitoba-hockey-hazing-1.1042770.

—. 2011b. "Hockey Coach Gets 5 Years for Sex Abuse." April 5. https://www.cbc.ca/news/canada/montreal/hockey-coach-gets-5-years-for-sex-abuse-1.1026722.

—. 2014a. "Heidi Ferber, Ex-Hockey Coach, Gets 1 Year in Jail in Teen Sex Case." April 3. https://www.cbc.ca/news/canada/british-columbia/heidi-ferber-ex-hockey-coach-gets-1-year-in-jail-in-teen-sex-case-1.2595085.

—. 2014b. "Hockey Coach Kelly Jones Sentenced to 8 Years for Sexual Assaults." August 8. https://www.cbc.ca/news/canada/ottawa/hockey-coach-kelly-jones-sentenced-to-8-years-for-sexual-assaults-1.2739066.

—. 2014c. "Kelly Jones 'Deserves the Maximum,' Says Sexual Assault Victim." June 25. http://www.cbc.ca/news/canada/ottawa/kelly-jones-deserves-the-maximum-says-sexual-assault-victim-1.2687170.

—. 2016a. "Greenham Now Facing a Total of 55 Charges Involving 14 Alleged Victims, Police Say." November 17. http://www.cbc.ca/news/canada/ottawa/donald-greenham-sexual-assault-nov-17-1.3854860.

—. 2016b. "U of O Men's Hockey Players Had Sex While Others Watched, University Claims." January 26. https://www.cbc.ca/news/canada/ottawa/u-of-o-sexual-assault-statement-defence-1.3420053.

—. 2018. "Ottawa Redblacks Cut Player Facing Sexual Assault Charges." July 18. https://www.cbc.ca/news/canada/ottawa/teague-sherman-redblacks-sexual-assault-1.4751787.

—. 2020. "U of O Settles Men's Hockey Lawsuit for Nearly $350k." March 31. https://www.cbc.ca/news/canada/ottawa/ottawa-geegee-mens-hockey-lawsuit-1.5516293.

CBC Sports. 2000. "Charges Dropped against Colts." July 10. https://www.cbc.ca/sports/hockey/charges-dropped-against-colts-1.206568.

—. 2005. "McGill Scraps Football Season over Hazing." October 18. https://www.cbc.ca/sports/football/mcgill-scraps-football-season-over-hazing-1.553792.

—. 2019. "Ottawa Announces Steps to Eliminate Abuse in Sport." February 21. https://www.cbc.ca/sports/federal-sport-minister-new-steps-eliminate-abuse-sport-1.5026911.

Chandler, Steve, DeWayne Johnson, and Pamela Carroll. 1999. "Abusive Behaviors of College Athletes." *College Student Journal* 33(4): 638–45.

Charlottetown Guardian. 2000. "Crown Drops Charges against Hockey Players: Former Teammates on the Antigonish Bulldogs Had Faced Sexual Assault Charges." January 22.

—. 2002. "Ex-College Hockey Star Not Guilty of Raping Woman." August 14, A5.

—. 2005. "Charges against Hockey Player from P.E.I. Dismissed by Judge." December 14, B3.

Chavaz, Chris. 2018. "Victims Share Stories of Abuse at Former USA Gymnastics Doctor Larry Nassar's Sentencing." *Sports Illustrated,* January 16. https://www.si.com/olympics/2018/01/16/larry-nassar-sentencing-victims-abuse-stories.

Cheedle, Bruce, and Jim Bronskill. 2011. "Accuser Who Revealed Graham James Pardon Sparked Changes to System." *Global News*, December 7. https://globalnews.ca/news/186823/accuser-who-revealed-graham-james-pardon-sparked-changes-to-system/.

Cheever, Jamie, and Marla Eisenberg. 2020. "Team Sports and Sexual Violence: Examining Perpetration by and Victimization of Adolescent Males and Females." *Journal of Interpersonal Violence* 37(1): 400–22.

Cherry, Paul. 2020. "Former National Ski Coach Bertrand Charest Granted Full Parole." *Gazette* [Montreal], March 31. https://montrealgazette.com/news/former-national-ski-coach-bertrand-charest-granted-full-parole.

Chidley-Hill, John. 2018. "More Sting Alum Open Up about Alleged Hazing in Early 2000s." *Hamilton Spectator*, November 28. https://www.thespec.com/sports/hockey/2018/11/28/more-sting-alum-open-up-about-alleged-hazing-in-early-2000s.html.

–. 2019. "Canada's Minister of Sport Kirsty Duncan: More Anti-Abuse Work to Be Done." *CBC News*, August 16. https://www.cbc.ca/sports/kirsty-duncan-anti-abuse-more-work-to-be-done-1.5249378.

Chin, Jessica, and jay johnson. 2011. "Making the Team: Threats to Health and Wellness within Sport Hazing Cultures." *International Journal of Health, Wellness and Society* 1(2): 29–38.

Chin, Jessica, jay johnson, Mary Anne Signer-Kroeker, and Margery Holman. 2019. "From the Bottom of the Bottle: A Sociological Examination of the Use of Alcohol in Varsity Sport Hazing." *International Review for the Sociology of Sport* 55(7): 991–1008. https://doi.org/10.1177%2F1012690219861607.

Chowdhury, Elora Halim. 2015. "Rethinking Patriarchy, Culture, and Masculinity: Transnational Narratives of Gender Violence and Human Rights Advocacy." *Journal of International Women's Studies* 16(2): 98–114.

CityNews. 2014. "Kamloops Hockey Coach Sentenced for Sexually Abusing Player." April 2. https://www.citynews1130.com/2014/04/02/kamloops-hockey-coach-sentenced-for-sexually-abusing-player/.

Clark, Lorenne, and Debra Lewis. 1977. *Rape: The Price of Coercive Sexuality*. Toronto: Women's Press.

Clarridge, Christine. 2008. "Man Fights 'Predator' Label." *Seattle Times*, March 26. https://www.seattletimes.com/seattle-news/man-fights-predator-label/.

Clayton, Ben. 2012. "Initiate: Constructing the 'Reality' of Male Team Sport Initiation Rituals." *International Review for the Sociology of Sport* 48(2): 204–19.

Coleman, Madeline. 2022. "ESPN, ABC Report Shows U.S. SafeSport Failures in Sexual Misconduct Investigations." *Sports Illustrated*, February 23. https://www.si.com/olympics/2022/02/23/us-safesport-espn-abc-report-shows-failures-in-investigations-trust-wavering.

Colton, M.J., and Maurice Vanstone. 1996. *Betrayal of Trust: Sexual Abuse by Men Who Work with Children … In Their Own Words*. New York: Free Association Books.

Connell, R.W. 1987. *Gender and Power*. Sydney: Allen and Unwin.

–. 1995. *Masculinities*. Berkeley: University of California Press.

Connell, R.W., and James W. Messerschmidt. 2005. "Hegemonic Masculinity: Rethinking the Concept." *Gender and Society* 19: 829–59.

Connor, Tracy. 2016. "FBI Says Gymnastics Doctor Larry Nassar Recorded Abuse on Go Pro." *NBC News*, December 21. https://www.nbcnews.com/news/us-news/gymnastics-doctor-larry-nassar-hit-new-sex-abuse-claim-n698741.

Cossins, Anne. 2000. *Masculinities, Sexualities and Child Sexual Abuse.* The Hague: Kluwer Law.

Crabb, Josh. 2016. "Female Football Players Allege Harassment, Assault by Members of Opposing Team." *CTVNews,* October 24. https://winnipeg.ctvnews.ca/female-footb all-players-allege-harassment-assault-by-members-of-opposing-team-1.3129213.

Craig, Elaine. 2018. *Putting Trials on Trial: Sexual Assault and the Failure of the Legal Profession.* Montreal and Kingston: McGill-Queen's University Press.

Craig, Kat. 2020. "Survivor and Victim-Centred Approaches to Responding to Abuse in Sport." IOC SafeSport 2020 Webinar Series. https://olympics.com/athlete365/ integrity/prioritising-survivors-within-safe-sport/.

Craven, Samantha, Sarah Brown, and Elizabeth Gilchrist. 2006. "Sexual Grooming of Children: Review of Literature and Theoretical Considerations." *Journal of Sexual Aggression* 12(3): 287–99.

Crew, A. Blair. 2012. "Striking Back: The Viability of a Civil Action against the Police for the 'Wrongful Unfounding' of Reported Rapes." In *Sexual Assault Law in Canada: Law, Legal Practice and Women's Activism,* edited by Elizabeth Sheehy, 211–39. Ottawa: University of Ottawa Press.

Critical Resistance and INCITE! Women of Color against Violence. 2016. "Gender Violence and the Prison-Industrial Complex." In *Color of Violence: The INCITE! Anthology,* edited by INCITE! Women of Color against Violence, 223–26. Durham, NC: Duke University Press.

Crooks, Claire, Peter Jaffe, Caely Dunlop, Amanda Kerry, Bridget Houston, Deinera Exner-Cortens, and Lana Wells. 2020. *Primary Prevention of Violence against Women and Girls: Current Knowledge about Program Effectiveness.* Centre for Research and Education on Violence against Women and Children. https://www. learningtoendabuse.ca/resources-events/pdfs/Report-Crooks_Jaffe-Primary_ Prevention_VAW_Update.pdf.

Crosset, Todd, Jeff Benedict, and Mark McDonald. 1995. "Male Student-Athletes Reported for Sexual Assault: A Survey of Campus Police Departments and Judicial Affairs Offices." *Journal of Sport and Social Issues* 19(2): 126–40.

Crow, Brian, and Eric MacIntosh. 2009. "Conceptualizing a Meaningful Definition of Hazing in Sport." *European Sport Management Quarterly* 9(4): 433–51.

Crow, Brian, and Dennis Phillips. 2004. "Hazing – What the Law Says." In *Making the Team: Inside the World of Sport Initiations and Hazing,* edited by jay johnson and Margery Holman, 19–31. Toronto: Canadian Scholars Press.

Crow, Brian, and Scott Rosner. 2002. "Institutional and Organizational Liability for Hazing in Intercollegiate and Professional Team Sports." *St. John's University Law Review* 76: 87–114.

CTV Atlantic. 2011. "School Board Admits It Didn't Check Potvin's Record." May 18. https://atlantic.ctvnews.ca/school-board-admits-it-didn-t-check-potvin-s-record-1.645801.

CTV News. 2010. "Soccer Coach Gets 6 Years for Sexual Assault." October 1. https:// www.ctvnews.ca/soccer-coach-gets-6-years-for-sexual-assault-1.558655.

–. 2011. "Hockey Coach Sentenced to Five Years for Sexual Assault." April 5. https://montreal.ctvnews.ca/hockey-coach-sentenced-to-five-years-for-sexual-assault-1.627794.

Cunningham, George, Na Young Ahn, Arden Anderson, and Marlene Dixon. 2019. "Gender, Coaching, and Occupational Turnover." *Women in Sport and Physical Activity Journal* 27: 63–72.

Currie, Bill. 1996. "Wolves Player Acquitted." *Chicago Tribune,* February 29. https://www.chicagotribune.com/news/ct-xpm-1996-02-29-9602290148-story.html.

Curtis, Christopher. 2015. "Do Sports Teams Have an Obligation to Better Inform Their Players about Sexual Consent?" *Gazette* [Montreal], March 17. https://montrealgazette.com/sports/hockey/do-sports-teams-have-an-obligation-to-better-inform-their-players-about-sexual-consent.

Dakin, Dan. 2012. "Jury Finds Yetman Guilty of Sexual Assaults." *Niagara Falls Review,* October 24. http://www.niagarafallsreview.ca/2012/10/23/jury-finds-yetman-guilty-of-sexual-assaults.

–. 2013. "Mark Yetman Pleads to Sexual Assault." *Niagara Fall Review,* April 5. http://www.niagarafallsreview.ca/2013/04/05/mark-yetman-pleads-to-sexual-assault.

Dambrofsky, Gwen. 1995. "Sex Dangerous Game in the World of Junior Hockey; Girl's Accusations Put Problem Back in Spotlight." *Ottawa Citizen,* February 11, G2.

Davidson, Jonathan, Dana Hughes, Linda George, and Dan Blazer. 1996. "The Association of Sexual Assault and Attempted Suicide within the Community." *Archives of General Psychiatry* 53(6): 550–55.

Davis, Angela. 1983. *Women, Race, and Class.* New York: Vintage Books.

Davis, Rob, Bruce Taylor, and Sarah Bench. 1995. "Impact of Sexual and Nonsexual Assault on Secondary Victims." *Violence and Victims* 10(1): 73–84.

Deacon, James. 1997. "The Secret Gardens: Charges of Abuse Taint Toronto's Hockey Shrine." *Maclean's,* March 3. https://archive.macleans.ca/article/1997/3/3/the-secret-gardens.

Deibert, Dave. 2018. "Coach's Recruitment of Player Facing Sex Assault Charge 'Was the Wrong Decision,' Say U of S Officials." *StarPhoenix* [Saskatoon], May 18. https://thestarphoenix.com/news/local-news/coachs-recruitment-of-player-facing-sex-assault-charge-was-the-wrong-decision-say-u-of-s-officials.

Denzin, Norman. 1978. *The Research Act: A Theoretical Introduction to Sociological Methods.* New York: McGraw-Hill.

Department of Justice. 2019a. "JustFacts: Indigenous Overrepresentation in the Criminal Justice System." May. https://www.justice.gc.ca/eng/rp-pr/jr/jf-pf/2019/docs/may01.pdf.

–. 2019b. "JustFacts: Sexual Assault." April. https://www.justice.gc.ca/eng/rp-pr/jr/jf-pf/2019/docs/apr01.pdf.

Diaczuk, Doug. 2018. "Former Ottawa Hockey Players Found Not Guilty of Sexual Assault." *Thunder Bay News Watch,* June 25. https://www.tbnewswatch.com/local-news/breaking-former-ottawa-hockey-players-found-not-guilty-of-sexual-assault-965833.

Dias, Diana, and Maria Jose Sa. 2012. "Initiation Rituals in University as Lever for Group Cohesion." *Journal of Further and Higher Education* 38(4): 447–64.

Dockterman, Eliana. 2019. "These Men Say the Boy Scouts' Sex Abuse Problem Is Worse Than Anyone Knew." *Time,* June 1. https://time.com/longform/boy-scouts-sex-abuse/.

Doe, Jane. 2012. "Who Benefits from the Sexual Assault Evidence Kit?" In *Sexual Assault in Canada: Law, Legal Practice and Women's Activism,* edited by Elizabeth Sheehy, 355–88. Ottawa: University of Ottawa Press.

Donnelly, Peter. 1997. "Child Labour, Sport Labour: Applying Child Labour Laws to Sport." *International Review for the Sociology of Sport* 32(4): 389–406.

–. 1999. "Who's Fair Game? Sport, Sexual Harassment, and Abuse." In *Sport and Gender in Canada,* edited by Philip White and Kevin Young, 107–28. Toronto: Oxford University Press.

Donnelly, Peter, Gretchen Kerr, Amanda Heron, and Danielle DiCarlo. 2016. "Protecting Youth in Sport: An Examination of Harassment Policies." *International Journal of Sport Policy and Politics* 8(1): 33–50.

Doolittle, Robyn. 2017. "Unfounded: Police Dismiss 1 in 5 Sexual Assault Claims as Baseless." *Globe and Mail,* February 3. https://www.theglobeandmail.com/news/investigations/unfounded-sexual-assault-canada-main/article33891309/.

Dowbiggin, Bruce. 2005. "In Matters of Morality, Not All Our Heroes Are Equal." *Calgary Herald,* December 8.

Doyle, Jennifer. 2019. "Harassment and the Privilege of Unknowing: The Case of Larry Nassar." *Differences* 30(1): 157–88.

Draper, Kevin. 2021. "Blackhawks Ignored 2010 Sexual Assault Accusation, an Investigation Says." *New York Times,* October 26. https://www.nytimes.com/2021/10/26/sports/hockey/blackhawks-investigation-sex-assault-bowman.html.

Drolet, Daniel. 2006. "When Rites Go Wrong." *University Affairs,* October 10. http://www.universityaffairs.ca/when-rites-go-wrong.aspx.

DuBois, Teresa. 2012. "Police Investigations of Sexual Assault Complaints: How Far Have We Come since Jane Doe?" In *Sexual Assault Law in Canada: Law, Legal Practice and Women's Activism,* edited by Elizabeth Sheehy, 191–209. Ottawa: University of Ottawa Press.

Duffy, Andrew. 2018a. "Historic Sex Abuse Probe Launched after Stories Surfaced at Bayshore Public School Reunion." *Ottawa Citizen,* April 2. https://ottawacitizen.com/news/local-news/historic-sex-abuse-probe-launched-after-stories-surfaced-at-bayshore-public-school-reunion.

Duffy, Andrew. 2018b. "Ottawa School Board Facing $8M in Lawsuits after Sex Abuse Claims, Former Basketball Players Share Their Stories." *Ottawa Citizen,* March 21. https://ottawacitizen.com/news/local-news/ottawa-school-board-facing-8m-in-lawsuits-after-sex-abuse-claims-former-basketball-players-share-their-stories.

Duffy, Andrew. 2021. "Former Carleton University Basketball Star Acquitted of Sexual Assault." *Ottawa Citizen,* October 1. https://ottawacitizen.com/news/local-news/former-carleton-university-basketball-star-acquitted-of-sexual-assault.

Du Mont, Janice, Karen-Lee Miller, and Terri Myhr. 2003. "The Role of 'Real Rape' and 'Real Victim' Stereotypes in the Police Reporting Practices of Sexually Assaulted Victims." *Violence against Women* 9(4): 466–86.

Dunning, Eric, Patrick Murphy, and John Williams. 1988. *The Roots of Football Hooliganism.* New York: Routledge.

Durkheim, Émile. 1968. *The Division of Labor in Society.* Translated by George Sampson. New York: Free Press. First published in 1893.

Edwards, Drew. 2018a. "CFL Reviewing What Went Wrong in Euclid Cummings Case." *3DownNation,* March 24. https://3downnation.com/2018/03/24/cfl-review-went-wrong-euclid-cummings-case/.

–. 2018b. "Euclid Cummings Facing Sexual Assault Charge in B.C." *3DownNation,* March 7. https://3downnation.com/2018/03/07/euclid-cummings-facing-sexual-assault-charge-b-c-report/.

Elliott, Diana, Doris Mok, and John Briere. 2004. "Adult Sexual Assault: Prevalence, Symptomatology, and Sex Differences in the General Population." *Journal of Traumatic Stress* 17: 203–11.

Elliott, R. Douglas, Daniel Hershkop, Michael Motala, and Maurice Tomlinson. 2016. *Grossly Indecent: Confronting the Legacy of State Sponsored Discrimination against Canada's LGBTQ2SI Communities.* Toronto: Egale Canada Human Rights Trust.

Ellis, Steven. 2022. "As U Sports Players Sit Sidelined, Two Alumni Make NHL Impact." *Hockey News,* January 5. https://thehockeynews.com/news/as-u-sports-players-sit-sidelined-two-alumni-make-nhl-impact.

Engman, Kathy. 1997a. "Ex-Coach Acquitted of Sexual Assault on Girl, 14." *Edmonton Journal,* February 22, B3.

—. 1997b. "Molestation Denied, Coach Told Girl to 'Forget It.'" *Edmonton Journal.* February 20, B3.

Epp, Sharie. 2006. "Grizz Focused on Task at Hand." *Times Colonist* [Victoria], November 3, D2.

Erikson, Kai. 1966. *Wayward Puritans: A Study in the Sociology of Deviance.* New York: Wiley.

ESPN. 2023. Anthony Blondell player profile. https://www.espn.com/soccer/player/_/id/157153/anthony-blondell.

Estrich, Susan. 1986. "Rape." *Yale Law Journal* 95: 127–77.

Ewing, Lori. 2022a. "Canadian Bobsled, Skeleton Athletes Call for Resignation of Program's Top Staff amid Toxic Culture Allegations." *Globe and Mail,* March 7. https://www.theglobeandmail.com/sports/article-canadian-bobsled-skeleton-athletes-call-for-resignation-of-programs/.

—. 2022b. "Canadian Experts Say Sexual Violence in Hockey, Other Sports Has Existed for Decades." *CBC News,* July 27. https://www.cbc.ca/sports/experts-say-sexual-violence-existed-decades-1.6533945.

Fagan, Jeffrey, and Sandra Wexler. 1988. "Explanations of Sexual Assault among Violent Delinquents." *Journal of Adolescent Research* 3: 363–85.

Farr, Kathryn. 1988. "Dominance Bonding through the Good Old Boys Sociability Group." *Sex Roles* 18: 259–77.

Farrey, Tom. 2002. "Like Fighting, Part of the Game." *ESPN,* June 3. http://www.espn.com/otl/hazing/thursday.html.

Fasting, Kari, Celia Brackenridge, and Jorunn Sundgot Borgen. 2000. *Sexual Harassment in and outside Sport.* Oslo: Norwegian Olympic Committee.

Fasting, Kari, Celia Brackenridge, and G. Kjølberg. 2013. "Using Court Reports to Enhance Knowledge of Sexual Abuse in Sport." *Scandinavian Sport Studies Forum* 4: 49–67.

Favero, Marisalva, Sofia Pinto, Fatima Ferreira, Francisco Machado, and Amaia Del Campo Sanchez. 2018. "Hazing Violence: Practices of Domination and Coercion in Hazing in Portugal." *Journal of Interpersonal Violence* 33(11): 1830–51.

Fazioli, Domenic. 2014. "'It's Hard to Move On': Alleged Victim in McGill Sex Scandal Speaks Out." *Global News,* November 18. http://globalnews.ca/news/1679223/its-hard-to-move-on-alleged-victim-in-mcgill-sex-scandal-speaks-out/.

Feinauer, Leslie, Eddy Callahan, and H. Gill Hilton. 1996. "Positive Intimate Relationships Decrease Depression in Sexually Abused Women." *American Journal of Family Therapy* 24(2): 99–106.

Findlay, Martha Hall, and Vania Grandi. 2018. "Statement from Alpine Canada." Alpine Canada, June 4. https://alpinecanada.org/news/statement-from-alpine-canada.

Finley, Laura. 2018. "Engaging College Men in Conversations and Activities Related to Dating and Domestic Violence." In *Social Isolation: An Interdisciplinary Review,* edited by Rosalba Morese, Sara Palermo, and Raffaella Fiorella. London: Intechopen. https://www.intechopen.com/books/social-isola-

tion-an-interdisciplinary-view/engaging-college-men-in-conversations-and-acti
vities-related-to-dating-and-domestic-violence.

Fitzgerald, Louise. 2017. "Still the Last Great Open Secret: Sexual Harassment as
Systemic Trauma." *Journal of Trauma and Dissociation* 18(4): 483–89.

Fleming, Grant. 2015a. "Guilty: The Trial of Mitchell Vandergunst, Star Hockey
Player for the Stratford Cullitons." *Grant Fleming* (blog), May 1. http://
grantfleming.ca/guilty-the-trial-of-mitchell-vandergunst-star-hockey-p
layer-for-the-stratford-cullitons/.

—. 2015b. "Parents of Victim Don't Believe Team Execs." *Grant Fleming* (blog), March
30. http://grantfleming.ca/exclusive-parents-of-victim/.

Fleury, Theoren. 2009. *Playing with Fire*. Toronto: HarperCollins.

—. 2012. "Fleury's Victim Impact Statement." *CBC News*, February 22. https://www.
cbc.ca/player/play/2200289106.

Fogel, Curtis. 2012. "Snow on the Gridiron: A Brief History of Canadian Football."
Physical Culture and Sport 54: 49–54.

—. 2013. *Game-Day Gangsters: Crime and Deviance in Canadian Football*. Edmonton: Athabasca University Press.

—. 2017. "Precarious Masculinity and Rape Culture in Canadian University Sport." In
*Sexual Violence at Canadian Universities: Activism, Institutional Responses, and
Strategies for Change,* edited by Elizabeth Quinlan, Andrea Quinlan, Curtis Fogel,
and Gail Taylor, 139–58. Waterloo, ON: Wilfrid Laurier University Press.

Fogel, Curtis, and Andrea Quinlan. 2021. "Sexual Assault in the Locker Room:
Sexually Violent Hazing in Canadian Sport." *Journal of Sexual Aggression* 27(3):
353–72.

Forbes, Gordon, Leah Adams-Curtis, Alexis Pakalka, and Kay White. 2006. "Dating
Aggression, Sexual Coercion, and Aggression-Supporting Attitudes among College Men as a Function of Participation in Aggressive High School Sports." *Violence against Women* 12: 441–55.

Fortier, Kristine, Sylvie Parent, and Geneviève Lessard. 2020. "Child Maltreatment
in Sport: Smashing the Wall of Silence: A Narrative Review of Physical, Sexual,
Psychological Abuses and Neglect." *British Journal of Sports Medicine* 54: 4–7.

Foucault, Michel. 1995. *Discipline and Punish: The Birth of the Prison*. New York:
Vintage Books.

Fowlie, Jonathan. 2003. "Morin Gets Three Years for Assaulting Boys." *Globe and
Mail,* January 22, A5.

Franklin, Karen. 2004. "Enacting Masculinity: Antigay Violence and Group Rape as
Participatory Theater." *Sexuality Research and Social Policy* 1: 25–40.

Fraser, Keith. 2021. "Former B.C. Lion Josh Boden Guilty of 2009 Murder of Former
Girlfriend." *Vancouver Sun,* November 4. https://vancouversun.com/news/former
-b-c-lion-josh-boden-guilty-of-2009-murder-of-former-girlfriend.

Freeman, Joshua. 2020. "Maple Leaf Gardens Sex Offender Gordon Stuckless
Released from Jail." *CTV News,* January 14. https://toronto.ctvnews.ca/maple-lea
f-gardens-sex-offender-gordon-stuckless-released-from-jail-1.4767852.

Friesen, Joe. 2022. "London Police to Review Its Investigation of Sexual-Assault
Allegations following a 2018 Hockey Canada Event." *Globe and Mail,* July 21.
https://www.theglobeandmail.com/canada/article-london-police-to-review-its
-investigation-of-sexual-assault/.

Fruman, Leslie. 1996. "Thin Ice" (television documentary). *The Fifth Estate*. Canadian Broadcasting Corporation.

Ganson, Kyle, Rachel Rodgers, Sarah Lipson, Tamara Cadet, and Michelle Putnam. 2020. "Sexual Assault Victimization and Eating Disorders among College-Enrolled Men." *Journal of Interpersonal Violence* 37(7): NP5143–NP5166.

Gardiner, Andy. 2001. "Hazing Scandal Rips Apart Town, School: University of Vermont Still Has Scars." *USA Today*, February 5, C1.

Garland, Randall, and Michael Dougher. 1990. "The Abused/Abuser Hypothesis of Child Sexual Abuse: A Critical Review of Theory and Research." In *Pedophilia: Biosocial Dimensions*, edited by Jay Feierman, 488–519. New York: Springer-Verlag.

Gavey, Nicola. 2005. *Just Sex? The Cultural Scaffolding of Rape*. London: Routledge.

Gerell, Manne. 2016. "Hot Spot Policing with Actively Monitored CCTV Cameras: Does It Reduce Assaults in Public Places?" *International Criminal Justice Review* 26(2): 187–201.

Gibson, Victoria. 2017. "'I Thought I Was Safe,' Victim in Kingston Assault Case Says." *Toronto Star*, October 19. https://www.thestar.com/news/gta/2017/09/05/i-thought-i-was-safe-victim-in-kingston-assault-case-says.html.

Gidycz, Christine, and Mary Koss. 1990. "A Comparison of Group and Individual Sexual Assault Victims." *Psychology of Women Quarterly* 14: 325–42.

Gilhooly, Greg. 2018. *I Am Nobody: Confronting the Sexually Abusive Coach Who Stole My Life*. Vancouver: Greystone Books.

Gill, Jordan, and Karissa Donkin. 2017. "Convicted Sex Offender Removed from Coaching Position in Fredericton." *CBC News*, June 29. http://www.cbc.ca/news/canada/new-brunswick/sex-offender-basketball-coach-1.4182554.

Gillespie, Kerry. 2022. "Canadian Gymnastics Federation Vows to Do More to Protect Athletes." *Toronto Star*, March 29. https://www.thestar.com/sports/amateur/2022/03/29/canadian-gymnastics-federation-vows-to-do-more-to-protect-athletes.html.

Gillis, Charlie. 2014. "How Parents (and Their Lawyers) Are Killing Minor Hockey." *Maclean's*, April 4. https://www.macleans.ca/society/life/the-new-minor-hockey-fights/.

Globe and Mail. 2005a. "Diver's Suspension Lifted in Sex Scandal Case." October 8, S7.

–. 2005b. "Otters 2, Rangers 1." March 26, S3.

Goffman, Erving. 1961. *Asylums*. New York: First Anchor Books.

Goldsmith, Rachel, Christina Gamache Martin, and Carly Parnitzke Smith. 2014. "Systemic Trauma." *Journal of Trauma and Disassociation* 15(2): 117–32.

Goodmark, Leigh. 2018. *Decriminalizing Domestic Violence: A Balanced Policy Approach to Intimate Partner Violence*. Oakland: University of California Press.

Graham, Kevin. 1996. "The Childhood Victimization of Sex Offenders: An Underestimated Issue." *International Journal of Offender Therapy and Comparative Criminology* 40(3): 192–203.

Gravelin, Claire, Monica Biernat, and Caroline Bucher. 2019. "Blaming the Victim of Acquaintance Rape: Individual, Situational, and Sociocultural Factors." *Frontiers in Psychology* 9. https://www.frontiersin.org/articles/10.3389/fpsyg.2018.02422/full.

Gray, Mandi. 2016. "Six Lessons I Learned from My Rape Case." *Now News*, July 26. https://nowtoronto.com/mandi-gray-six-lessons-i-learned-from-my-rape-case.

Green, Sara Jean. 2008. "Jury Rejects Predator Label for Rapist." *Seattle Times*, April 11. https://www.seattletimes.com/seattle-news/jury-rejects-predator-label-for-rapist/.

Greene, Saara, Apondi Odhiambo, Marvelous Muchenje, Alison Symington, Jasmine Cotnam, Kristin Dunn, Margaret Frank, Shelly Glum, Rebecca Gormley, Allyson Ion, Valerie Nicholson, Krista Shore, and Angela Kaida. 2019. "How Women Living with HIV React and Respond to Learning about Canadian Law That Criminalises HIV Non-Disclosure: 'How Do You Prove That You Told?'" *Culture, Health and Sexuality* 21(10): 1087–1102.

Greenland, Jacob, and Adam Cotter. 2018. "Unfounded Criminal Incidents in Canada, 2017." Statistics Canada. https://www150.statcan.gc.ca/n1/pub/85-002-x/2018001/article/54975-eng.htm.

Grillo, Chantel. 2018. "The Acquittal of 4 Former High School Football Players Charged with Sexual Assault Sparks Controversy." *CHCH News*, July 20. https://www.chch.com/acquittal-4-former-high-school-football-players-charged-sexual-assault-sparks-controversy/.

Groves, Mark, Gerald Griggs, and Kathryn Leflay. 2012. "Hazing and Initiation Ceremonies in University Sport: Setting the Scene for Further Research in the United Kingdom." *Sport in Society* 15(1): 117–31.

Gruber, Aya. 2020. *The Feminist War on Crime: The Unexpected Role of Women's Liberation in Mass Incarceration.* Oakland: University of California Press.

Guiora, Amos. 2020. *Armies of Enablers: Survivor Stories of Complicity and Betrayal in Sexual Assaults.* Washington, DC: American Bar Association.

Guynn, Kevin, and Frank Aquila. 2004. *Hazing in High Schools: Causes and Consequences.* Bloomington, IN: Phi Delta Kappa Educational Foundation.

Hachey, Michel. 2018. "Creating a Safer Sport Environment with the Rule of Two." Sport Information Resource Centre. https://sirc.ca/blog/creating-a-safer-sport-environment-with-the-rule-of-two/.

Halifax City News. 2011. "Volleyball Coach Facing Sex-Related Charges Was Charged Once Before." May 17. https://halifax.citynews.ca/2011/05/17/volleyball-coach-facing-sex-related-charges-was-charged-once-before/.

Hall, M. Ann. 1996. *Feminism and Sporting Bodies: Essays on Theory and Practice.* Champaign, IL: Human Kinetics.

–. 2016. *Girl in the Game: A History of Women's Sport in Canada.* 2nd ed. Toronto: University of Toronto Press.

Hall, M. Ann, and Dorothy Richardson. 1982. *Fair Ball: Towards Sex Equality in Canadian Sport.* Ottawa: Canadian Advisory Council on the Status of Women.

Hamilton, Ryan, David Scott, L. O'Sullivan, and D. LaChapelle. 2013. "An Examination of the Rookie Hazing Experiences of University Athletes in Canada." *Canadian Journal for Social Research* 3(1): 35–48.

Hancock, Meg, and Mary Hums. 2016. "A 'Leaky Pipeline'? Factors Affecting the Career Development of Senior-Level Female Administrators in NCAA Division I Athletic Departments." *Sport Management Review* 19(2): 198–210.

Hanes, Allison. 2005. "Skate Coach Jailed for Sex Abuse." *Vancouver Sun,* April 23, A12.

Harris, Andrew, and R. Karl Hanson. 2004. "Sex Offender Recidivism: A Simple Question." Report prepared for Public Safety and Emergency Preparedness Canada.

Hartill, Michael. 2017. *Sexual Abuse in Youth Sport: A Sociocultural Analysis.* New York: Routledge.

Hartman, Marilyn, Stephen Finn, and Gloria Leon. 1987. "Sexual-Abuse Experiences in a Clinical Population: Comparisons of Familial and Nonfamilial Abuse." *Psychotherapy: Theory, Research, Practice, Training* 24(2): 154–59.

Hassija, Christina, and Matt Gray. 2013. "Adaptive Variants of Controllability Attributions among Survivors of Sexual Assault." *International Journal of Cognitive Therapy* 6: 342–57.

Hauser, Christine, and Maggie Astor. 2018. "The Larry Nassar Case: What Happened and How the Fallout Is Spreading." *New York Times,* January 25. https://www.nytimes.com/2018/01/25/sports/larry-nassar-gymnastics-abuse.html.

Hayes, Kelly, and Wayne Moore. 2008. "Tyler Stephens Aftermath." *Castanet Kelowna News,* October 27. https://www.castanet.net/news/Kelowna/42735/Tyler-Stephens-aftermath.

Heenan, Melanie, and Suellen Murray. 2006. *Study of Reported Rapes in Victoria 2000–2003: Summary Research Report.* Melbourne: Victoria Police. http://www.police.vic.gov.au/retrievemedia.asp?Media_ID=19462.

Heesacker, Martin, and Steven Snowden. 2013. "Pay No Attention to That Man behind the Curtain: The Challenges, Causes, and Consequences of Precarious Manhood." *Psychology of Men and Masculinity* 14(2): 121–24.

Heise, Lori. 1997. "Violence, Sexuality, and Women's Lives." In *The Gender and Sexuality Reader: Culture, History, Political Economy,* edited by Roger Lancaster and Micaela di Leonardo, 110–34. London: Routledge.

Hempstead, Doug. 2015a. "Gatineau Olympiques Subject of Sex Complaint." *Kingston Whig Standard,* March 11. https://www.thewhig.com/2015/03/10/gatineau-olympiques-subject-of-sex-complaint/wcm/9377aefc-6991-4097-a256-0e8ddf10933d.

–. 2015b. "No Charges Involving Olympiques Players and Drunk Woman." *Chatham Daily News,* April 30. https://www.chathamdailynews.ca/2015/04/30/no-charges-involving-olympiques-players-and-drunk-woman/wcm/06962879-3392-4e10-b4d8-a6b021d38101.

Hernandez, Jon. 2021. "Misogyny, Racism and Bullying Prevalent across Canadian Youth Hockey, Survey Finds." *CBC News,* May 4. https://www.cbc.ca/news/canada/british-columbia/misogyny-racism-bullying-across-canadian-youth-hockey-1.6014070.

Heroux, Devin, and Lori Ward. 2019. "'It Isn't Up to Children to Protect Themselves': How to Keep Kids Safe from Sexual Abuse in Sports." *CBC News,* February 12. https://www.cbc.ca/sports/sexual-abuse-amateur-sports-canada-protecting-kids-1.5014330.

Hirsley, Michael. 1996. "Wolves' Wiseman Faces Trial for 1991 Assault." *Chicago Tribune,* February 17. https://www.chicagotribune.com/news/ct-xpm-1996-02-17-9602170118-story.html.

Hobson, Will, and Cindy Boren. 2018. "Michigan State Settles with Larry Nassar Victims for $500 Million." *Washington Post,* May 16. https://www.washingtonpost.com/news/early-lead/wp/2018/05/16/michigan-state-settles-larry-nassar-lawsuits-for-500-million/.

Hockey Canada. 2022. "Hockey Canada Statement." July 22. https://www.hockey-canada.ca/en-ca/news/hockey-canada-july-22-statement-2022-news.

Hoffman, Jennifer. 2010. "The Dilemma of the Senior Woman Administrator Role in Intercollegiate Athletics." *Journal of Issues in Intercollegiate Athletics* 3(5): 53–75.

Hoffman, Kristy. 2015. "York University's Sexual Assault Policy Sparks Human-Rights Complaint." *Globe and Mail,* June 15. https://www.theglobeandmail.com/news/national

/education/york-universitys-sexual-assault-policy-sparks-human-rights-complaint/article25194134/.

Holman, Margery. 2004. "A Search for a Theoretical Understanding of Hazing Practices in Athletics." In *Making the Team: The Inside World of Sport Initiations and Hazing,* edited by jay johnson and Margery Holman, 61–82. Toronto: Canadian Scholars Press.

Holman, Margery, and jay johnson. 2015. "Moving from Awareness towards Prevention." *Physical and Health Education Journal* 82(2): 1–27.

Holmstrom, Lynda, and Ann Burgess. 1980. "Sexual Behavior of Assailants during Reported Rapes." *Archives of Sexual Behavior* 9: 427–39.

Honderich, Holly. 2021. "Canada Apologises for 'Scourge' of Military Sexual Misconduct." *BBC News,* December 13. https://www.bbc.com/news/world-us-canada-59632657.

Hooper, Tom. 2019. "Queering '69: The Recriminalization of Homosexuality in Canada." *Canadian Historical Review* 100(2): 257–73.

Hoover, Nadine. 1999. "National Survey: Initiation Rites and Athletics for NCAA Sports Teams." Alfred University. https://fliphtml5.com/yyhu/swkv.

Hoover, Nadine, and Norm Pollard. 2000. "Initiation Rites in American High Schools: A National Survey." Alfred University. https://files.eric.ed.gov/fulltext/ED445809.pdf.

Hornberger, Rob. 1995. "Hockey Hazing Brings Fines, Censure." *Windsor Star,* June 30.

Howard, Adam, and Elizabeth England Kennedy. 2006. "Breaking the Silence: Power, Conflict, and Contested Frames within an Affluent High School." *Anthropology and Education Quarterly* 37(4): 347–65.

Huffman, Tracy. 2002. "'Justice' in Gardens Sex Case; Maple Leaf Gardens Guard Assaulted Youths; Third Sex Crime Conviction of a Rink Worker." *Toronto Star,* December 13, B4.

Hutchinson, Brian, and Gerry Bellett. 2005. "CFL Player Gets Bail in Alleged HIV Sex Assault." *National Post,* November 3. https://www.pressreader.com/canada/national-post-latest-edition/20051103/281513631551411.

International Olympic Committee. 2021. "IOC Launches the International Safeguarding Officer in Sport Certificate." May 31. https://olympics.com/ioc/news/ioc-launches-the-international-safeguarding-officer-in-sport-certificate.

Isaac, Dave. 2013. "Sexual Assault Charges Dropped against Hockey Trio." *USA Today,* April 4. https://www.usatoday.com/story/sports/hockey/juniors/2013/04/04/nhl-prospects-junior-hockey-sexual-assault-charges-dropped/2054559/.

Iveson, Ali. 2022. "Hockey Canada Publishes Action Plan Tackling 'Toxic Behavior' and Pledges Further Reforms." *Inside the Games,* July 25. https://www.insidethe-games.biz/articles/1126165/hockey-canada.

Jeckell, Aaron, Elizabeth Copenhaver, and Alex Diamond. 2018. "The Spectrum of Hazing and Peer Sexual Abuse in Sports: A Current Perspective." *Sports Health* 10(6): 558–64.

Johal, Har. 2021. "Arrest Warrant Issued for Former Whitecaps Player Anthony Blondell." *Offside,* November 12. https://dailyhive.com/vancouver/arrest-warrant-whitecaps-anthony-blondell.

Johnson, Holly. 2012. "Limits of a Criminal Justice Response: Trends in Police and Court Processing of Sexual Assault." In *Sexual Assault Law in Canada: Law, Legal*

Practice and Women's Activism, edited by Elizabeth Sheehy, 613–34. Ottawa: University of Ottawa Press.

Johnson, Holly, and Myrna Dawson. 2011. *Violence against Women in Canada: Research and Policy Perspectives.* New York: Oxford University Press.

johnson, jay. 2001. "Taking It Like a Man: Re-Examining the Power Structure in Sport Initiations." *Culture and Tradition* 23: 10–31.

–. 2007. "The Effectiveness of Orientations as an Alternative to Traditional Hazing Practices." PhD diss., University of Toronto.

–. 2009. "From the Sidelines: The Role of the Coach in Affecting Team Unity and Cohesion in Place of Hazing Traditions." *Journal of Coaching Education* 2(1): 46–72.

–. 2011. "Across the Threshold: A Comparative Analysis of Communitas and Rites of Passage in Sport Hazing and Initiations." *Canadian Journal of Sociology* 36(3): 199–227.

johnson, jay, and Jessica Chin. 2016a. "Hazing Rites/Rights: Using Outdoor- and Adventure Education-Based Orientation to Effect Positive Change for First-Year Athletes." *Journal of Adventure Education and Outdoor Learning* 16(1): 16–30.

–. 2016b. "Seeking New Glory (D)Haze: A Qualitative Examination of Adventure-Based, Team Orientation Rituals as an Alternative to Traditional Sport Hazing for Athletes and Coaches." *International Journal of Sports Science and Coaching* 11(3): 1–15.

johnson, jay, Michelle Guerrero, Margery Holman, Jessica Chin, and Mary Ann Signer-Kroeker. 2018. "An Examination of Hazing in Canadian Intercollegiate Sports." *Journal of Clinical Sport Psychology* 12: 144–59.

johnson, jay, and Patricia Miller. 2004. "Changing the Initiation Ceremony." In *Making the Team: Inside the World of Sport Initiations and Hazing,* edited by jay johnson and Margery Holman, 155–75. Toronto: Canadian Scholars Press.

Joy, Barbara. 2016. "Joint Statement from York University and Mandi Gray, Human Rights Tribunal Settlement." York University, December 12. https://news.yorku.ca/2016/12/12/joint-statement-york-university-mandi-gray-human-rights-tribunal-settlement/.

Joyce, Gare. 2008. "Catching Hell." *Gare Joyce* (blog). http://garejoyce.blogspot.com.

–. 2017. "The Full Cost." *Sportsnet.* https://www.sportsnet.ca/hockey/nhl/akim-aliu-hockey-hazing-big-read/.

Kaida, Angela, and Sarah Spencer. 2019. "Recommendations on Changes to HIV Criminalization Don't Go Far Enough." *Conversation,* September 5. https://theconversation.com/recommendations-on-changes-to-hiv-criminalization-dont-go-far-enough-121397.

Kaiser, David, and Lovisa Stannow. 2011. "Prison Rape and the Government." *New York Review of Books,* March 24. http://www.nybooks.com/articles/2011/03/24/prison-rape-and-government/?pagination=false.

Kanters, Michael, Jason Bocarro, and Jonathan Casper. 2008. "Supported or Pressured? An Examination of Agreement among Parents and Children on Parent's Role in Youth Sports." *Journal of Sport Behaviour* 31(1): 64–80.

Kaplan, Anna. 2021. "USA Gymnastics, U.S. Olympic Committee Agree to $380 Million Settlement with Nassar Victims." *Forbes,* December 13. https://www.forbes.com/sites/annakaplan/2021/12/13/usa-gymnastics-us-olympic-committee-agree-to-380-million-settlement-with-nassar-victims-report-says/?sh=6248122556da.

Kari, Shannon. 2009. "Former Argo Williams Acquitted of Sexual Assault." *Vancouver Sun,* February 24. http://www.vancouversun.com/Former+Argo+Williams+acquitted+sexual+assault/1328641/story.html.

Katz, Jackson. 2019. *The Macho Paradox: Why Some Men Hurt Women and How All Men Can Help*. Naperville, IL: Sourcebooks.

Kaufman, Michael. 1987. "The Construction of Masculinity and the Triad of Men's Violence." In *Beyond Patriarchy: Essays on Pleasure, Power, and Change*, edited by Michael Kaufman, 2–29. Toronto: Oxford University Press.

—. 1999. "Men and Violence." *International Association for Studies of Men Newsletter* 6: 16–23.

Kay, Jason. 2013. "Graham James not The Hockey News 1989 Man of the Year: THN Stripped Graham James of the Award We Had Given Him in 1989." *Hockey News*, November 21. https://www.si.com/hockey/news/graham-james-not-the-hockey-news-1989-man-of-the-year.

Kelly, Liz. 1988. *Surviving Sexual Violence*. Minneapolis: University of Minnesota Press.

Kennedy, Sheldon. 2006. *Why I Didn't Say Anything: The Sheldon Kennedy Story*. Toronto: Insomniac Press.

Kerr, Gretchen, Bruce Kidd, and Peter Donnelly. 2020. "One Step Forward, Two Steps Back: The Struggle for Child Protection in Canadian Sport." *Social Sciences* 9(5): 68–84.

Kerr, Gretchen, and Ashley Stirling. 2008. "Child Protection in Sport: Implications of an Athlete-Centred Philosophy." *Quest* 60(2): 307–23.

Kerr, Gretchen, Ashley Stirling, and Ellen McPherson. 2014. "A Critical Examination of Child Protection Initiatives in Sport Contexts." *Social Sciences* 3(4): 742–57.

Kidd, Bruce. 1987. "Sports and Masculinity." In *Beyond Patriarchy: Essays by Men on Pleasure, Power and Change*, edited by Michael Kaufman, 250–65. Oxford: Oxford University Press.

—. 2013. "The Canadian State and Sport: The Dilemma of Intervention." *Sport in Society* 16(4): 362–71.

Kilpatrick, Dean, Heidi Resnick, Kenneth Ruggiero, Lauren Conoscenti, and Jenna McCauley. 2007. *Drug-Facilitated, Incapacitated, and Forcible Rape: A National Study*. Final report submitted to the National Institute of Justice. Washington, DC: US Department of Justice, National Institute of Justice.

Kimmel, Michael. 1994. "Masculinity as Homophobia: Fear, Shame, and Silence in the Construction of Gender Identity." In *Theorizing Masculinities*, edited by Harry Brod and Michael Kaufman, 119–41. Thousand Oaks, CA: Sage.

—. 2018. *Guyland: The Perilous World Where Boys Become Men*. 2nd ed. New York: HarperCollins.

Kimmel, Michael, and Michael Messner. 1995. "Introduction." In *Men's Lives*, edited by Michael Kimmel and Michael Messner, xiii–xxiii. Boston: Allyn and Bacon.

King, Mike. 1995. "Volunteers May Require Screening from Police." *Ottawa Citizen*, February 17, B3.

—. 2005. "Coach Broke Trust." *Gazette* [Montreal], April 5, A8.

Kirby, Sandra. 1995. "Not in My Backyard: Sexual Harassment and Abuse in Sport." *Canadian Woman Studies* 15(4): 58–62.

Kirby, Sandra, Guylaine Demers, and Sylvie Parent. 2008. "Vulnerability/Prevention: Considering the Needs of Disabled and Gay Athletes in the Context of Sexual Harassment and Abuse." *International Journal of Sport and Exercise Psychology* 6: 407–26.

Kirby, Sandra, and Lorraine Greaves. 1997. "Le jeu interdit: Le harcelement sexuel dans le sport." *Recherches féministes* 10(1): 5–33.

Kirby, Sandra, Lorraine Greaves, and Olena Hankivsky. 2000. *The Dome of Silence: Sexual Harassment and Abuse in Sport*. Halifax: Fernwood.

–. 2002. "Women under the Dome of Silence: Sexual Harassment and Abuse of Female Athletes." *Canadian Woman Studies* 21(3): 132–38.

Kirby, Sandra, and Glen Wintrup. 2004. "Running the Gauntlet: An Examination of Initiation/Hazing and Sexual Abuse in Sport." *Journal of Sexual Aggression* 8(2): 49–68.

Kirke, Gordon. 1997. *Players First Report.* Commissioned by the Canadian Junior Hockey League.

Klowak, Marianne. 2018. "2 Skiers Abused by Former Coach as Teens Tell Their Story in Winnipeg." *CBC News,* June 7. https://www.cbc.ca/news/canada/manitoba/amelie-frederique-gagnon-genevieve-simard-sex-abuse-skier-bertrand-charest-1.4696238.

Knoppers, Annelies. 1992. "Explaining Male Dominance and Sex Segregation in Coaching: Three Approaches." *Quest* 44(2): 210–27.

Kornik, Slav. 2013. "Former Eskimo Adam Braidwood Sentenced for Sexual Assault." *Global News,* April 19. https://globalnews.ca/news/495848/former-eskimo-adam-braidwood-sentenced-for-sexual-assault/.

Koshan, Terry. 2000. "3 Barrie Colts Charged with Sexual Assault." *Toronto Sun,* March 18. https://www.tapatalk.com/groups/whlmessageboard/3-barrie-colts-charged-with-sexual-assault-t1577.html.

Kozlowski, Kim. 2017. "Nassar Expected to Take Plea Deal on Child Porn Charges." *Detroit News,* July 7. https://www.detroitnews.com/story/news/local/michigan/2017/07/07/nassar-prepares-guilty-plea-child-porn-case/103514940/.

Krahn, Alixandra. 2019. "Sport Policy Praxis: Examining How Canadian Sport Policy Practically Advances the Careers of Nascent Female Coaches." *Women in Sport and Physical Activity Journal* 27(2): 118–27.

Krakauer, Jon. 2015. *Missoula: Rape and the Justice System in a College Town.* New York: Doubleday.

Krakow, Barry, Anne Germain, Teddy Warner, Ron Schrader, Mary Koss, Michael Hollifield, Dan Tandberg, Dominic Melendrez, and Lisa Johnston. 2001. "The Relationship of Sleep Quality and Posttraumatic Stress to Potential Sleep Disorders in Sexual Assault Survivors with Nightmares, Insomnia, and PTSD." *Journal of Traumatic Stress* 14: 647–65.

Krein, Anna. 2013. *Night Games: Sex, Power and Sport.* Collingwood, Australia: Black Inc.

Krishnan, Manisha. 2017. "A Hockey Player's Assault Sentence Was Postponed So It Wouldn't Hurt His Internship." *Vice,* September 1. https://www.vice.com/en/article/qvv5zv/a-hockey-players-assault-sentence-was-postponed-so-it-wouldnt-hurt-his-internship.

Kwan, Matthew, Sarah Bobko, Guy Faulkner, Peter Donnelly, and John Cairney. 2014. "Sport Participation and Alcohol and Illicit Drug Use in Adolescents and Young Adults: A Systematic Review of Longitudinal Studies." *Addictive Behaviors* 39(3): 497–506.

Labhardt, Danielle, Emma Holdsworth, Sarah Brown, and Douglas Howat. 2016. "You See but You Do Not Observe: A Review of Bystander Intervention and Sexual Assault on University Campuses." *Aggression and Violent Behaviour* 35: 13–25.

Lafferty, M.E., C. Wakefield, and H. Brown. 2017. "'We Do It for the Team': Student-Athletes' Initiation Practices and Their Impact on Group Cohesion." *International Journal of Sport and Exercise Psychology* 15(4): 438–46.

Laframboise, Kalina. 2021. "Canadian Artistic Swimmers File Lawsuit against Governing Body over Abuse, Harassment Allegations." *Global News*, March 9. https://globalnews.ca/news/7685854/canada-artistic-swimmers-lawsuit/.

Larocque, Corey. 2015. "A Year of Allegations of Misbehaving." *Ottawa Sun*, March 21. https://ottawasun.com/2015/03/21/a-year-of-allegations-of-misbehaving.

Larsen, Karin. 2018. "New Evidence Key in Charging Former B.C. Lions Player with 9-Year-Old Cold Case Murder." *CBC News*, November 5. https://www.cbc.ca/news/canada/british-columbia/new-evidence-key-in-charging-former-b-c-lions-player-with-9-year-old-cold-case-murder-1.4892624.

Larsen, Leslie, and Christopher Clayton. 2019. "Career Pathways to NCAA Division I Women's Basketball Head Coach Positions: Do Race and Gender Matter?" *Women in Sport and Physical Activity Journal* 27: 94–100.

Lavigne, Paula. 2020. "NCAA Sued by 7 Women for Failure to Protect in Alleged Sexual Assaults." *ESPN*, April 29. https://www.espn.com/college-sports/story/_/id/29114869/ncaa-sued-7-women-failure-protect-alleged-sexual-assaults.

Lavigne, Paula, and Mark Schlabach. 2017. *Violated: Exposing Rape at Baylor University amid College Football's Sexual Assault Crisis*. New York: Center Street.

LaVoi, Nicole M. 2016. *Women in Sports Coaching*. London: Routledge.

Layes, Cavelle. 2014. "Prison Sentence Likely for Female Hockey Coach Who Preyed on Player." *Info News*, February 22. https://infotel.ca/newsitem/likely-prison-sentence-for-female-hockey-coach-who-had-sex-with-girl/it8097.

Leahy, Trisha, Grace Pretty, and Gershon Tenenbaum. 2002. "Prevalence of Sexual Abuse in Organised Competitive Sport in Australia." *Journal of Sexual Aggression* 8(2): 16–36.

Leavitt, Sarah. 2017. "Ex-Ski Coach Bertrand Charest Sentenced to 12 Years in Prison for Sex Crimes." *CBC News*, December 8. https://www.cbc.ca/news/canada/montreal/bertrand-charest-sentenced-1.4438348.

Leclerc, Martin. 2022. "Quebec Junior Hockey Players Accused of Group Sexual Assault." *CBC News*, December 13. https://www.cbc.ca/news/canada/montreal/quebec-hockey-culture-toxic-1.6684059.

Lee-Olukoya, Eugena. 2009. "Sisterhood: Hazing and Other Membership Experiences of Women Belonging to Historically African American Sororities." PhD diss., Illinois State University.

Leff, Lisa. 2012. "High School's Athletes Formed 'Fantasy Slut League,' Awarding Points for Sex." *Toronto Star*, October 23. http://www.thestar.com/news/world/2012/10/23/high_schools_athletes_formed_fantasy_slut_league_awarding_points_for_sex.html.

Leithwood, Stephen. 2019. "Sold Out Show as Brock Badgers Bitten by Guelph Gryphons." *Brock News*, September 13. https://brocku.ca/brock-news/2019/09/sold-out-show-as-brock-badgers-bitten-by-guelph-gryphons/.

Lenskyj, Helen Jefferson. 2004. "What's Sex Got to Do with It? Analyzing the Sex + Violence Agenda in Sport Hazing Practices." In *Making the Team: Inside the World of Sport Initiations and Hazing*, edited by jay johnson and Margery Holman, 83–96. Toronto: Canadian Scholars Press.

–. 2012. "Reflections on Communication and Sport: On Heteronormativity and Gender Identities." *Communication and Sport* 1(1): 1–13.

Leroux, Jacki. 1999. "Gary Blair Walker." *Ottawa Sun*, June 19. http://cancrime.com/walker.gary.blair.html.

Let's Go Pens. 1997. "Nedved's Sexual Assault Charges Are on Hold." February 4. http://letsgopens.com/index96.htm.

Lisak, David, Lori Gardinier, Sarah Nicksa, and Ashley Cote. 2010. "False Allegations of Sexual Assault: An Analysis of Ten Years of Reported Cases." *Violence against Women* 16(12): 1318–34.

Little, Lyndon. 2008. "Lions Make Tough Decision to Cut Boden." *Vancouver Sun,* May 15. https://www.pressreader.com/canada/vancouver-sun/20080515/282424164957056.

Long, Jamie. 2018. "Gymnastics Bodies Never Told of Allegations against Ottawa Coach." *CBC News,* February 2. https://www.cbc.ca/news/canada/ottawa/gymnastics-canada-ontario-coach-allegations-2013-ottawa-1.4515262.

–. 2022. "Gymnastics Coach Scott McFarlane Acquitted on Sexual Assault-Related Charges." *CBC News,* November 22. https://www.cbc.ca/news/canada/ottawa/gymnastics-coach-scott-mcfarlane-not-guilty-1.6657190.

Long, Lynn, Judith Burnett, and R. Valorie Thomas. 2006. *Sexuality Counseling: An Integrative Approach.* Upper Saddle River, NJ: Pearson.

Longwell, Karen. 2015. "OPP Keeping Quiet on Northumberland House Party Investigation." *Northumberland News,* March 11. https://www.northumberland-news.com/news-story/5471007-update-opp-keeping-quiet-on-northumberland-house-party-investigation/.

Lorrigio, Paola. 2009. "Friend Not Told of Alleged Rape till Later, Ex-Argo's Trial Hears." *Toronto Star,* February 24. https://www.thestar.com/news/crime/2009/02/24/friend_not_told_of_alleged_rape_till_later_exargos_trial_hears.html.

Lowthers, Drake. 2019a. "Former Student-Athlete Suspended, Facing Criminal Sexual Assault Charges." *Port Hawkesbury Reporter,* March 20. http://porthawkesburyreporter.com/former-student-athlete-suspended-facing-criminal-sexual-assault-charges/.

–. 2019b. "Supreme Court Judge Not Convinced beyond a Reasonable Doubt in Case of Sexual Assault Charges against Former StFX Football Players by Another Student." *Port Hawkesbury Reporter,* December 3. https://porthawkesburyreporter.com/supreme-court-judge-not-convinced-beyond-a-reasonable-doubt-in-case-of-sexual-assault-charges-against-former-stfx-football-players-by-another-student/.

Lyon, Matthew. 2004. "No Means No? Withdrawal of Consent during Intercourse and the Continuing Evolution of the Definition of Rape." *Journal of Criminal Law and Criminology* 95: 277–314.

MacDonald, Cheryl. 2018. "Insert Name of Openly Gay Hockey Player Here: Attitudes towards Homosexuality among Canadian Male Major Midget AAA Ice Hockey Players." *Sociology of Sport Journal* 35: 347–57.

MacDonald, Darren. 2016. "LU Hockey Player Faces Sexual Assault Charge." *Sudbury.com,* November 28. https://www.sudbury.com/local-news/lu-hockey-player-faces-sexual-assault-charge-475871.

–. 2018. "Former LU Hockey Player Has Sex Assault Charge Withdrawn." *Sudbury.com,* August 17. https://www.sudbury.com/police/former-lu-hockey-player-has-sex-assault-charges-withdrawn-1019035.

MacGregor, Roy. 2013. "How Hazing Nearly Ended This Junior Hockey Star's Life." *Globe and Mail,* December 14. https://www.theglobeandmail.com/sports/hockey/macgregor-hockey-was-his-life-but-hazing-nearly-ended-it/article15971781/.

MacKinnon, Catharine. 2005. *Women's Lives, Men's Laws.* Cambridge, MA: Harvard University Press.

MacLeod, Robert. 1996. "Universities March Madness Sports Black Eye." *The Globe and Mail*, March 7, C6.

MacPherson, Taylor. 2017a. "Former Nanaimo Hockey Player Acquitted of Sexual Assault in Saskatchewan." *Nanaimo News*, April 13. https://nanaimonewsnow.com/2017/04/13/update-former-nanaimo-hockey-player-acquitted-of-sexual-assault-in-saskatchewan/.

MacPherson, Taylor. 2017b. "Former Nipawin Hawks Star Testifies at His Sexual Assault Trial." *Prince Albert Now*, April 12. https://panow.com/2017/04/12/former-nipawin-hawks-star-testifies-at-his-sexual-assault-trial/.

Maki, Allan. 2005. "Sidelined for Standing Up for Teammates." *Globe and Mail*, October 19. https://www.theglobeandmail.com/sports/sidelined-for-standing-up-to-teammates/article739600/.

Malszecki, Greg. 2004. "'No Mercy Shown nor Asked' – Toughness Test or Torture: Hazing in Military Combat Units and Its 'Collateral Damage.'" In *Making the Team: Inside the World of Sport Initiations and Hazing*, edited by jay johnson and Margery Holman, 32–49. Toronto: Canadian Scholars Press.

Maltz, Wendy. 2002. "Treating the Sexual Intimacy Concerns of Sexual Abuse Survivors." *Sexual and Relationship Therapy* 17(4): 321–27.

Mandel, Michele. 2019. "Victim in St. Michael's Sex Attack to Sue School, Coaches." *Toronto Sun*, October 17. https://torontosun.com/news/local-news/mandel-victim-in-st-michaels-sex-attack-to-sue-school-coaches.

Mann, Arshy. 2016. "The History of Gross Indecency in Canada." *Xtra Magazine*, February 5. https://xtramagazine.com/power/the-history-of-gross-indecency-in-canada-70136.

Mann, Liesbeth, Allard Feddes, Bertjan Doosje, and Agneta Fischer. 2015. "Withdraw or Affiliate? The Role of Humiliation during Initiation Rituals." *Cognition and Emotion* 30(1): 80–100.

Manne, Kate. 2018. *Down Girl: The Logic of Misogyny.* New York: Oxford University Press.

–. 2020. *Entitled: How Male Privilege Hurts Women.* New York: Crown.

Marowits, Ross. 2006. "Sex Tape Leads to Hockey Players' Arrest." *Halifax Daily News*, December 22, 15.

Martin, Patricia. 2005. *Rape Work: Victims, Gender, and Emotions in Organization and Community Context.* New York: Routledge.

Martin, Patricia, and R.M. Powell. 1994. "Accounting for the 'Second Assault': Legal Organizations' Framing of Rape Victims." *Law and Social Inquiry* 19(4): 853–90.

Mascoll, Philip. 1994. "Portrait of a Pedophile." *Toronto Star*, June 23, A25.

Massey, Kyle, and Jennifer Massey. 2017. "It Happens, Just Not to Me: Hazing on a Canadian University Campus." *Journal of College and Character* 18(1): 46–63.

Mathers, Scott, and Jackie Chavez. 2018. "When Hazing Is Not Hazing: Media Portrayal of Hazing." *Social Sciences* 7: 158–70.

Maynard, Robyn. 2017. *Policing Black Lives: State Violence in Canada from Slavery to Present.* Halifax: Fernwood.

McCarthy, Eugene. 1997. "Former Player Sues Team, University for Negligence." *Ottawa Citizen*, January 29, D3.

McEwan, Todd. 2015. "No Charges Laid against Cobourg Cougars Players after Police Investigation into House Party." *Northumberland News*, September 15. https://

www.northumberlandnews.com/news-story/5839811-update-no-charges-laid-ag
ainst-cobourg-cougars-players-after-police-investigation-into-house-party/.

McGlone, Colleen. 2005. "Hazing in N.C.A.A. Division I Women's Athletics: An
Exploratory Analysis." PhD diss., University of New Mexico.

McGouran, Kathleen. 2015. "Victim Testifies at Hick's Sexual Assault Sentencing:
Skating Coach Faces Jail Time." *Windsor Star,* April 25, A6.

McGran, Kevin, and Kieran Leavitt. 2022. "TSN Reports on Shocking Video from
2003 as Hockey Canada Confirms Two Police Investigations of Sex-Assault Claims."
Toronto Star, July 25. https://www.thestar.com/sports/hockey/2022/07/22/
hockey-canada-says-2003-world-junior-team-also-accused-of-group-se
xual-assault.html.

McIntyre, Mike. 2008a. "Sex Charges against Wrestler Dismissed." *Winnipeg Free
Press,* May 28, A3.

–. 2008b. "Sex Scandal Rocks Wrestling Community." *Winnipeg Free Press,* May 27, B1.

McKenzie, Julian. 2022. "Hockey Canada Timeline: 'Federal Government Let Victims Down' by Not Acting on Assault Allegations, MP Says." *Athletic,* July 20.
https://theathletic.com/3437209/2022/07/20/hockey-canada-lawsuit-
investigation-timeline/.

McLaughlin, Tracy. 2000. "Crown Drops Sex Case against OHL Players." *Globe
and Mail,* July 11. https://www.theglobeandmail.com/news/national/crown-
drops-sex-case-against-ohl-players/article25466544/.

Meadows, Cui Zhang, and Charles Meadows. 2019. "He Will Never Walk outside of
a Prison Again: An Examination of Twitter Users' Responses to the Larry Nassar
Case." *Communication and Sport* 8(2): 188–214.

Messerschmidt, James. 1993. *Masculinities and Crime: Critique and Reconceptual-
ization.* Lanham, MD: Rowman and Littlefield.

–. 1997. *Crime as Structured Action: Gender, Race, Class, and Crime in the Making.*
Thousand Oaks, CA: Sage.

Messner, Michael. 1995. *Power at Play: Sports and the Problem of Masculinity.* Boston: Beacon Press.

–. 2002. *Taking the Field: Women, Men, and Sport.* Minneapolis: University of Minnesota Press.

–. 2007. *Out of Play: Critical Essays on Gender and Sport.* Albany: SUNY Press.

Messner, Michael, Max Greenberg, and Tal Peretz. 2015. *Some Men: Feminist Allies and
the Movement to End Violence against Women.* New York: Oxford University Press.

Messner, Michael, and Don Sabo. 1994. *Sex, Violence and Power in Sports: Rethinking Masculinity.* Freedom, CA: Crossing Press.

Meyer, Barbara. 2000. "The Ropes and Challenge Course: A Quasi-Experimental
Examination." *Perceptual and Motor Skills* 90: 1249–57.

Midwestern Newspapers. 2016. "Vandergunst Wins Appeal, Could Face New
Trial." May 4. https://midwesternnewspapers.com/vandergunst-wins-appeal-
could-face-new-trial/.

Milano, Alyssa (@Alyssa_Milano). 2017. "If you've been sexually harassed or
assaulted write 'me too' as a reply to this tweet." Twitter, October 15. https://
twitter.com/Alyssa_Milano/status/919659438700670976.

Montgomery, Sue. 2011. "Hockey Coach Gilbert Dubé Sentenced to 5 Years for Sex
Abuse." *Gazette* [Montreal], April 5. http://www.montrealgazette.com/story_
print.html?id=4561818andsponsor=.

–. 2014. "Sexual Assault Charges Dropped against McGill Redmen." *Gazette* [Montreal], November 17. http://montrealgazette.com/news/local-news/sexual-assault-charges-dropped-against-mcgill-redmen.

Moodie, Jim. 2016. "Laurentian U Suspends Hockey Player." *Sudbury Star*, November 29. https://www.thesudburystar.com/2016/11/30/laurentian-u-suspends-hockey-player/wcm/0bb92f27-8e2d-d82e-c732-775e2e51cb01.

Moore, Oliver. 2006. "Argos Bail Out Williams in Sexual Assault Case." *Globe and Mail*, September 1. https://www.theglobeandmail.com/sports/argos-bail-out-williams-in-sexual-assault-case/article18172477/.

Moore, Shannon, Teresa Anne Fowler, and Tim Skuce. 2022. "Showered in Sexism: Hockey Culture Needs a Reckoning." *Conversation*, July 5. https://theconversation.com/showered-in-sexism-hockey-culture-needs-a-reckoning-186002.

Moore, Wayne. 2008. "Suspect Arrested in Rutland Rapes." *Castanet Kelowna News*, October 23. https://www.castanet.net/news/Kelowna/42665/Suspect-arrested-in-Rutland-Rapes.

Morris, Chris. 2003. "PEI's Star Baseball Prospect Found Guilty of Sex Charge Involving Young Girls under 14." *Globe and Mail*, October 23. https://www.theglobeandmail.com/news/national/peis-star-baseball-prospect-found-guilty-of-sex-charge-involving-young-girls-under-14/article1047581/.

Morton, Haley. 2016. "License to Abuse: Confronting Coach-Inflicted Sexual Assault in American Olympic Sports." *William and Mary Journal of Women and the Law* 23(1): 141–74.

Mountjoy, Margo. 2018. "'Only by Speaking Out Can We Create Lasting Change': What Can We Learn from the Dr Larry Nassar Tragedy?" *British Journal of Sports Medicine* 53(1): 57–60.

Mountjoy, Margo, Celia Brackenridge, Malia Arrington, Cheri Blauwet, Andrea Carska-Sheppard, Kari Fasting, Sandra Kirby, et al. 2016. "International Olympic Committee Consensus Statement: Harassment and Abuse (Non-Accidental Violence) in Sport." *British Journal of Sports Medicine* 50: 1019–29.

Muir, Allan. 2015. "Junior Hockey Players under Investigation for Public Sex Acts." *Sports Illustrated*, February 23. https://www.si.com/nhl/2015/02/23/junior-hockey-players-public-sex-investigation-qmjhl-gatineau-olympiques.

Mulvaney, Kieran. 2007. "No Winners: The Davey Hilton Story." *ESPN*, June 5. https://www.espn.com/sports/boxing/news/story?id=2872638.

Murnen, Sarah K., and Marla H. Kohlman. 2007. "Athletic Participation, Fraternity Membership, and Sexual Aggression among College Men: A Meta-Analytic Review." *Sex Roles* 57(1–2): 145–57.

Murphy, William F. 2019. "Investigating the Incidence of Sexual Assault in Martial Arts Coaching Using Media Reports." *Digital Investigation* 30: 90–93.

Murray, Ray. 1995a. "Image Rocked: Franchise Shooting Itself in Foot." *Calgary Herald*, June 10, D1.

–. 1995b. "Jovanovski Charges Withdrawn." *Sun-Sentinel*, August 12. https://www.sun-sentinel.com/news/fl-xpm-1995-08-12-9508120041-story.html.

–. 1995c. "Jovanovski Must Stand Trial in Sexual Assault." *Sun-Sentinel*, July 15. https://www.sun-sentinel.com/news/fl-xpm-1995-06-15-9506150092-story.html.

Nash, James. 1994. "Former 'M' Hockey Player to Face Trial for Sexual Assault." *Michigan Daily*, May 18, S3.

National Parole Board. 2009. "NPB Pre-release Decision Sheet: Gary Blair Walker." June 4. https://pdfslide.net/documents/pedophile-gary-blair-walker-denied-parole-2009.html.

National Post. 1999. "Hockey Players in Sex Case." March 31, A5.

–. 2006. "Four Junior Hockey Players Arrested in Sex-Related Case." December 22, A5.

Neugebauer, Robynne, ed. 2000. *Criminal Injustice: Racism in the Criminal Justice System.* Toronto: Canadian Scholars Press.

Nielsen, Jan Toftegaard. 2001. "The Forbidden Zone: Intimacy, Sexual Relations and Misconduct in the Relationship between Coaches and Athletes." *International Review for the Sociology of Sport* 36(2): 165–82.

–. 2004. *Idraettens illusoriske intimitet.* Copenhagen: Kobenhavns Universitet.

Norman, Mark, Peter Donnelly, and Bruce Kidd. 2021. "Gender Inequality in Canadian Interuniversity Sport: Participation Opportunities and Leadership Positions from 2010–11 to 2016–17." *International Journal of Sport Policy and Politics* 13(2): 207–23.

Nuwer, Hank. 2000. *High School Hazing: When Rites Become Wrongs.* New York: Franklin Watts.

–. 2001. *Wrongs of Passage: Fraternities, Sororities, Hazing and Binge Drinking.* Bloomington: Indiana University Press.

–. 2004a. *The Hazing Reader.* Bloomington: Indiana University Press.

–. 2004b. "How Sportswriters Contribute to Hazing Culture in Athletics." In *Making the Team: Inside the World of Sport Initiations and Hazing,* edited by jay johnson and Margery Holman, 118–31. Toronto: Canadian Scholars Press.

–. 2017. "Hazing Deaths in American College Campuses Remain Far Too Common." *Economist,* October 13. https://www.economist.com/graphic-detail/2017/10/13/hazing-deaths-on-american-college-campuses-remain-far-too-common.

O'Grady, William. 2007. *Crime in Canadian Context: Debates and Controversies.* Toronto: Oxford University Press.

O'Hara, Jane. 2000. "The Hell of Hazing." *Maclean's,* March 6, 50–52.

Ohlheiser, Abby. 2017. "The Woman behind 'Me Too' Knew the Power of the Phrase When She Created It – 10 Years Ago." *Washington Post,* October 19. https://www.washingtonpost.com/news/the-intersect/wp/2017/10/19/the-woman-behind-me-too-knew-the-power-of-the-phrase-when-she-created-it-10-years-ago/.

Oleksyn, Michael. 2017. "Former Nipawin Hockey Player Garrett Dunlop Acquitted of Sexual Assault, Interference Charges." *StarPhoenix* [Saskatoon], April 13. https://thestarphoenix.com/news/local-news/former-nipawin-hockey-player-garrett-dunlop-acquitted-of-sexual-assault-interference-charges.

Ontario Coalition of Rape Crisis Centres. 2015. "About Us: Sexual Assault Centres in Your Communities." http://www.sexualassaultsupport.ca/page-411845.

O'Reilly, Maureen. 2017. "Queen's Student Avoids Sexual Assault Charge, Convicted of Common Assault." *Queen's Journal,* August 31. https://www.queensjournal.ca/story/2017-08-31/news/queens-student-avoids-sexual-assault-charge-convicted-of-common-assault/.

Orlando Sentinel. 1996. "Nedved Accused of Sexual Assault." February 27. https://www.orlandosentinel.com/news/os-xpm-1996-02-27-9602270109-story.html.

Osborne, Judith. 1984. "Rape Law Reform: The New Cosmetic for Canadian Women." *Criminal Justice Politics and Women* 4(3): 49–64.

O'Sullivan, C.S. 1991. "Acquaintance Gang Rape on Campus." In *Acquaintance Rape: The Hidden Crime,* edited by Andrea Parrot and Laurie Bechhofer, 140–56. New York: Wiley.

Ottawa Citizen. 2007. "Sex Charges Dropped." February 10, C3.

Owton, Helen. 2016. *Sexual Abuse in Sport: A Qualitative Case Study*. Cham, Switzerland: Palgrave Macmillan.

Owton, Helen, and Andrew Sparkes. 2017. "Sexual Abuse and the Grooming Process in Sport: Learning from Bella's Story." *Sport, Education and Society* 22(6): 732–43.

Owusu-Bempah, Akwasi, Maria Jung, Firdaous Sbai, Andrew Wilton, and Fiona Kouyoumdjian. 2021. "Race and Incarceration: The Representation and Characteristics of Black People in Provincial Correctional Facilities in Ontario, Canada." *Race and Justice*. https://doi.org/10.1177%2F21533687211006461.

Owusu-Bempah, Akwasi, and Scot Wortley. 2013. "Race, Criminality and Criminal Justice in Canada." In *The Oxford Handbook on Ethnicity, Crime and Immigration*, edited by Sandra Bucerious and Michael Tonry, 281–320. New York: Oxford University Press.

Page, Amy Dellinger. 2010. "True Colors: Police Officers and Rape Myth Acceptance." *Feminist Criminology* 5(4): 315–34.

Paolucci, Elizabeth, Mark Genuis, and Claudio Violato. 2001. "A Meta-Analysis of the Published Research on the Effects of Child Sexual Abuse." *Journal of Psychology* 135(1): 17–36.

Pappas, Nick. 2012. *The Dark Side of Sports: Exposing the Sexual Culture of Collegiate and Professional Athletes*. Maidenhead, UK: Meyer and Meyer Sport.

Parent, Sylvie. 2010. "Prevention and Management of Sexual Harassment and Abuse in Quebec Sport Organizations." In *Elite Child Athlete Welfare: International Perspectives*, edited by Celia Brackenridge, 138–47. London: Brunel University Press.

—. 2011. "Disclosure of Sexual Abuse in Sport Organizations: A Case Study." *Journal of Child Sexual Abuse* 20: 322–37.

Parent, Sylvie, and Joelle Bannon. 2011. "Sexual Abuse in Sport: What about Boys?" *Child and Youth Services Review* 34: 354–59.

Parent, Sylvie, and Karim El Hlimi. 2012. "Athlete Protection in Quebec's Sport System: Assessments, Problems and Challenges." *Journal of Sport and Social Issues* 37(3): 284–96.

Parent, Sylvie, and Kristine Fortier. 2018. "Comprehensive Overview of the Problem of Violence against Athletes in Sport." *Journal of Sport and Social Issues* 42(4): 227–46.

Parent, Sylvie, Francine Lavoie, Marie-Eve Thibodeau, Martine Hébert, and Martin Blais. 2016. "Sexual Violence Experienced in the Sport Context by a Representative Sample of Quebec Adolescents." *Journal of Interpersonal Violence* 31(16): 2666–86.

Parnis, Deborah, and Janice Du Mont. 1999. "Rape Laws and Rape Processing: The Contradictory Nature of Corroboration." *Canadian Woman Studies* 19(1): 74–78.

Parrish, Julia. 2013. "Former Eskimo Braidwood Sentenced for Sexual Assault, Firearm Charges." *CTV News*, April 19. https://edmonton.ctvnews.ca/former-eski mo-braidwood-sentenced-for-sexual-assault-firearm-charges-1.1245633.

Parton, Nicole. 1995. "Hazing Was a Rite of Passage in Hockey, but Now It's Taboo." *Vancouver Sun*, October 26, B1.

Pazzano, Sam. 2017. "Spitfire Johnson Loses Appeal of Sexually Assaulting Drunken Teen in Bar." *Toronto Sun*, November 21. https://torontosun.com/news/crime/ spitfire-johnson-loses-appeal-of-sexually-assaulting-drunken-teen-in-bar.

—. 2019. "Lacrosse Player-Rapist Nets Two Years in Prison." *Toronto Sun*, November 21. https://torontosun.com/news/crime/lacrosse-player-rapist-nets-two-years-b efore-judge-hugs-his-parents-in-court.

Pearson, Quinn. 1994. "Treatment Techniques for Adult Female Survivors of Childhood Sexual Abuse." *Journal of Counseling and Development* 73(1): 32–37.

Pépin-Gagné, Joannie, and Sylvie Parent. 2016. "Coaching, Touching, and False Allegations of Sexual Abuse in Canada." *Journal of Sport and Social Issues* 40(2): 162–72.

Perreault, Samuel. 2015. "Criminal Victimization in Canada, 2014." Statistics Canada. https://www150.statcan.gc.ca/n1/pub/85-002-x/2015001/article/14241-eng.htm.

Powell, Anastasia, and Nicola Henry. 2017. *Sexual Violence in a Digital Age.* London: Palgrave Macmillan.

Powell, Betsy. 2018. "Student on Trial for Sexual Assault Says Accuser Initiated Their 'Hookup.'" *Toronto Star,* September 24. https://www.thestar.com/news/gta/2018/09/24/student-on-trial-for-sex-assault-says-accuser-initiated-their-hookup.html.

–. 2019. "Toronto Judge Gives Book to Man in Unusual Move after Sentencing Him for Sex Assault." *Toronto Star,* February 19. https://www.thestar.com/news/gta/2019/02/19/toronto-judge-gives-book-to-man-after-sentencing-him-for-sex-assault-in-unusual-move.html.

Prest, Ashley. 2016. "Youth Football Organizers Fumble Harassment, Sex Allegations, Father Says." *Winnipeg Free Press,* October 25. https://www.winnipegfreepress.com/breakingnews/2016/10/24/youth-football-officials-fumble-harassment-sex-allegations-father-says.

Preston, M.B. 2006. "Sheldon Kennedy and a Canadian Tragedy Revisited: A Comparative Look at U.S. and Canadian Jurisprudence on Youth Sports Organizations' Civil Liability for Child Sexual Exploitation." *Vanderbilt Journal of Transnational Law* 39(4): 1333–72.

Pringle, Josh. 2020. "UOttawa Settles Class-Action Lawsuit with Members of Gee-Gees Hockey Team." *CTV News,* March 30. https://ottawa.ctvnews.ca/uottawa-settles-class-action-lawsuit-with-members-of-gee-gees-hockey-team-1.4874990.

Pron, Nick. 2001 "Gardens Molester Dies in Prison." *Toronto Star,* February 28, B1.

Province. 1992. "Ottawa Eyeing King." March 26, B4.

Pruden, Jana. 2013. "Father Raised Concerns about Coach in 1996." *Edmonton Journal,* May 13, A4.

Putnam, Frank. 2003. "Ten-Year Research Update Review: Child Sexual Abuse." *Journal of the American Academy of Child Adolescent Psychiatry* 42(3): 269–78.

QMI Agency. 2015. "House Party Allegations." *Belleville Intelligencer,* March 11. https://www.intelligencer.ca/2015/03/11/sexual-assault-accusations-against-cobourg-hockey-players/wcm/bd4c0a92-68b3-ea6c-7b41-85e32d22470f.

Quigley, Joseph. 2015. "Tweet with '#consentisoverrated' Sparks Outcry, Response." *QNet News,* March 12. http://www.qnetnews.ca/?p=51709.

Quinlan, Andrea. 2016. "Suspect Survivors: Police Investigation Practices in Sexual Assault Cases in Ontario, Canada." *Women and Criminal Justice* 26(4): 301–18.

–. 2017. *The Technoscientific Witness of Rape: Contentious Histories of Law, Feminism, and Forensic Science.* Toronto: University of Toronto Press.

Quinlan, Elizabeth. 2017. "Introduction: Sexual Violence in the Ivory Tower." In *Sexual Violence at Canadian Universities: Activism, Institutional Responses, and Strategies for Change,* edited by Elizabeth Quinlan, Andrea Quinlan, Curtis Fogel, and Gail Taylor, 1–23. Waterloo, ON: Wilfrid Laurier University Press.

Quinlan, Elizabeth, Andrea Quinlan, Curtis Fogel, and Gail Taylor, eds. 2017. *Sexual Violence at Canadian Universities: Activism, Institutional Responses, and Strategies for Change.* Waterloo, ON: Wilfrid Laurier University Press.

Rahill, Brian, and Elizabeth Allan. 2005. "Hazing Defined." Stop Hazing. http://www.stophazing.org.

Ralph, Dan. 2021. "National Survey Indicates Many Canadians Don't Want NFL Here at the Expense of CFL." *Yahoo Sports,* December 2. https://ca.sports.yahoo.com/news/national-survey-indicates-many-canadians-164601293.html.

Ratican, Kathleen. 1992. "Sexual Abuse Survivors: Identifying Symptoms and Special Treatment Considerations." *Journal of Counseling and Development* 71(1): 33–38.

Rau, Nate, and Anita Wadhwani. 2016. "Tennessee Settles Sexual Assault Suit for $2.48 Million." *Tennessean,* July 5. https://www.tennessean.com/story/news/crime/2016/07/05/tennessee-settles-sexual-assault-suit-248-million/86708442/.

Raycraft, Richard. 2022. "Hockey Canada Paid Out $8.9 Million in Sexual Abuse Settlements since 1989." *CBC News,* July 27. https://www.cbc.ca/news/politics/hockey-canada-house-of-commons-committee-1.6533439.

Reade, Ian, Wendy Rodgers, and Leanne Norman. 2009. "The Under-Representation of Women in Coaching: A Comparison of Male and Female Canadian Coaches at Low and High Levels of Coaching." *International Journal of Sports Science and Coaching* 4(4): 505–20.

Reigeluth, Christopher, and Michael Addis. 2016. "Adolescent Boys' Experiences with Policing of Masculinity: Forms, Functions, and Consequences." *Psychology of Men and Masculinity* 17: 74–83.

Revell, Peggy. 2018. "Prince Albertan Sentenced to Two Years for Sexual Assault in Alberta Court." *Prince Albert Daily Herald,* May 15. https://paherald.sk.ca/2018/05/15/prince-albertan-sentenced-to-two-years-for-sexual-assault-in-alberta-court/.

Rhodes, Blair. 2014. "Luc Potvin, Coach Convicted of Sex Assault, to Be Released." *CBC News,* May 21. https://www.cbc.ca/news/canada/nova-scotia/luc-potvin-coach-convicted-of-sex-assault-to-be-released-1.2649490.

Richie, Beth. 2012. *Arrested Justice: Black Women, Violence, and America's Prison Nation.* New York: New York University Press.

Robertson, Grant. 2022a. "Canada's Sport System Must Confront Growing Complaints of Athlete Abuse, Sport Minister Says." *Globe and Mail,* April 1. https://www.theglobeandmail.com/canada/article-canadas-sport-system-must-confront-growing-complaints-of-athlete-abuse/?cmpid=rss.

–. 2022b. "Canadian Gymnasts Call on Ottawa to Launch Probe into What They Say Is Sport's Toxic Culture." *Globe and Mail,* March 28. https://www.theglobe-andmail.com/canada/article-canadian-gymnasts-call-on-ottawa-to-investigate-abuse-and-toxic/.

–. 2022c. "Hockey Canada Used Health Fund for Lawsuits, Documents Say." *Globe and Mail,* July 25. https://www.theglobeandmail.com/canada/article-hockey-can-ada-also-used-health-fund-for-lawsuits-documents-say/.

Robertson, Grant, and Rachel Brady. 2022a. "Canadian Gymnasts Launch Class-Action Lawsuit Alleging Years of Physical and Sexual Abuse." *Globe and Mail,* May 11. https://www.theglobeandmail.com/sports/olympics/article-canadian-gymnasts-class-action-lawsuit-abuse-allegations/.

–. 2022b. "Researchers Outline Path to Fix Flaws in Ottawa's Plan to Address Abuse in Sport." *Globe and Mail,* January 17. https://www.theglobeandmail.com/canada/article-sport-minister-given-options-on-how-to-fix-holes-in-system-to-prevent/.

Robidoux, Michael, and Jochen Bocksnick. 2010. "Playing beyond the Glass: How Parents Support Violence in Minor Hockey." In *Sexual Sports Rhetoric: Historical and Media Contexts of Violence,* edited by Linda Fuller, 15–30. New York: Peter Lang.

Robinson, Laura. 1998. *Crossing the Line: Sexual Harassment and Abuse in Canada's National Sport.* Toronto: McClelland and Stewart.

—. 2000. "Code of Silence: Hockey's Dark Side." *Globe and Mail,* April 25. https://www.theglobeandmail.com/opinion/code-of-silence-hockeys-dark-side/article767309/.

—. 2002. "Crossing the Line: Violence and Sexual Assault in Canada's National Sport." *Play the Game,* November 9. https://www.playthegame.org/news/news-articles/2002/crossing-the-line-violence-and-sexual-assualt-in-canadas-national-sport/.

—. 2004. "Hazing – A Story." In *Making the Team: Inside the World of Sport Initiations and Hazing,* edited by jay johnson and Margery Holman, 1–18. Toronto: Canadian Scholars Press.

—. 2005. "Gods and Monsters: More Disturbing Stories about Hockey Violence against Women." *Play the Game,* April 29. https://www.playthegame.org/news/news-articles/2005/gods-and-monsters-more-disturbing-stories-about-hockey-violence-against-women/.

—. 2006. "In Sport and Sex, the Objective of Male Teams Is Conquest." *Ottawa Citizen,* December 22, A19.

—. 2008. "Another Canadian Hockey Scandal." *Play the Game,* December 1. https://www.playthegame.org/news/news-articles/2008/another-canadian-hockey-scandal/.

—. 2011a. "Hockey Promotes Violence." *Winnipeg Free Press,* September 6. https://www.winnipegfreepress.com/opinion/analysis/hockey-promotes-violence-129285213.html.

—. 2011b. "Reports Ignore the Hockey-Violence Relationship." *Vancouver Sun,* September 7. https://www.pressreader.com/canada/vancouver-sun/20110907/283570922202631.

—. 2016. "A Canadian Game in Which 'No' Means 'Yes.'" *Truthdig,* June 30. https://www.truthdig.com/articles/a-canadian-game-in-which-no-means-yes/page/2/.

Ross, MacIntosh. 2022. "Hockey Trouble: Can the Sport Overcome Its History of Neglect and Abuse?" *Conversation,* July 17. https://theconversation.com/hockey-trouble-can-the-sport-overcome-its-history-of-neglect-and-abuse-187062.

Ross, Rob J. 2019. "Sweep Creates Dynasty in the Stars." *Hometown Play,* March 26. https://hometownplay.ca/MAR25OMHAFinalSTTDynasty.php.

Rotenberg, Cristine. 2017. "From Arrest to Conviction: Court Outcomes of Police-Reported Sexual Assaults in Canada, 2009 to 2014." Statistics Canada. https://www150.statcan.gc.ca/n1/pub/85-002-x/2017001/article/54870-eng.htm.

Roy, Jonathan, and Martin Camire. 2017. "A Season-Long Case Study Examining Alcohol Use and Misuse in Canadian Junior Hockey." *Qualitative Research in Sport, Exercise, and Health* 9(3): 354–71.

Ruicci, Peter. 2012. "Greyhounds Players Charged with Sexual Assault." *North Bay Nugget,* August 26. https://www.nugget.ca/2012/08/26/players-on-ohls-greyhounds-accused-of-sex-assault/wcm/ddf634a4-57ca-4195-b6ec-c92d1c6c58b5.

Rupert, Jake. 2001a. "Alleged Victim Lying: Lawyer: False Complaint against Ex-67's Player Meant to Cover Embarrassment." *Ottawa Citizen,* October 11, B3.

—. 2001b. "Woman Testifies She Refused to Have Sex: Ex-67's Player Charged with Assault." *Ottawa Citizen,* October 10, B3.

—. 2002. "Hockey Player Wants Date Rape Charge Stayed: Ex-67's Galbraith Argues Excessive Delay under Charter." *Ottawa Citizen,* August 13, C1.

Russell, Louisa. 2010. "What Women Need Now from Police and Prosecutors: 35 Years of Working to Improve Police Response to Male Violence against Women." *Canadian Woman Studies* 28(1): 28–36.

Sabo, Don. 1985. "Pigskin, Patriarchy and Male Identity." *Arena Review* 9(2): 1–30.

Sacheli, Sarah. 2016. "Ben Johnson Sentenced to Three Years for 'Forcible, Criminal' Sexual Assault." *Windsor Star,* October 25. https://windsorstar.com/news/local-news/ben-johnson-sentenced-to-three-years-for-forcible-criminal-sexual-assault.

—. 2017. "Ex-Spitfire Ben Johnson Loses Appeal on Sexual Assault Conviction." *Windsor Star,* October 25. https://windsorstar.com/news/local-news/ex-spitfire-ben-johnson-loses-appeal-on-sexual-assault-conviction.

Sadler, Emily. 2022. "Sheldon Kennedy Calls for Hockey Canada Leadership to Step Down." *Sportsnet,* July 26. https://www.sportsnet.ca/juniors/article/sheldon-kennedy-calls-for-hockey-canada-leadership-to-step-down/.

Safai, Parissa. 2013. "Women in Sport Policy." In *Sport Policy in Canada,* edited by Lucie Thibault and Jean Harvey, 317–49. Ottawa: University of Ottawa Press.

Samson, Samantha. 2015. "What's Wrong with Male Athletes?" *Winnipeg Free Press,* June 8. https://www.winnipegfreepress.com/opinion/analysis/Whats-wrong-with-male-athletes-306559571.html.

Sanday, Peggy. 1981. "The Socio-Cultural Context of Rape: A Cross-Cultural Study." *Journal of Social Issues* 37: 5–27.

—. 1990. *Fraternity Gang Rapes: Sex, Brotherhood, and Privilege on Campus.* New York: New York University Press.

Sanderson, Jimmy, and Melinda Weathers. 2020. "Snapchat and Child Sexual Abuse in Sport: Protecting Child Athletes in the Social Media Age." *Sport Management Review* 23: 81–94.

Sands, Aaron. 2000. "Popular 67's Star Faces Sexual-Assault Charge." *Ottawa Citizen,* October 15, A12.

Sartore, Melanie, and George Cunningham. 2007. "Examining the Under-Representation of Women in Leadership Positions of Sport Organizations: A Symbolic Interactionist Perspective." *Quest* 59: 244–65.

Sawchuk, Bill. 2018. "Teen Football Players Acquitted of Sexual Assault." *St. Catharines Standard,* July 20. https://www.stcatharinesstandard.ca/news/niagara-region/2018/07/20/teen-football-players-acquitted-of-sexual-assault.html.

Scarce, Michael. 1998. *Male on Male Rape: The Hidden Toll of Stigma and Shame.* Cambridge, MA: Perseus.

Seattle Times. 1996. "NHL Stars Accused of Assault." August 12. https://archive.seattletimes.com/archive/?date=19960812andslug=2343844.

Senn, Charene, and Anne Forrest. 2016. "'And Then One Night I Went to Class …': The Impact of Sexual Assault Bystander Intervention Workshops Incorporated in Academic Courses." *Psychology of Violence* 6(4): 607–18.

Seymour, Andrew. 2015. "Report Alleges Four Gatineau Olympiques Players Face Sexual Assault Complaint." *Ottawa Citizen,* March 10. https://ottawacitizen.

com/news/local-news/report-alleges-four-gatineau-olympiques-players-face-sexual-assault-complaint.

Sgroi, Suzanne M. 1982. *Handbook of Clinical Intervention in Child Sexual Abuse.* Lexington, MA: Lexington Books.

Shaw, Rob. 2006. "Crown Gets Salmon Kings' Evidence." *Times Colonist* [Victoria], November 10, B1.

Sheehy, Elizabeth. 1999. "Legal Responses to Violence against Women in Canada." *Canadian Woman Studies* 19(1): 62–73.

—. 2014. *Defending Battered Women on Trial: Lessons from the Transcripts.* Vancouver: UBC Press.

Shields, Billy. 2013. "McGill Campus Football Team at Centre of Sex Assault Controversy." *Global News,* November 22. http://globalnews.ca/news/985364/mcgill-campus-football-team-the-centre-of-sex-assault-controversy/.

Silva, Edilson J. 2019. "All-Canadian Eddie Ekiyor Leaves Carleton Ravens for Pro Ranks." *Basketball Buzz,* August 9. https://basketballbuzz.ca/usports/all-canadian-eddie-ekiyor-leaves-carleton-ravens-for-pro-ranks.

Slade, Daryl. 2002a. "Alleged Attack Recalled: SAIT Hockey Star on Trial for Sex Assault." *Calgary Herald,* August 8, B3.

—. 2002b. "Hockey Star Accused of Sexual Assault: Member of Women's Team Had Been at Party in Home of the Accused." *Edmonton Journal,* August 8, A7.

—. 2002c. "SAIT Sex Assault Case Goes to Jury." *Calgary Herald,* August 13, B1.

Smart, Carol. 1989. *Feminism and the Power of Law.* London: Routledge.

Smiley, Brian. 2013. "I'm Just So Glad It's Over." *Brantford Expositor,* April 5. https://www.brantfordexpositor.ca/2013/04/05/im-just-so-glad-its-over/wcm/9a6e08b8-42af-eea6-485e-ff3c9f2f441c.

Smith, Lauren Reichart, and Ann Pegararo. 2020. "Media Framing of Larry Nassar and the USA Gymnastics Child Sex Abuse Scandal." *Journal of Child Sexual Abuse* 29(4): 373–92.

Smrke, Jacqueline. 1998. "No Charges in Hazing: Police Have Ruled None of the Hockey Players Involved Had Criminal Intent." *Windsor Star,* May 5, A5.

Soo Today. 2008. "Jarrett Reid's Past Comes Back to Haunt Him." November 15. https://www.sootoday.com/local-news/jarrett-reids-past-comes-back-to-haunt-him-120140.

Spears, Tony. 2015. "Sex Predator Coach Kelly Jones Sued for $3.1M." *Ottawa Sun,* October 9. http://www.ottawasun.com/2015/10/09/sex-predator-coach-kelly-jones-sued-for-31m.

Spokesman-Review. 1995a. "NHL Player off Hook." August 13. https://www.spokesman.com/stories/1995/aug/13/nhl-player-off-hook/.

—. 1995b. "NHL's Top Pick Arrested." February 27. https://www.spokesman.com/stories/1995/feb/27/nhls-top-pick-arrested/.

Sport Canada. 1986. *Sport Canada Policy on Women in Sport.* Ottawa: Fitness and Amateur Sport.

Spry, Tami. 1995. "In the Absence of Word and Body: Hegemonic Implications of 'Victim' and 'Survivor' in Women's Narratives of Sexual Violence." *Women and Language* 18(2): 27–32.

Srabstein, Jorge. 2008. "Deaths Linked to Bullying and Hazing." *International Journal of Adolescent Medicine and Health* 20(2): 235–39.

Statistics Canada. 2018. "Victims of Police-Reported Sexual Assault." https://www150.
    statcan.gc.ca/n1/pub/85-002 x/2018001/article/54979/tbl/tbl03-eng.htm.
Stebbins, Robert. 1996. *Tolerable Differences: Living with Deviance.* Toronto:
    McGraw-Hill Ryerson.
Stermac, Lana, Sarah Horowitz, and Sheena Bance. 2017. "Sexual Coercion on Cam-
    pus: The Impact of Victimization and Disclosure on the Educational Experiences
    of Canadian Women." In *Sexual Violence at Canadian Universities: Activism,
    Institutional Responses, and Strategies for Change,* edited by Elizabeth Quinlan,
    Andrea Quinlan, Curtis Fogel, and Gail Taylor, 27–43. Waterloo, ON: Wilfrid Lau-
    rier University Press.
Stewart, Andrew L. 2013. "The Men's Project: A Sexual Assault Prevention Program
    Targeting College Men." *Psychology of Men and Masculinity* 15(4): 481–85.
Stinson, Scott. 2022. "Why Did Hockey Canada Stay Silent for So Long?" *Vancou-
    ver Sun,* July 27. https://www.pressreader.com/canada/vancouver-sun/20220727
    /281973201400164.
Storer, Heather L., Erin Casey, and Todd Herrenkohl. 2016. "Efficacy of Bystander
    Programs to Prevent Dating Abuse among Youth and Young Adults: A Review of
    the Literature." *Trauma, Violence, and Abuse* 17(3): 256–69.
Strashin, Jamie, and Lori Ward. 2019. "Local Sports Clubs Say They're Left on Their
    Own to Protect Young Athletes from Abuse." *CBC News,* February 11. https://
    www.cbc.ca/sports/amateur-sport-abuse-local-clubs-1.5006510.
Sudbury Star. 2004. "Otters Player Charged." July 30, B1.
Sussberg, Joshua. 2002. "Shattered Dreams: Hazing in College Athletics." *Cardozo
    Law Review* 24: 1421–91.
Sutherland, Anne. 2014. "Former Boxer Dave Hilton Jr. in Hot Water Again." *Gazette*
    [Montreal], November 14. https://montrealgazette.com/news/local-news/former
    -boxer-dave-hilton-jr-in-trouble-with-the-law-again.
Sweet, Stephen. 1999. "Understanding Fraternity Hazing: Insights from Symbolic
    Interactionist Theory." *Journal of College Student Development* 40(4): 355–63.
Szklarski, Cassandra. 2017. "The Reasons Some Victims of Sexual Assault Choose
    to Sue in Civil Court." *Global News,* November 3. https://globalnews.ca/news/
    3842846/the-reasons-some-victims-of-sexual-assault-choose-to-sue-in-civil-court/.
Tasca, Melinda, Nancy Rodriguez, Cassia Spohn, and Mary Koss. 2012. "Police
    Decision Making in Sexual Assault Cases: Predictors of Suspect Identification and
    Arrest." *Journal of Interpersonal Violence* 28(6): 1157–77.
Temple, Jeff, Rebecca Weston, Benjamin Rodriguez, and Linda Marshall. 2016. "Dif-
    fering Effects of Partner and Nonpartner Sexual Assault on Women's Mental
    Health." *Violence against Women* 13(3): 285–97.
Theberge, Nancy. 1981. "A Critique of Critiques: Radical and Feminist Writings on
    Sport." *Social Forces* 60(2): 341–53.
–. 2000. *Higher Goals: Women's Ice Hockey and the Politics of Gender.* Albany: SUNY
    Press.
Thomas, Renu, David DiLillo, Kate Walsh, and Melissa Polusny. 2011. "Pathways
    from Child Sexual Abuse to Adult Depression." *Psychology of Violence* 1(2):
    121–35.

Thompson, Charles. 2017. "Jury Reaches Split Verdict in Trial of Ex-PSU President Graham Spanier." *Pennsylvania Real-Time News,* March 24. https://www.penn-live.com/news/2017/03/jury_reaches_verdict_in_trial.html#incart_election.

Thompson, Jamie, James Johnstone, and Curt Banks. 2018. "An Examination of Initiation Rituals in a UK Sporting Institution and the Impact on Group Development." *European Sport Management Quarterly* 18(5): 544–62.

3DownNation. 2021. "Former CFLer Teague Sherman Pleads Guilty to Assault after 'Significant Compromise' Results in Sexual Assault Charges Being Dropped." December 18. https://3downnation.com/2021/12/18/former-cfler-teague-sherman-pleads-guilty-to-assault-after-significant-compromise-resu lts-in-sexual-assault-charges-being-dropped/.

Todd, Jack. 1996. "Disturbing Documentary on Junior Hockey." *Gazette,* October 26, C1.

Tokar, Krzysztof, and Craig Stewart. 2010. "Defining High School Hazing: Control through Clarity." *Physical Educator* 67(4): 204–8.

Tomlinson, Alan, and Ilkay Yorganci. 1997. "Male Coach/Female Athlete Relations: Gender and Power Relations in Competitive Sport." *Journal of Sport and Social Issues* 21(2): 134–55.

Top Shelf Hockey. 2020. "The Bible." Accessed July 5, 2020. https://tshockey.word-press.com/the-bible/.

Toronto Star. 1995. "Hazing Controversy." October 30, B2.

Trota, Brian, and jay johnson. 2004. "A Brief History of Hazing." In *Making the Team: The Inside World of Sport Initiations and Hazing,* edited by jay johnson and Margery Holman, x–xvi. Toronto: Canadian Scholars Press.

Turner, Randy. 2011. "Hazing Victim Had Water Bottles Tied to Genitals." *Calgary Herald,* October 27, A8.

Turnpenney, Rachel. 2022. *Report on the CHL's Well-Being Programs and Related Recommendations.* Turnpenney Milne LLP. https://cdn.chl.ca/uploads/chl/2022/01/21095713/PlayerWellbeingUpdate_FINAL.pdf.

Twin, Stephanie. 1979. *Out of the Bleachers: Writings on Women and Sport.* New York: Feminist Press.

Tylock, Angela. 2021. "A 50-State Summary of Hazing Laws." https://system.suny.edu/media/suny/content-assets/documents/sci/A-50-State-Summary-of-Hazing-Laws.pdf.

Ullman, Sarah E. 1999. "A Comparison of Gang and Individual Rape Incidents." *Violence and Victims* 14: 123–33.

–. 2010. *Talking about Sexual Assault: Society's Response to Survivors.* Washington, DC: APA PsycBooks.

Ulmer, Mike. 2005. "Hazing Sadly Commonplace." *Toronto Sun,* October 19. http://slam.canoe.com/Slam/Columnists/Ulmer/2005/10/19/1269039-sun.html.

Valiante, Giuseppe. 2017. "Witness Testifies Former Ski Coach Fondled Teammate's Breasts to Humiliate Her." *CBC News,* March 13. https://www.cbc.ca/news/canada/montreal/witness-testifies-former-ski-coach-fondled-teammate-s-breasts-to-humiliate-her-1.4023035.

Vancouver Island University Athletics. 2022. "Garrett Dunlop Hockey Bio." https://mariners.viu.ca/sports/cice/2018-19/bios/dunlop_garrett_qmnd?view=bio.

Vancouver Sun. 1990. "Eskimo Footballer among 5 under Investigation for Rape." November 27, A11.

Van Raalte, Judy, Allen Cornelius, Darwyn Linder, and Britton Brewer. 2007. "The Relationship between Hazing and Team Cohesion." *Journal of Sport Behavior* 30: 491–507.

Vertommen, Tine, Nicolette Schipper-van Veldhoven, Michael Hartill, and Filip Van Den Eede. 2015. "Sexual Harassment and Abuse in Sport: The NOC*NSF Helpline." *International Review of the Sociology of Sport* 50(7): 822–39.

Vertommen, Tine, Nicolette Schipper-van Veldhoven, Kristien Wouters, Jarl Kampen, Celia Brackenridge, Daniel Rhind, and Filip Van Den Eede. 2016. "Interpersonal Violence against Children in Sport in the Netherlands and Belgium." *Child Abuse and Neglect* 51: 223–36.

Vine, Cathy, and Paul Challen. 2002. *Gardens of Shame: The Tragedy of Martin Kruze and the Sexual Abuse at Maple Leaf Gardens*. Vancouver: Greystone Books.

Volkwein-Caplan, Karin, and Gopal Sankaran. 2002. *Sexual Harassment in Sport: Impact, Issues, and Challenges*. Oxford: Meyer and Meyer Sport.

Volkwein-Caplan, Karin, Frauke Schnell, Dennis Sherwood, and Anne Livezey. 1997. "Sexual Harassment in Sport: Perceptions and Experiences of American Female Student-Athletes." *International Review for the Sociology of Sport* 32(3): 283–95.

von der Lippe, Gerda. 1997. "Gender Discrimination in Norwegian Academia: A Hidden Male Game or an Inspiration for Postmodern Feminist Praxis?" In *Critical Postmodernism in Human Movement, Physical Education and Sport*, edited by Juan-Miguel Fernandez-Balboa, 27–39. New York: SUNY Press.

Waldron, Jennifer, and Christopher Kowalski. 2009. "Crossing the Line: Rites of Passage, Team Aspects, and Ambiguity of Hazing." *Research Quarterly for Exercise and Sport* 80(2): 291–302.

Waldron, Jennifer, Quinten Lynn, and Vikki Krane. 2011. "Duct Tape, Icy Hot and Paddles: Narratives of Initiation onto US Male Sport Teams." *Sport, Education and Society* 16(1): 111–25.

Walker, Nefertiti, and Trevor Bopp. 2010. "The Underrepresentation of Women in the Male-Dominated Sport Workplace: Perspectives of Female Coaches." *Journal of Workplace Rights* 15(1): 47–64.

Walter, Karena. 2012. "Second Woman Testifies Ex-Brock Goalie Assaulted Her." *Niagara Falls Review*, October 17. http://www.niagarafallsreview.ca/2012/10/17/second-woman-testifies-ex-brock-goalie-assaulted-her.

Walton, Dawn, and Allan Maki. 2007. "Trevis Smith: Anatomy of a Sexual Assault." *Globe and Mail*, February 25. https://www.theglobeandmail.com/sports/trevis-smith-anatomy-of-sexual-assault/article1070818/.

Ward, Doug. 2009. "Former B.C. Lion Josh Boden Faces New Sexual Assault Charge, Is Taken into Custody." *Vancouver Sun*, October 17. https://www.pressreader.com/canada/vancouver-sun/20091017/281865819533098.

Ward, Elizabeth. 1985. *Father-Daughter Rape*. New York: Grove Press.

Ward, Lori, and Jamie Strashin. 2019. "Sex Offences against Minors: Investigation Reveals More Than 200 Canadian Coaches Convicted in Last 20 Years." *CBC News*, February 10. https://www.cbc.ca/sports/amateur-sport s-coaches-sexual-offences-minors-1.5006609.

Warick, Jason. 2005. "The Secret Life of Trevis Smith: Women Who Dated Football Player Offer Glimpse into His Private Life." *StarPhoenix* [Saskatoon], December 3. https://thestarphoenix.com/news/local-news/the-secret-life-of-trevis-smith-women-who-dated-football-player-offer-glimpse-into-his-private-life.

Warren, May. 2018. "What We Know and Don't Know about the Scandal at St. Michael's College School – and What We Can't Report." *Toronto Star*, December 19. https://www.thestar.com/news/gta/2018/12/19/what-we-know-and-dont-know -about-the-scandal-at-st-michaels-college-school-and-what-we-cant-report.html.

Warshaw, Robin. 1988. *I Never Called It Rape*. New York: Harper and Row.

Waterhouse-Watson, Deb. 2013. *Athletes, Sexual Assault, and Trials by Media: Narrative Immunity*. New York: Routledge.

Webb, Danielle. 2010. "Did Canada's First Hazing Death Happen at STU?" *Maclean's*, December 10. https://www.macleans.ca/education/university/ did-canadas-first-hazing-death-happen-at-stu/.

Webb, Eugene, Donald Campbell, Richard Schwartz, and Lee Sechrest. 2000. *Unobtrusive Measures*. Thousand Oaks, CA: Sage.

Wegman, Josh. 2022. "Players Will Cooperate in NHL's Investigation of Hockey Canada Scandal." *Score*, July 17. https://www.thescore.com/nhl/news/2382831.

Wendell, Bryan. 2018. "What's the Difference between 'Two-Deep Leadership' and 'No One-on-One Contact'?" *Scouting Magazine*, January 19. https://blog. scoutingmagazine.org/2018/01/19/whats-the-difference-between-two-deep -leadership-and-no-one-on-one-contact/.

Werner, Eric M. 2021. "Avoiding the Second Assault: A Guidebook for Trauma-Informed Prosecutors." *Lewis and Clark Law Review* 25(2): 573–605.

West, Candace, and Don Zimmerman. 1987. "Doing Gender." *Gender and Society* 1(2): 125–51.

West, Carolyn M., and Kalimah Johnson. 2013. "Sexual Violence in the Lives of African American Women." National Online Resource Center on Violence against Women. https://vawnet.org/sites/default/files/materials/files/2016-09/AR_SVAA-WomenRevised.pdf.

Westhead, Rick. 2007. "New Sex Lawsuits Hit Leafs' Empire." *Toronto Star*, March 29. https://www.thestar.com/news/2007/03/29/new_sex_lawsuits_hit_leafs_empire.html.

–. 2022a. "Hockey Canada, CHL Settle Lawsuit over Alleged Sexual Assault Involving World Junior Players." *TSN*, May 26. https://www.tsn.ca/hock ey-canada-chl-settle-lawsuit-over-alleged-sexual-assault-involving-world-junior-players-1.1804861.

–. 2022b. "Sexual Assault Allegations Related to 2003 World Junior Team under Investigation." *TSN*, July 22. https://www.tsn.ca/sexual-assault-allegations-2003-worl d-juniors-team-1.1828253.

White, Mervyn F. 2005. "Supreme Court of Canada Brings Clarity to Vicarious Liability of Churches in Canada." *Church Law Bulletin*, May 31. https://www.cart-ers.ca/pub/bulletin/church/2005/chchlb11.htm.

White, Spencer. 2018. "Hockey's Unnoticed Problem." *Puck Stuff*, May 31. https:// puckstuff.wordpress.com/2018/05/31/hockeys-unnoticed-problem/.

Whitlock, Kay, and Michael Bronski. 2016. *Considering Hate: Violence, Goodness, and Justice in American Culture and Politics*. Boston: Beacon Press.

Whynacht, Ardath. 2021. *Insurgent Love: Abolition and Domestic Homicide*. Halifax: Fernwood.

Wilson, Brian. 2006. "Selective Memory in a Global Culture: Reconsidering Links between Youth, Hockey, and Canadian Identity." In *Artificial Ice: Hockey, Culture, and Commerce*, edited by David Whitson and Richard Gruneau, 53–70. Toronto: University of Toronto Press.

Wolf, Naomi. 1993. *Fire with Fire: The New Female Power and How to Use It.* New York: Fawcett Columbine.

World Health Organization. 2002. "Sexual Violence." In *World Report on Violence and Health.* https://www.who.int/violence_injury_prevention/violence/world_report/en/full_en.pdf.

Yanagisawa, Sue. 2017. "Sentencing Postponed for Business Student Who Assaulted Girl, 16, So It Wouldn't Affect His Internship." *National Post,* August 30. https://nationalpost.com/news/canada/sentencing-postponed-for-business-student-who-assaulted-girl-16-so-it-wouldnt-affect-his-internship.

Yard, Briget. 2018. "Volleyball Player Spent Season with U of S Huskies While on Bail, Facing Sexual Assault Charges." *CBC News,* May 16. https://www.cbc.ca/news/canada/saskatoon/matthew-meyer-sex-assault-huskies-1.4665660.

Yogaretnam, Shaamini. 2018. "Update: Redblacks Defensive Back Charged with Sex Assault, Let Go from Team." *Ottawa Citizen,* July 19. https://ottawacitizen.com/news/local-news/redblacks-defensive-back-charged-with-sex-assault-let-go-from-team.

Yonack, Lyn. 2017. "Sexual Assault Is about Power." *Psychology Today,* November 14. https://www.psychologytoday.com/ca/blog/psychoanalysis-unplugged/201711/sexual-assault-is-about-power.

Young, Belinda-Rose, Sarah Desmarais, Julie Baldwin, and Rasheeta Chandler. 2016. "Sexual Coercion Practices among Undergraduate Male Recreational Athletes, Intercollegiate Athletes, and Non-Athletes." *Violence against Women* 23(7): 795–812.

Legislation

An Act to Amend the Criminal Code and the Canada Evidence Act, SC 1987 c C-24.

An Act to Amend the Criminal Code (Unconstitutional Provisions) and to Make Consequential Amendments to Other Acts, SC 2017, c C-39.

Child and Family Services Act, RSO 1990, c C-11.

Criminal Code, SC 1892, c 29.

Criminal Code, RSC 1970, c C-34.

Criminal Code of Canada, RSC 1985, c C-46.

Criminal Law Amendment Act, SC 1985, c 19.

Jurisprudence

Berg v Canadian Hockey League, 2017 ONSC 2608.

Berg v Canadian Hockey League, 2020 ONSC 2608.

Blainey v OHA, 1986 7 CHRR 3529.

Carcillo v Canadian Hockey League, 2023 ONSC 886.

Creppin v University of Ottawa, 2015 ONSC 4449.

Guillemette c Verreault, 1994 QC CM 1786.

LSJPA – 1954, 2019 QCCQ 10339.

R v AGA, 2010 ABCA 61.

R v Anderson, 2009 PECA 04.

R v Cedeno, 2005 195 CCC (3d) 468 (OCJ).

R v Chase, 1987 23 SC 2 SCR 293.

R v Cornejo, 2003 68 OR (3d) 117 (CA).

R v DVV, 2005 BCPC 88.

R v Ewanchuk, 1999 1 SCR 330.
R v GJD, 1995 PEIJ 173 (SCTD).
R v Hall, 2000 BCCA 148.
R v Haugo, 2006 BCPC 0319.
R v Higginbottom, 2001 CanLII 3989.
R v Innerebner, 2010 ABQB 188.
R v James, 2012 MBPC 31.
R v James, 2013 MBCA 14.
R v JMA, 2009 283 NFLD 179.
R v Johnson, 2016 ONSC 3947.
R v Kaija, 2006 ONCJ 193.
R v Kienapple, 1974 1 SCR 729.
R v Laude, 1965 51 WWR 175.
R v McFarlane, 2020 ONSC 5194.
R v McNutt, 2020 NSSC 219.
R v NB, 2018 ONCJ 527.
R v Richardson, 2009 ONSC 80253.
R v Sazant, 2002 OTC 203.
R v Sazant, 2004 SCC 77.
R v Smith, 2008 SKCA 61.
R v Stuckless, 2016 ONCJ 338.
R v Stuckless, 2019 ONCA 504.
R v S (VCA), 2001 MBCA 85.
R v Swietlinski, 1980 53 SCC 2 SCR 956.
R v Triller, 1980 2850 BCSC.
R v Vandergunst, 2014 [unreported; summary retrieved from Fleming 2015a].
R v Vigon, 2016 ABCA 75.
R v Williams, 2019 NSSC 352.
R v Williams, 2019 NSSC 399.
Simpson v University of Colorado, 500 F (3d) 1170 (10th Cir 2007).

Index

Note: (t) after a page number indicates a table.

Printed and bound in Canada by Friesens

Set in Warnock Pro and Futura by Apex CoVantage, LLC
Copy editor: Dallas Harrison
Proofreader: Judith Earnshaw
Indexer: Patti Phillips
Cover designer: Martyn Schmoll
Cover image: janiecbros/iStock